STUDIES IN GLOBA

DIASPORAS

—— AND ——

DEVELOPMENT

STUDIES IN GLOBAL EQUITY

DIASPORAS
AND
DEVELOPMENT

EDITORS

BARBARA J. MERZ
LINCOLN C. CHEN
PETER F. GEITHNER

PUBLISHED BY
GLOBAL EQUITY INITIATIVE
ASIA CENTER
HARVARD UNIVERSITY

DISTRIBUTED BY HARVARD UNIVERSITY PRESS
CAMBRIDGE, MASSACHUSETTS, AND LONDON, ENGLAND 2007

Library of Congress Cataloging-in-Publication Data

Diaspora Philanthropy and Equitable Development Conference
(2006 : Harvard University)
  Diasporas and development / editors Barbara J. Merz, Lincoln C.
Chen, Peter F. Geithner.
      p. cm. -- (Studies in global equity)
The chapters in this volume were presented at the Diaspora
Philanthropy and Equitable Development Conference organized
by the Harvard Global Equity Initiative in May 2006. Contributors
highlight diaspora activity in Africa, Asia, Central America, and the
Caribbean
  Includes bibliographical references and index.
  ISBN-13: 978-0-674-02455-7
  ISBN-10: 0-674-02455-9
  1. Emigrant remittances--Developing countries--Congresses. 2.
Labor mobility--Developing countries--Congresses. 3. Equality--De-
veloping countries--Congresses. 4. Economic growth--Congresses.
5. Emigration and immigration--Economic aspects--Developing
countries--Congresses. I. Merz, Barbara J. (Barbara Jean), 1974– II.
Chen, Lincoln C. III. Geithner, Peter F. IV. Harvard University. Global
Equity Initiative. V. Title.
  HG3877.D5 2007
  338.9009172′4--dc22

                                                        2006102558

Cover design by Jill Feron / FeronDesign, South Hamilton, MA.
Interior text design by Oona Patrick.

CONTENTS

PREFACE

In our search for a more equitable world, the Global Equity Initiative pursues scholarship and promotes policies that advance fairness in health, education, and economic opportunities worldwide. The programs launched by the Initiative address concrete aspects of global equity, such as global health, primary education, human capabilities, and human security. One cross-cutting thematic program focuses on global philanthropy and examines the way private giving can catalyze action for equity.

In exploring the terrain of global philanthropy, the program increasingly became aware of the dynamism of diaspora communities in contributing to equitable development of their countries of origin. Thus, the program initially commissioned a series of papers on diaspora giving of the Chinese and Indian diaspora that eventually culminated in a conference and an edited volume. This Asian work was subsequently buttressed with studies of diaspora philanthropy in other regions—Mexico, the Caribbean, and Pakistan.[1]

By bringing together a series of papers on key issues and regional patterns of diaspora philanthropy around the world, this volume is a natural culmination of these earlier efforts.

1. *Diaspora Philanthropy and Equitable Development in China and India*, edited by Lincoln Chen, Peter Geithner, and Paula Johnson (2005); *New Patterns for Mexico: Observations on Remittances, Philanthropic Giving, and Equitable Development*, edited by Barbara J. Merz (2006); and *Portrait of a Giving Community: Philanthropy by the Pakistani-American Diaspora* by Adil Najam (2006).

Indeed, our aspiration is to provide, for the first time, a truly global perspective on the diversity, richness, and issues associated with what is clearly a growing philanthropic phenomenon in our globalizing world.

The papers together provide a special lens on the implications of diaspora philanthropy for equitable development. While diaspora giving is an important subset of global giving, it carries distinctive dimensions, especially the non-financial impacts of diaspora relationships with their home societies. This volume aimed to bring together diverse national patterns of diaspora giving to provide information for a more informed public dialogue on questions such as: How can the equity impact of this global giving be maximized? Might creative intermediary mechanisms or public policies help channel diaspora philanthropy in positive directions? What can be done to promote trust in these mechanisms and to improve their transparency, accountability, and performance? *Diasporas and Development* aims to deepen the understanding of the promise and pitfalls of diaspora engagement in their countries of origin and how this activity might help bridge the distances between societies in an unequal world.

The chapters in this volume were presented in a conference organized by the Harvard Global Equity Initiative in May 2006 (see participant list). The conference benefited from the enormous diversity of the over forty participants coming from major geographic regions with backgrounds in academia, policymaking, and philanthropic practice. The participants raised a number of significant questions about how to consider various forms of diaspora engagement and whether diasporas have an impact on equitable development in sending and receiving communities. These discussions have been further explored and expanded by the contributors to this volume.

We are grateful to the authors who joined us in this volume and shared their knowledge and talents. In addition, we would like to thank those who provided guidance to the Global Equity

Initiative's Philanthropy Program on this project, including Akwasi Aidoo, Barry Gaberman, Natalia Kanem, Sal LaSpada, and Adele Simmons. We are also deeply indebted to our present and past colleagues at Harvard who have provided intellectual fellowship: Sudhir Anand, Sabina Alkire, Alex de Waal, Christina Doyle, Colleen Gross, John Hammock, Piya Hanvoravongchai, Paula Johnson, Erin Judge, Peggy Levitt, Tony Saich, and Cynthia Sanborn. We would also like to thank Iris Tuomenoksa, Ginger Tanton, and Brian Na for helping to organize the conference, and we offer special thanks to Oona Patrick, who managed the copyediting and publication of this volume.

The Global Equity Initiative is grateful to sponsors of this work: the William and Flora Hewlett Foundation, the Rockefeller Foundation, the Ford Foundation, and the Canadian International Development Agency.

We have been privileged to work with so many dedicated scholars and practitioners to proactively address issues related to equitable development. We hope that this volume will be of use to those many new and inspired voices who will continue to carry this work forward.

BARBARA J. MERZ
LINCOLN C. CHEN
PETER F. GEITHNER
Cambridge, Mass.
October 2006

CONFERENCE PARTICIPANTS

Diaspora Philanthropy and Equitable Development
Conference
Harvard University, May 2006

Hector Almendrades, Policy Analyst, Canadian International Development Agency

Suzy Antounian, Vice President, the World Affairs Council of Northern California

Charles Bailey, Program Officer, Ford Foundation, Hanoi

Barnett F. Baron, Executive Vice President, the Asia Foundation

Kofi A. Boateng, Chief Operating Officer, The Africa-America Institute

Cristina de Borbón y Grecia, Her Royal Highness the Princess of Spain

Katrina Burgess, Associate Professor, Fletcher School of Law and Diplomacy, Tufts University

Alix Cantave, Program Officer, Local Initiatives Support Corporation

Lincoln C. Chen, founding Director, Global Equity Initiative, Harvard University; President, China Medical Board

Ana Criquillion, Director, Central American Women's Fund

Rafael Fernández de Castro, Head of the Department of International Studies, Instituto Tecnológico Autónomo de México

David de Ferranti, Senior Fellow, the United Nations Foundation; Distinguished Visiting Fellow, Brookings Institution

Leona S. Forman, founder, the Brazil Foundation

Victoria Pineda Garchitorena, President, Ayala Foundation, the Philippines

Peter F. Geithner, Advisor to the Global Equity Initiative, Harvard University

Rajat Gupta, Senior Partner, McKinsey & Company; Co-Chair, American India Foundation

Christopher M. Harris, Program Officer, Ford Foundation

John Harvey, Executive Director, Grantmakers Without Borders

Paula Johnson, Senior Fellow, the Philanthropic Initiative; Research Fellow, Global Equity Initiative, Harvard University

Devesh Kapur, Director, Center for the Advanced Study of India and Madan Lal Sobti Professor for the Study of Contemporary India, University of Pennsylvania

Pradeep Kashyap, Executive Director, American India Foundation

Mark R. Kramer, Managing Director, Foundation Strategy Group

Peggy Levitt, Chair of the Sociology Department, Wellesley College; Research Fellow, Hauser Center for Nonprofit Organizations, Harvard University

Janet Maughan, Deputy Director, Global Inclusion, Rockefeller Foundation

Felipe Medina, Director, Latin America Private Wealth Management, Goldman Sachs

Barbara J. Merz, Philanthropy Program Director, Global Equity Initiative, Harvard University

Diana Molina, Program Officer, Fundació la Caixa, Spain

Adil Najam, Professor of International Negotiation and Diplomacy, Fletcher School of Law and Diplomacy, Tufts University

Anthony J. Ody, Consultant, United Nations Foundation; Adjunct Professor, Georgetown University Public Policy Institute

Mojúbàolú Olúfúnké Okome, Associate Professor, Department of Political Science, Brooklyn College, CUNY

Manuel Orozco, Director of Remittances and Development, Inter-American Dialogue

Sushma Raman, Program Manager of the International Initiative to Strengthen Philanthropy, Ford Foundation

Tony Saich, Daewoo Professor of International Affairs, Harvard University; Director, Asia Center and Global Equity Initiative, Harvard University

Gerry Salole, Chief Executive, European Foundation Centre, Belgium

Cynthia Sanborn, Chair of Social and Political Science, Universidad del Pacífico, Perú

Mark Sidel, Professor of Law and International Affairs, University of Iowa; Research Scholar, Obermann Center for Advanced Studies

Naresh Singh, Executive Director, UNDP Commission on Legal Empowerment of the Poor

Anh K. Tran, co-founder, Pacific Links Foundation

Diep Ngoc Vuong, co-founder, Pacific Links Foundation, Vietnam

CONTRIBUTORS

Lincoln C. Chen is the founding Director of Harvard's Global Equity Initiative. He now serves as President of the China Medical Board, an independent foundation that seeks to advance health in China and Asia through medical education and research.

David de Ferranti headed up the World Bank's Latin America group as Regional Vice President until his retirement from the Bank in 2005. He is currently at the Brookings Institution and the United Nations Foundation.

Peter F. Geithner is an advisor to the Global Equity Initiative and the Ash Institute at Harvard University and serves as a consultant to the Rockefeller Foundation, Sasakawa Peace Foundation, and other nonprofit organizations.

Devesh Kapur is Director of the Center for the Advanced Study of India and holds the Madan Lal Sobti Professorship for the Study of Contemporary India at the University of Pennsylvania.

Barbara J. Merz directs the Philanthropy Program at Harvard's Global Equity Initiative and holds a research appointment at the Hauser Center for Nonprofit Organizations.

Adil Najam is Professor of International Negotiation and Diplomacy at the Fletcher School of Law and Diplomacy, Tufts University.

Anthony J. Ody is a consultant to the United Nations Foundation and Adjunct Professor at Georgetown University's Public Policy Institute.

Mojúbàolú Olúfúnké Okome is an international political economist whose specialization is on the African continent as Associate Professor in the Department of Political Science at Brooklyn College, CUNY.

Manuel Orozco is Director of Remittances and Development at the Inter-American Dialogue. He conducts policy analysis and advocacy on issues relating to remittances.

Mark Sidel is Professor of Law and International Affairs at the University of Iowa and a research scholar at the University's Obermann Center for Advanced Studies.

CHAPTER 1

Overview:
Diasporas and Development

Barbara J. Merz
Lincoln C. Chen
Peter F. Geithner

Our global era has spawned unprecedented transnational movements across traditional political and geographic boundaries.
Just as money, goods, information, and technologies are flowing
rapidly across borders, so too are people driven by insecurity due
to conflict and workers in search of jobs in expanding global labor
markets. Human mobility is creating new transnational migrant
communities that retain varying social, financial, and cultural
linkages with their countries of origin. Increasingly, these communities are sending financial resources back to their families and
communities in the form of household remittances, commercial
investments, and philanthropy. They are also sharing knowledge,
skills, attitudes, and values learned or acquired abroad.

Diasporas and Development addresses one central question
about diaspora flows: Is global equity an inevitable consequence
of diaspora transfers or might these flows actually aggravate inequity? The volume examines the mostly positive, but sometimes
negative, influences of diaspora engagement in the development
of home countries. The individual chapters examine both philanthropic policies and modalities of given global diaspora communities as well as regional patterns of diaspora engagement.

Engagement of diaspora communities with their country
of origin is of course not new. Recent developments, however,
have heightened interest in the links between diaspora and

1

development. High rates of migration have important implications for economic development, labor markets, ethnic diversity, and social equity. Skilled migrants who move from low-income sending countries to wealthy receiving nations often, although not invariably, improve their life choices. In so doing, they may widen disparities between those who are fortunate enough to emigrate and those who are not. Those left behind may face heavier familial burdens, fragmented and imbalanced households, and an increasing dependence on cash transfers from abroad. Remittances may also provide a welfare safety net in receiving communities as well as provide for public goods such as basic education and health. Invested wisely, resources from abroad can in addition stimulate entrepreneurship and economic gains. This volume highlights these complex contrasts so as to provide an informed view on the impact of diaspora investments on equitable development.

CONCEPTS AND DEFINITIONS

At the outset, it is useful to clarify three terms that serve as touchstones for this volume: diaspora, philanthropy, and equitable development. None of these terms enjoys complete consensus in definition. Indeed, each concept is embedded in controversy and is linked to such contentious subjects as globalization, human identity, ethics and fairness, and collective responsibility.

DIASPORA

By diaspora we refer broadly to communities of individuals residing and working outside their country of origin. These individuals often maintain social, financial, and cultural connections to their country of origin usually mediated through family and friends in the homeland. The ancient Greek derivation of the word diaspora connotes a spreading or scattering of seeds. Historic diasporas were often forcibly expelled, although many modern diasporas are formed by those who have elected to search for opportunities abroad. Diaspora communities have different origins. While some communities, for example, are born in exile, their historic lack of statehood does not necessarily exclude ties with countries of origin. Suzy Antounian points out that "the Armenian and Jewish diasporas predate the independence and founding of their countries as they exist today. Members of these diasporas may not even have visited Israel or Armenia. Yet, they often choose to support various causes and institutions that directly benefit these countries. For these diasporas the home countries are a symbol of national survival and the individual's identification with them is both historical and political. Their motivation for giving is not the result of family needs, nor is it rooted in the geographic identification with a village or a region but stems from a broad desire to build a collective home and nation" (Antounian 2006).

Despite the similarity of challenges faced by diasporas in their host countries, individual diasporas differ in how they were created, how they define themselves, and how their diasporic identities are shaped. These factors influence the way members of a diaspora relate to each other, to the larger transnational community, and to their home country. They also affect the allocation of individual and collective philanthropic resources back to their country of origin.

PHILANTHROPY

We define philanthropy as private giving for public purposes. Under this definition, philanthropy is shaped by the motivation of the giver. Transfers to countries of origin may include goods and services, investments, and remittances, as well as intangible aspects such as knowledge, contacts, and values. These flows are not necessarily mutually exclusive nor collectively exhaustive. The spectrum of diaspora engagements described in this volume underscores the blurred boundaries among and between philanthropic giving, transfers to fulfill familial obligations, and other forms of contributions in terms of time, money, or services.

Sometimes philanthropic investments generate unintended consequences. For example, Mexican hometown associations donate funds for social projects that are matched by the Mexican government. The public matching of hometown donations may increase political accountability and transparency for such projects. Some even argue that any form of engagement by the diaspora advances development whether through travel back to their country of origin, trade in goods and services with their homeland, telecommunications with friends and family who still reside there, or private investment in business ventures in home communities.

Equitable Development

Equitable development is the expansion of human choice widely shared across members of a community or a nation. As such, equitable development is based on normative notions of fairness in the distribution of opportunities for achieving human advancement. In the context of development, equity fosters a focus on those aspects of inequality that violate notions of fairness. Examples of severe inequity include a child who does not have the opportunity to go to school, basic medical treatments that are withheld or unavailable, or court systems that are corrupt or unaccountable. These challenges are disproportionately, though not exclusively, borne by the most vulnerable members of society. Equitable development, thus, includes the tackling of poverty by removing obstacles, such as illiteracy, ill health, lack of access to basic resources, or lack of civil and political freedoms. Indicators of equitable development are those that reflect the quality of people's lives and human capabilities, such as adequate nourishment, a respectable standard of living, good health and longevity, opportunities to acquire individually and socially valuable knowledge, basic human rights protections, and the ability to participate meaningfully in community life.

THIS VOLUME

Diasporas and Development is organized into two parts. The first half of the volume explores several key themes that relate to diaspora flows: What is the role of the state in supporting or regulating diaspora engagement? What is the role of financing and remittances in development? What are the risks—political, social, and cultural—of diaspora engagement? The second half of the volume examines patterns of diaspora giving in different world regions: Asia, Africa, the Caribbean, and Central America. These chapters address such key questions as: What are the patterns of diaspora philanthropy among the regions? In what ways are the patterns similar across regions? How do they differ? What are the trends within and across regions? By presenting empirical patterns of diaspora philanthropy on a broad global canvas, the chapters offer an unprecedented worldwide view of diaspora philanthropy.

THEMATIC CHAPTERS

The three thematically oriented chapters offer the reader overarching frameworks for considering key policies and challenges raised by diaspora activity. These themes are revisited within specific contexts in the regional chapters that follow.

Role of the State

In his chapter, "Focusing on the State," Mark Sidel underscores the importance of state regulations in governing diaspora philanthropy. The chapter opens a discussion of the many ways in which the current norms of diaspora giving largely bypass the state, with potential negative consequences on equity in the home country. Sidel argues that many states have been overgeneralized or stereotyped in their reactions to their diaspora populations. Better understanding the state's nuanced role and reaction in each country is crucial to understanding diaspora impact on equity in the country of origin. He also warns us that leaving the state out may increase inequity, since one of the primary responsibilities accorded to governments is reallocation of resources for equity.

Some governments have only recently begun to grapple with the role they would like to see their diasporas play. Many are actively considering best approaches to channel diaspora interest. Foreign direct investments (FDI) provide a natural window for diasporas to invest in the development of the private sector of their home countries. In some countries, like China, FDI is a particularly important feature and there is a long history of diaspora investment. Other countries are creating diaspora-specific investment opportunities and "one-stop-shopping" for making investment easier for interested diaspora members. Local connections and networks within the country often give diaspora members a particular interest in funding business endeavors or supporting fledgling industries.

Financing

In their chapter, David de Ferranti and Anthony Ody ask: "What can remittances and other migrant flows do for equitable development?" Given that migrants' remittances now constitute one of the most important forms of financial transfer to developing countries—twice the size of official development assistance—it is important to explore how remittances affect equitable development. They find that remittances often exacerbate inequity during the early years of migration since it is not the poorest that can afford to send a family member to emigrate. However, remittance flows may enhance equity over the long term through greater financial flows among a broader base of participants. Increased competition among financial institutions can expand the base of people who have access to financial services in the developing world, thereby decreasing inequity. Diaspora can and should play a role in ensuring these positive aspects of equitable development.

Risks of Diaspora Engagement

Devesh Kapur turns the table on assumptions about the positive roles of the diaspora in equity in home countries. He urges caution regarding the "Janus face of diasporas" and the negative impact that ideologically extreme expatriates can have on democracy in both the country of origin and the larger world. He highlights some of the world's largest criminal organizations and the diaspora groups that create or sustain them, arguing that diasporas in fact tend to be more extreme than their home country compatriots for two reasons. First, in the world's most volatile regions, diasporas tend to be largely composed of the individuals who are most at odds with the current government, thus explaining much of their reason for living outside their homeland. Second, because they do not live with the day-to-day conflict or the constant struggle for survival, it is easier for them to discourage compromise and maintain a hard-line stance.

It is particularly disturbing that some of these diaspora groups have created "charities" that mix philanthropic giving and relief efforts with violent movements. As funds given for aid purposes are siphoned off for militant uses, donors may unwittingly become the financiers of criminal activity. Citing case studies of the Indian, Sri Lankan Tamil, and Pan-Islamic diasporas, Kapur questions the "unbridled euphoria" that has accompanied the rise of the "third sector" and the increase of diaspora engagement in and financial transfers to their countries of origin.

Regional Perspectives

The four regionally oriented chapters highlight similarities and differences in diaspora activities among countries in Asia, Africa, the Caribbean, and Central America. In comparing diaspora approaches and strategies, context is a critical factor in determining effectiveness. What works in Mexico would not necessarily be applicable in China. Major differences may arise within as well as among countries. In focusing on similarities and differences, the chapters are intended to facilitate comparisons across regions and offer for the first time a global view of diaspora philanthropy.

Asia

In his chapter, Adil Najam tackles the incredible vastness and diversity that is Asia. The chapter focuses on four diaspora groups in the US: Chinese, Filipinos, Indians, and Pakistanis—posing questions about why these diasporas give, how they give, and what challenges they face in so doing. For example, most Asian diasporas evidence a strong desire to give to individuals rather than institutions, reflecting the importance of familial ties and low trust in governments and nongovernmental institutions. Najam finds that for diaspora communities, giving back to their countries of origin fulfills a desire for identity with their homelands. Furthermore, the major obstacles to giving are neither interest nor capability but limited mechanisms or modalities to facilitate safe and effective diaspora transfers. Although these lessons are derived from the Asian experience, Najam argues that they are likely to be broadly applicable to our general understanding of diaspora engagements and their philanthropic practices.

Africa

Mojúbàolú Olúfúnké Okome, in her chapter on "African Diasporas," reminds us that Africa is experiencing a development crisis where diaspora engagement is woefully inadequate to meet Africa's needs. Private giving to Africa has not been enough, and certainly will not be enough, to lift the continent out of poverty. Deep structural barriers continue to plague African economic development. Migration has become a survival strategy for many Africans, giving rise to diaspora communities throughout the world. These diasporas share communal obligations to their families in Africa. Obligations are fulfilled through individual remittances, in-kind transfers, and traditions like the group savings pot, a concept used for community projects both in Africa and by the diaspora. However, Okome cautions, whatever good is engendered through diaspora engagement should only be considered an adjunct to significant and sustained state efforts to combat the poverty and marginalization of the African continent.

Caribbean

Caribbean nations have among the highest proportion of diaspora populations relative to their home population. Because of their size and the proximity between sending and receiving countries, diaspora groups in the Caribbean tend to be actively engaged with their home country. In this chapter, Barbara Merz highlights survey findings from diaspora groups from Guyana, Haiti, and Jamaica. These findings point to the gap between stated development priorities and diaspora contributions. She argues that, because diaspora giving is often based on personal preference, it is crucial to clarify local priorities before promoting greater diaspora involvement. In other words, local priorities, participation, and accountability should be incorporated into projects financed by the diaspora. However, diaspora members report that the greatest obstacle to larger contributions is their distrust of local government. Diaspora members also face resistance from those in the country of origin who view diaspora activity as a threat to their power. Diaspora engagement in the Caribbean is largely driven by community and familial attachments. Therefore, divisions and inequalities inherent to socio-economic status within the home country may be perpetuated through diaspora contributions. These realities pose challenges for development agencies that aim to expand opportunities in the most vulnerable populations throughout the Caribbean.

Central America

Hometown associations are models of engagement prevalent in Central American diaspora communities. Manuel Orozco describes these relatively informal, volunteer-based groups. He notes that Central American hometown association participants tend to be heavily involved with their families both in the US and abroad. This dual-community orientation is reflected in the way in which fundraising for development projects back home often comes from community events that celebrate shared culture like traditional dances, pageants, or festivals. Central American hometown associations are organized to work in specific geographic areas. Some associations choose to work with government, while others find it unproductive to engage the state. Most partner at least with other organizations, groups, or coalitions in the home country. Orozco notes that diaspora remittances are, at the most basic level, foreign savings that interact with the structure of the local economy—with net positive or negative impact. Understanding the vulnerability of the local economy is required if diasporas are to support long-term equitable development of their hometowns.

ISSUES AND CHALLENGES

The policy and regional chapters in this volume highlight many issues associated with diaspora and equitable development. During the Harvard conference where these chapter papers were presented and discussed, many issues arose. Conceptual clarity and definitions emerged. So did many positive and negative examples of diaspora philanthropy for equitable development. The conference also highlighted such issues as the role of remittances, diaspora and migration, and gender and the diaspora.

One of the key themes of the conference related to the role of remittances, the largest category of diaspora transfers. World Bank estimates for worldwide remittance flows exceed $232 billion in 2005 with $167 billion flowing to developing countries. These estimates do not incorporate unrecorded flows, which are believed to be at least 50 percent higher than recorded flows. Even without counting unofficial flows, remittances are now more than twice the level of development aid from all sources and comparable to the level of foreign direct investment. The top three remittance receiving nations are India, China, and Mexico. Rich countries are the main source of remittances with the United States as the largest source, followed by Saudi Arabia and Switzerland.

Remittances are defined as private resources earned by migrants and sent predominantly to relatives for private consumption in their country of origin. These are not public funds; they belong to the migrants who worked to earn them or to the family members to whom they are sent. Because they are money transfers within families, remittances are not usually considered philanthropy nor should they be counted as international aid. Nevertheless, they may have positive public externalities. Remittances can buttress a country's foreign exchange reserves, improve its creditworthiness, enhance access to international capital, and thus reduce poverty as demonstrated in several low-income countries (Ratha 2005).

While many institutional stakeholders—governments, multilateral agencies, and businesses alike—have a stated interest in the growing phenomenon of remittances, far less attention is being paid to whether and how the non-monetary contributions of diaspora might impact development. In the areas of health and education, diaspora leaders have established professional organizations such as the New York Association of Jamaican Physicians and the Guyanese Legal Society of the UK to share information, best-practices, professional advances, and skills with their colleagues in their countries of origin. Other examples of non-monetary contributions can be found in governance, the arts, and culture. At the same time, some in-country leaders report that they are uneasy about the diaspora coming home bearing "gifts." The receptivity to non-monetary diaspora interventions varies and should be balanced by the strength and health of local government to meet citizen needs.

Diasporas and Migration

A book about diasporas and development would be incomplete without a discussion of their relationship to migration policies and practices. Three trends are strongly influencing both immigration policy in receiving nations, as well as migrants' ongoing relationship with their countries of origin. These are: the brain drain that often results as well-educated citizens of developing countries leave for higher paying jobs in wealthy nations; the increased scrutiny of financial flows in the wake of the September 11, 2001, terrorist attacks in the United States; and deepening concern about the perceived intrusion of foreign cultures and values in home countries.

The rate of migration has increased in recent years, especially the migration of better-educated citizens from developing countries to wealthier developed nations. Approximately 30 to 50 percent of science and technology professionals from the developing world are now living in industrialized countries (Meyer and Brown 1999). A recent World Bank report, "International Migration, Remittances, and the Brain Drain," finds that, while bigger countries experience larger absolute numbers of out-migration, small countries tend to feel the effect more acutely due to loss of a higher percentage of better-educated migrants: "The [skilled] emigration rate exceeds 80 percent in nations such as Guyana, Jamaica, Haiti, Grenada, and St. Vincent and the Grenadines . . . and exceeds 50 percent in five African countries—Cape Verde, The Gambia, Mauritius, the Seychelles, and Sierra Leone" (World Bank 2006). Central America, the Caribbean, and Africa see higher percentages of their skilled workers leave than any other regions in the world (see Orozco, Merz, and Okome chapters).

Particularly worrisome, most of the countries experiencing this brain drain are among the poorest in the world with a desperate need for health workers, teachers, lawyers, and other professionals at home. This is particularly true in Africa, where the exploding AIDS epidemic, combined with the shortage of health workers as many leave for better paying jobs in developed countries, has had devastating and fatal consequences on much of the population. Only 1.3 percent of the world's health practitioners live in sub-Saharan Africa, despite its carrying 25 percent of the world's burden of disease (World Health Organization 2004). It is estimated that 20,000 health workers leave Africa annually (Stillwell 2004). Country leaders may exacerbate this problem by encouraging migration and diaspora relations in the hopes of gaining stronger remittance income from those who leave. Mexican President Vicente Fox, for example, frequently insists that "undocumented immigrants [are] heroes whose self-sacrifice and hard work in the United States produce cash that sustain entire communities in Mexico" (Dellios 2006). While this may be true, there is a danger that this increased dependence on "heroes" abroad could make the government complacent in its own responsibilities to its citizens.

Another factor in contemporary migration are new patterns and barriers to international philanthropic donations from certain communities to certain countries. After the September 11, 2001, terrorist attacks, the United States passed the US Patriot Act and the Treasury Department released "Anti-Terrorist Financing Guidelines: Voluntary Best Practices for US-Based Charities." Both sought stricter accountability for international charitable giving and monetary transfers, but the language was vague and created ambiguity about what exactly was expected of international organizations. Soon, 209 of the world's 219 countries followed suit, "express[ing] support in the war on terrorist financing—173 nations have implemented orders to freeze terrorist assets, more than 100 countries have introduced new legislation to fight terrorist financing, and 84 countries have established Financial Intelligence Units to share information" (US Treasury Department 2003). Further, UN Security Council Resolutions 1372 and 1390 "compel action by member states to combat terrorist financing." Thus far, anti-terrorist guidelines do not appear to have had a strong negative impact on international giving. In fact, the total value of such transactions has increased, from $4.2 billion in 2001 to $4.6 billion in 2002 to $5.3 billion in 2003 (AAFRC 2003 and 2004). However, there is anecdotal evidence that these regulations have chilled giving by particular segments of the international grant making community, "particularly US-based Muslim American and Arab American charities" (Baron 2005). In Adil Najam's chapter, he discusses this new climate of fear through the lens of the Pakistani-American diaspora.

As terrorism often breeds in regions wracked by poverty and lack of opportunity, accessible mechanisms for funding charitable organizations and development initiatives in these areas seem increasingly critical. Yet, as Devesh Kapur discusses in his chapter, there is real reason to be concerned about the negative and extremist influences diasporas sometimes have on their countries of origin. He cites examples of funding directed toward groups such as the Irish IRA and the Sri Lankan Tamil Tigers, as well as extremist Hindu and Islamist groups, such as Hamas and Hezbollah.

Finally, many countries are heatedly debating their immigration policies. As new immigrants change the racial, cultural, and religious face of the countries they enter, host nations struggle to define their collective identity. In the United States, the large number of undocumented Latino immigrants has infuriated some, as have claims that this wave of immigrants is not assimilating like previous immigrant groups. The influx of Latinos has proven a unique case in US immigration history due to the geographic proximity of their countries of origin and the cyclical and circular nature of migration patterns. Many come with the intention of staying just long enough to save up the money to fulfill a goal back in their home country. These intentions to return reduce the incentive to assimilate and learn English, yet many such immigrants stay longer than they originally planned.

In Europe, concern over the intrusion of foreign values and cultures is even more heated. In France, multiple generations of Muslim immigrants have long felt alienated from mainstream culture. Manifestations of this tension include the debates over headscarves in French schools and riots on the outskirts of Paris. Turkish immigrants have similarly felt excluded from German society. Only since 2000 has Germany changed its traditional citizenship laws based on descent (*jus sanguinis*) to permit citizenship based on birth (*jus soli*) and to grant citizenship to the children of long-term residents who are not ethnically German (German Embassy 2006). Previously, guest workers who had been living and working in the country for up to forty years had claim to few rights. Still, many native Germans are concerned about the lack of assimilation of their Turkish countrymen and are particularly outraged by the forty-five "honor killings" that police say have been carried out over the last eight years (Furlong 2005). Germans point to this as evidence that multiculturalism—allowing immigrants and natives to live by different rules and values—is unacceptable.

Unease with Muslim immigration has been especially strong in the Netherlands after the 2004 stabbing of filmmaker Theo Van Gogh in broad daylight in a busy part of town by a Moroccan-Dutch Islamic extremist. Pinned to Van Gogh's chest was a death threat against Ayaan Hirsi Ali, producer of the controversial documentary *Submission*, which Van Gogh filmed. A then-Member of the Dutch Parliament and a Somali-born Muslim atheist, Hirsi Ali has been an outspoken critic of Islam and its treatment of women. She is a compelling example of the culture clash that can arise within diaspora groups, particularly around issues of gender, between those who change and adapt to their new country and those who want to maintain the home country's traditions. As these culture and identity debates continue, it is clear that immigrants themselves are far from guaranteed an easy life in their new country.

Gender and Diasporas

Women in the diaspora may have unparalleled opportunity to influence gender norms in their home countries, a key lever for equitable development. Development scholars have long cited the important role of women, not only for the benefit of women themselves but for the well-being of the entire family and community. Women's empowerment within the family, particularly through education and literacy, tends to significantly reduce child mortality (Sen 1999). Nevertheless, in many countries, women are disproportionately denied education and economic opportunities. Thus, they often perform work that is underappreciated and underpaid, earning on average 20–30 percent less than men in developing countries (International Labour Organization 2004), despite working an estimated 30 percent more hours (Association for Women's Rights in Development 2004).

Seeking better opportunities abroad, women are migrating at increasing rates. Fifty-five percent of immigrants to the United States in 2000 were female (US Immigration and Naturalization Service 2000). In 1990, 30–45 percent of Mexican immigrants, the United States' largest immigrant group, were women, yet 76 percent had less than a high school education (US Census Bureau 1990). The challenges they face are many. The 2002 US Census found 31 percent of female-migrant–headed households are poor, compared with 15 percent of households headed by male migrants. Domestic abuse is particularly high among immigrant women, because they are often dependent upon their partner not only economically, but also for their ability to remain in the country. About half of Latina immigrants reported that domestic violence against them had increased since coming to the United States (Dutton, Orloff, and Aguilar Hass 2000). Women who marry citizens often derive their legal permission to live and work in the country through their husband, who might use this knowledge to control or wield power over them. Legal residents who are abusive to their undocumented wives or partners often threaten to report them to authorities if they complain about their abuse.

Still, despite the many risks confronting female migrants, these women often have access to greater opportunity in their host country due to the host country's more liberal views about women or from greater economic independence. Many women are remitting substantial sums of money to their home country economies. In Sri Lanka, women contributed more than 62 percent of the total of the $1 billion in private remittances (International Organization on Migration 2003). Women now make up 47 percent of migrants within Africa (Baruah 2006) and over 70 percent of migrants from Southeast Asia, mainly working temporarily in Japan, Hong Kong, or Singapore (Orozco 2006). A study of migrant remittances in South Africa concluded that "employed migrant men are 25 percent less likely than employed migrant women to remit" (Martin 2004:7). Beyond remittances, the larger influence of migration is likely to manifest itself in attitudinal changes about women and the level of opportunity and empowerment women achieve in both their home and host countries.

The effect of migration on women left at home is mixed. A study of women in Brazil whose husbands had migrated found no improvement in their social status, "even though they were de facto heads of household. Their domestic activities increased relative to the wives of non-migrating men and the psychological stress of the separation was significant" (Martin 2004:15). Yet studies in South Asia and Southeast Asia find that "while left-behind families encounter difficulties and adjustments, on the whole, families are coping well" (Asis 2004:11). In countries where women have limited freedom, male migration has, in some instances, allowed them to become more powerful players, with greater control and responsibility over finances and household decisions. In some towns, where males still migrate at much higher rates than females, the number of women taking on leadership positions in town governance has increased

(Kakad 2006). When women migrate, however, men are not as likely to take over traditionally female household responsibilities. These duties instead fall to other women in the household, thus increasing their workload without a corresponding increase in freedom or control (Asis 2004:12).

THE WAY AHEAD

The papers in this volume constitute a pioneering effort to bring together studies on the patterns and challenges in diaspora giving for equity in the major world regions. While selective and incomplete, the studies as a whole show that the global pattern of diaspora flows demonstrates enormous diversity with many diaspora communities engaged in many ways with their home countries—each shaped by history, time, and context. Given acceleration of international migration and transnational financial flows, diaspora giving may be expected to continue to grow as a significant social phenomenon in the years ahead.

A major theme echoed in this volume is that diaspora giving involves more than money. While financing can flow as family remittances, commercial investments, and social philanthropy, non-material flows of knowledge, connections, attitudes, and values also matter greatly. The equity impact of these diverse flows is complex, subtle, and difficult to fully explicate. It seems reasonable to assume that most flows exert positive equity effects in home countries, but there are many examples of negative and unintended consequences. Each of the flows should be considered in their specific temporal, cultural, and national contexts, avoiding over-generalizations. Case examples illustrate the full range of impact of diaspora flows—from safety net, poverty alleviation, and basic services to commercialism, elitism, and political intrusion.

Ultimately, the papers in the volume also demonstrate that global diaspora philanthropy can be a legitimate field of academic study as well as a vibrant field of professional practice. Because it is linked to so many intellectual fields—migration, economic development, cultural adaptation—diaspora philanthropy offers a window to advance understanding across a broad range of related fields. Because diaspora financing passes through many modalities and intermediaries for many different philanthropic purposes, with such diverse consequences, the field of diaspora philanthropy also engages professionalism in policies and practices. Our hope is that this volume, however modestly, will contribute to the growing field of diaspora philanthropy in the academy and in the professions.

References

AAFRC Trust for Philanthropy. 2003 and 2004. *Giving USA 2003* and *Giving USA 2004, Reporting on the Previous Year's Contributions from Individuals, Bequests, Foundations, and Corporations* (Giving USA 2004 online at: https://www.givinginstitute.org/secure/index. cfm?pg=proddetail.cfm&productID=9).

Antounian, Suzy M. 2006. Commentary at the Global Equity Initiative Conference on Diaspora Philanthropy and Global Equity, May 10–12, Harvard University, Cambridge.

Asis, Maruja M.B. 2004. "When Men and Women Migrate: Comparing Gendered Migration in Asia." United Nations Division for the Advancement of Women. January 14:11 (http://www.un.org/womenwatch/daw/meetings/consult/CM-Dec03-EP1.pdf).

Association for Women's Rights in Development (AWID). 2004. "Women's Work Exposed: New Trends and Their Implications." *Women's Rights and Economic Change* no. 10, August:1 (http://www.awid.org/publications/primers/women-work_en.pdf UNFPA).

Baron, Barnett F. 2005. "The Treasury Guidelines Have Had Little Impact Overall on US International Philanthropy, But They Have Had a Chilling Impact on US-Based Muslim Charities." *Pace Law Review* 25, no. 307, p. 314 (http://www.library.law.pace.edu/PLR/25-2/Baron.pdf).

Baruah, Nilim. 2006. "Remittances to Least Developed Countries." *Final Report on the Ministerial Conference of the Least-Developed Countries on Enhancing the Development Impact of Remittances.* P. 14. International Organization for Migration, Geneva.

Dellios, Hugh. 2006. "Mexico Pledges to Control Flow of Illegal Immigrants" *Chicago Tribune*. March 27.

Dutton, Mary, Leslye Orloff, and Giselle Aguilar Hass. 2000. "Characteristics of Help-Seeking Behaviors, Resources, and Services Needs of Battered Immigrant Latinas: Legal and Policy Implications." *Georgetown Journal on Poverty Law and Policy* 7, no. 2. Quoted from "Family Violence Prevention Fund: The Facts About Immigrant Women and Domestic Abuse" (http://www.endabuse.org/resources/facts/Immigrant.pdf#search=%22Leslye%20orloff%22).

Furlong, Ray. 2005. "'Honour Killing' Shocks Germany." BBC News, Berlin. March 14 (http://news.bbc.co.uk/2/hi/europe/4345459.stm).

German Embassy in London. 2006. "Reform of Germany's Citizenship and Nationality Law" (http://www.london.diplo.de/Vertretung/london/en/06/other__legal__matters/Reform__Germanys__citizenship__seite.html).

International Labour Organization (ILO). 2004. "Global Employment Trends for Women 2004." March:14 (http://kilm.ilo.org/GET2004/DOWNLOAD/trendsw.pdf#search=%22ilo%20global%20employment%20trends%20for%20women%22).

International Organization on Migration (IOM), 2003. Quoted from "Fact Sheet." The United Nations International Research and Training Institute for the Advancement of Women: 2006 (http://www.un-instraw.org/en/index.php?option=content&task=blogcategory&id=76&Itemid=110).

Kakad, Seema. 2006. "Women and Migration: The Rise of Women Leadership in Rural Communities in Guanajuato, Mexico as a

Result of NAFTA and US Free Trade Policies" (http://www.duke.edu/web/sow/Mexico%20Project.html).

Martin, Susan Forbes. 2004. "Women and Migration." The United Nations Division for the Advancement of Women, January 14 (http://www.un.org/womenwatch/daw/meetings/consult/CM-Dec03-WP1.pdf).

Meyer, Jean-Baptiste and Mercy Brown. 1999. "Scientific Diasporas: A New Approach to the Brain Drain." Management of Social Transformations (MOST) Discussion Paper No. 41, UNESCO, Geneva (http://www.unesco.org/most/meyer.htm). Cited from B. Linsdsay Lowell, Allan Findlay, and Emma Stewart. "Brain Strain: Optimising Highly Skilled Migration from Developing Countries." Institute for Public Policy Research, 2004:9 (http://www.ippr.org/ecomm/files/brainstrain.pdf).

Orozco, Manuel. 2006. "Gender Remittances: Preliminary Notes about Senders and Recipients in Latin America and the Caribbean." United Nations Commission on the Status of Women, Feb/March:3.

Ratha, Dilip. 2005. "Global Economic Prospects 2006: Economic Implications of Remittances and Migration." World Bank, Washington, DC.

Sen, Amartya. 1999. *Development as Freedom*. New York: Anchor Books, p. 195.

Stillwell, B., et al. 2004. "Managing Brain Drain and the Brain Waste of Health Workers in Nigeria." World Health Organization, Geneva (http://www.who.int/bulletin/bulletin_board/82/stilwell1/en/).

US Census Bureau. 1993. *1990 Census of the Population: The Foreign Born Population in the United States*. Washington, DC: US Government Printing Office.

US Immigration and Naturalization Service (INS). 2000. *Statistical Yearbook of the Immigration and Naturalization Service 2000*. Washington, DC: US Government Printing Office.

US Treasury Department. 2003. "Progress in the War on Terrorist Financing." September 11, 2003 (http://www.ustreas.gov/press/releases/reports/js721.pdf).

World Bank. 2006. "International Migration, Remittances, and the Brain Drain" (http://www-wds.worldbank.org/external/default/WDSContentServer/WDSP/IB/2003/07/08/000094946_03062104301450/Rendered/PDF/multi0page.pdf).

World Health Organization. 2004. "Addressing Africa's Health Workforce Crisis: An Avenue of Action." Paper prepared for the High-Level Forum on MDGs, Abuja (http://www.hlfhealthmdgs.org/Documents/AfricasWorkforce-Final.pdf#search=%22who%20Addressing%20Africa's%20Health%20Workforce%20Crisis%22).

CHAPTER 2

FOCUSING ON THE STATE:
GOVERNMENT RESPONSES TO DIASPORA GIVING
AND IMPLICATIONS FOR EQUITY

MARK SIDEL

Numerous efforts over the past decade have begun the process of mapping the new world of diaspora philanthropy, which we generally define as giving back by ethnic communities living abroad for social or public purposes in their countries of origin. In most cases these studies focused on the activities of the *donors* and, to some degree, their developing intermediaries. They explored how much diaspora donors are giving, through what mechanisms, toward what purposes, and, at least in some studies, whether the new phenomenon of diaspora philanthropy is promoting equitable or counter-equitable development in selected countries. Studies have also focused on *recipients*: educational, medical, charitable, nongovernmental, religious, and other organizations and projects within home countries. The initial wave of studies in this field, often scoping exercises intended to drill down to a level of detail that made discussion of the phenomenon feasible, largely skipped over a key actor in the diaspora philanthropy process: the receiving state.

I am grateful to Rafael Fernandez de Castro, Peter Geithner, Barbara Merz, and other participants in the May 2006 Global Equity Initiative Conference on Diaspora Philanthropy and Equitable Development for comments and discussions on these themes. I served as Visiting Professor of Law at Harvard Law School and Vermont Law School while this chapter was written and am grateful to colleagues at both institutions. Particular thanks to Bill Alford, Juliet Bowler, Laura Gillen, Emma Johnson, Tim Locher, Jeff Shields, Melissa Smith, and Stephanie Willbanks. Support for this chapter was also provided by the Office of the Provost Faculty Scholar support fund and the College of Law at the University of Iowa and by the Global Equity Initiative.

Through its attitudes, policies, laws, and regulations, the receiving state can play a decisive role in the scale, priorities, and directions for diaspora giving. Of course, the state was not entirely absent from the early studies of diaspora giving. In work largely focused on donors and recipients, there was some attention paid to state attitudes and policies in India, China, Mexico, and elsewhere. But much of this discussion of the role of receiving states lacked the detail of the finely tuned focus on donors and recipients (Young and Shih 2005; Kapur, Mehta, and Dutt 2005; Sidel 2005; Viswanath and Dadrawala 2005; Merz 2005; Zamora 2005; Burgess 2005; Orozco and Welle 2005).

THE STEREOTYPED STATE

In some cases the first wave of diaspora philanthropy studies not only under-studied receiving governments but also overly generalized and even stereotyped receiving governments' reactions to giving back from abroad. Earlier analyses did provide significant detail and some analysis of donor decision-making, as well as similar specificity on recipients. But the state was generally portrayed in only one of two ways: *eager governments* open to diaspora giving—the state of open arms and smiling officials; and *suspicious governments* who were apprehensive, guarded, and often more or less closed to external ethnic philanthropy—the state of crossed arms and glaring cadres.

There has always been a third generalization about receiving states as well, but one rarely discussed in explicit terms: confused governments. These lagged in their responses as sophisticated and even manipulative donors and recipients and their increasingly experienced intermediaries moved through and around the state like vehicles entering a traffic circle at high speed, making a momentary swerve past the state.

This chapter focuses a spotlight solely on the state and its reactions to diaspora engagement, while seeking to provide an initial framework for understanding and analyzing a state's

varying policies and mechanisms. It looks beyond the stereotypes of the initial research on diaspora giving, stereotypes that
have since disappeared in the increasingly subtle research on
diasporic remittances (Joint Conference on Remittances 2005;
Orozco 2000).

These government reactions are considerably more nuanced
than we have generally assumed. Diaspora philanthropy cannot
be isolated as a policy issue by itself—it is intimately bound up
with policy toward a state's diaspora, and toward remittances. In
many countries it is complicated by religion, politics, tax policy,
and other complex and controversial issues that implicate a
state's policies toward its emigrants and emigrants' ties to the
state (Barry 2006; Chander 2001; Chander 2006). Governments
can adopt overlapping, and sometimes even conflicting, policies
toward giving by their compatriots from abroad.

Here we will view state responses to diaspora engagement
along a spectrum, with the strongly supportive state at one end
and more controlling or restrictive states at the other. We must
bear in mind that the boundaries in these classifications are
highly permeable: in the typology used here, states can be at
once supportive, rent-seeking or inquisitive, and restrictive or
controlling, depending on the specific policy in question or the
state agency that is acting. India serves as an excellent example
for many of our purposes. It is a state that is strongly, rhetori-
cally, and yet also selectively supportive of diaspora giving. But
it also employs bans and licensing requirements—among the
most restrictive behaviors seen.

It is understandable that we find some complexity in what are
now, for the most part, eager government efforts to attract diaspora
philanthropy. State responses to diaspora giving are generally
characterized by the weakening controls and restrictions that
governments place on giving from ethnic populations overseas,
and a policy of welcome for diaspora philanthropic investment
that is, in many countries, considerably more pronounced than a

decade ago (Sidel 1997). This chapter identifies some of the factors affecting these responses. These include governments' needs for development funding and the failures of the state as a developmental actor in its own right; diaspora donors acting in alliance with each other, with increasingly powerful intermediaries, and with influential domestic actors; the rise of subnational (provincial and municipal) authorities as partners and targets for diaspora giving and their policies of welcome and state investment; and other factors in the weakening of government resistance.

This chapter also seeks to ask whether increasingly welcoming policies affect the equity implications of diaspora giving. Where national and local authorities work to actively encourage diaspora philanthropy, loosening legal and bureaucratic restrictions and allowing diaspora givers to promote development often entirely independent of the state, are there equity implications to the giving that results? Inevitably there must be, but identifying those implications is complex.

THE SUPPORTIVE STATE

State support for diaspora giving has become considerably more pronounced in many recipient countries over the past decade. A "supportive" policy takes many potential forms, some more supportive than others, and some more or less broadly tailored than others. If we seek to move beyond the stereotyped state in its reactions to diaspora giving, among the threads we first need to untangle are the various forms of the supportive state.

THE STRONGLY SUPPORTIVE STATE

At one end of the state spectrum are governments that back up a supportive attitude with actual investment in partnership with diaspora giving: real budget outlays, either at the national or subnational level. Mexico's "Three-for-One" policy of subsidizing philanthropic remittances is one example of the supportive state that actually supplements diaspora giving with government funds, despite specific problems in the program identified in earlier research (Zamora 2005; Burgess 2005; Orozco and Welle 2005). How the state provides budgetary support to diaspora giving is an important arena for further research as more countries devote resources directly to partnering with the diaspora.

Another form of the strongly supportive state directly encourages or even requires simplified and enhanced banking and financial services to facilitate diaspora remittances, including diaspora giving, and to increase access to financial services for the poor. This is occurring in Mexico, India, and many other countries. The reduction of financial and other barriers has been the subject of extensive research, both on the role of recipient states in facilitating financial services and the roles of emigrant states, the finance and banking industry, and other actors. Easing financial procedures may also include such important steps by recipient governments as issuing facilitative documents, such as the Mexican *matricula consular* (Bouquet 2005; Orozco 2004; Joint Conference on Remittances 2005; de Ferranti and Ody chapter in this volume). The relaxation of financial and banking barriers emerges as a priority in new studies of countries where little previous research has been conducted on diaspora giving and its obstacles. For example, a recent study of diaspora giving to Pakistan identified loosening financial and banking barriers as a key need (Najam 2006).

A related form of the strongly supportive state moves sharply and effectively to reduce or eliminate regulatory barriers to giving from abroad. This state lessens or ends the collection of taxes on philanthropic remittances, reporting requirements, and other "soft" legal barriers. The elimination of regulatory and fiscal barriers is under way in literally dozens of countries with significant diasporas.

This is a complex area, one in which both recipient and emigrant governments are promoting competition, transparency, and efficiency in money transfer and financial services. Recipient governments are adopting considerably broader policies to promote vibrancy and competition in the financial sector, as well as reducing investment barriers, strengthening the investment climate, and strengthening the legal and institutional framework for philanthropy.

As Anthony Ody puts it, more relaxed policies, additional subsidies, and more incentives adopted by governments "desperate for diaspora funds" and specifically targeted at the diaspora are a distinctly "second best approach" that can distort the domestic policy climate. The best approach is to "improve the climate for everyone." So while the relaxation of various obstacles for the diaspora looks like and often is a positive step, an even stronger approach involves reforming the policy environment for domestic and diaspora actors alike. And, of course, some of these developments are involuntary, at least in part: globalization and new technology are seriously weakening the capacity of governments to regulate incoming resource flows.

Strongly supportive states may also relax citizenship policies to allow for dual citizenship by their émigrés, a status that may directly facilitate diasporic engagement including giving. The dual citizenship trend is taking hold around the world, with dozens of governments now allowing it, and in some cases facilitating electoral rights for diaspora members as well (Barry 2006; Okome in this volume). Mojúbàolú Okome puts this clearly in her chapter in this volume: "Transnational migrants seek such policies to extend their power vis-à-vis the state."

Finally, the strongly supportive state may establish diaspora ministries or other state agencies; set up diaspora advisory councils; hold well-publicized annual or occasional meetings with diaspora investors (philanthropic and otherwise); enlist its embassies and consulates overseas to promote diaspora giving home; and utilize other means to provide both substantive and expressive support for diaspora philanthropic investment.

Jamaica, India, and many other countries have established such diaspora advisory councils, for example, and they can be useful feedback mechanisms for both government and compatriots overseas (see Merz chapter in this volume; Sidel 2004). Sometimes these are multi-pronged support initiatives, as in Jamaica, where a diaspora advisory board is but one of a number of diaspora linkage mechanisms that include a national diaspora conference, a website, a national diaspora day, and a foundation (Merz in this volume). A number of countries, including Haiti, India, Ghana, and others, have established diaspora ministries or other government agencies (see Merz and Okome chapters; Kapur, Mehta, and Dutt 2004). A wide variety of other such initiatives are under way around the world, from Central America to Eritrea, Nigeria, Ghana, and elsewhere.

For example, Filipino embassies and consulates in the United States—direct arms of the Philippine government—have organized " 'roadshows' that present to the FilAm community not just opportunities for investments but also selected [social] programs that have shown track records of success," including education, housing, and Internet access projects (Garchitorena 2006). Called "Bayan Ko, Bahay Ko" ("My Country, My Home") in Tagalog, the 2006 "roadshows" showcased investment projects in Honolulu, Los Angeles, San Francisco, Chicago, New York, and Washington, DC—all major centers of the Filipino diaspora. While the focus was clearly on land and other investment opportunities, there was discussion of opportunities for diaspora giving as well, particularly in corporate philanthropy projects linked to major land development companies such as Ayala (Department of Foreign Affairs 2006). The roadshows are not only occurring in the United States: perhaps the most ambitious efforts have been in Europe, where the Manila-based Economic Resource Center for Overseas Filipinos (ERCOF) sponsored a roadshow to showcase "hometown development" opportunities in Luxembourg, Brussels, Geneva,

Rotterdam, and The Hague in November 2005 (ERCOF 2006). Meetings at the Luxembourg roadshow, for example, began discussions on developing a microfinance investment fund involving diaspora investors, ERCOF, and the Manila-based rural Bankers Association of the Philippines (RBAP) (Opiniano 2005).

Even where these activities are merely expressive of governments' commitment to receiving diaspora funds and are without significant policy clout, these expressive activities can be important in the resulting policy environment for diaspora relations. This last form of the strongly supportive state illustrates the permeable spectrum of state response to the diaspora. The form of support that involves advisory councils, meetings with prominent members of the diaspora, annual conferences, well-publicized invitations home, invitations to consult on government policy, and the like, may reflect either a state that is strongly supportive of diaspora engagement (including giving), or one that is supportive but in a less concrete and more rhetorical sense. In both cases, the receiving state wants the philanthropic investment. And in virtually all these cases, the strongly supportive actions taken by recipient governments must be followed up for the longer term, often in the face of a skeptical or suspicious diaspora. As Merz puts it in her chapter in this volume, describing the Caribbean context but more generally applicable to other regions as well, "trust-building measures between diaspora and the home-country governments are essential."

The Rhetorically Supportive State

Some governments seek to encourage diaspora giving, but without utilizing the mechanisms of the strongly supportive state. India is a recent example, encouraging diaspora giving (and, of course, investment), without yet taking some of the necessary, specific steps either to subsidize giving or to reduce barriers that Mexico or other states have taken (Kapur, Mehta, and Dutt 2004; Viswanath and Dadrawala 2004). Other states also firmly express the desire to work with the diaspora but fail to follow those statements with a full range of amended policies.

But for some states that understand how useful the diaspora can be for national development, domestic conditions may not allow as much direct support as the government might like to provide. Haiti, for example, has opened a Ministry of Haitians Living Abroad to work with the diaspora. As Merz points out in this volume, the Haitian ministry is "one of the few such diaspora-specific posts in the Caribbean." But political, financial, and organizational problems have also prevented Haiti from sufficiently funding the Ministry and its activities or addressing a number of other problems in relations with the diaspora: "lack of dual citizenship . . . , lack of trust in policy-makers, lack of security, and the lack of political stability." And limited support can also mask a certain ambivalence as well. The Haitian experience, where "some in-country leaders [have] expressed doubt about greater diaspora involvement . . . due to concerns of corruption and elitism in the country" is repeated elsewhere as well (Merz, this volume).

The Selectively Supportive State

Governments may also support diaspora philanthropic investment, but with a preference for specific fields, seeking to "channel" diaspora giving into certain areas. The activities of the selectively supportive or "channeling" state can take many different forms, and can have positive or negative implications for equity. They include, among others,

- statements particularly welcoming philanthropic investment in certain priority fields such as primary health care, primary education, disaster relief, and other areas;

- official policies that seek to channel giving into certain arenas, such as differential tax policies for different forms of diaspora giving, including preferential tax deductions or other fiscal policies rewarding investment in preferred fields;

- policies that reduce regulatory barriers to giving in fields of particular importance as a way of channeling donations in those directions, especially streamlining or eliminating approval processes for such areas as disaster relief, primary health care, primary education, and other "channeled" priority fields;

- the establishment of preferred domestic intermediaries for diaspora giving that focus on areas of preferred donations, such as specialized government funds or specific approval authorities for preferred areas; and

- work with preferred overseas intermediaries that reflects domestic government priorities for diaspora investment, such as "authorized" or "approved" overseas intermediaries that reflect governments' priorities for diaspora giving.

Here India is a reasonable recent example, having more actively supported recent diaspora giving in the high technology, medical, and higher education sectors than in some other arenas. India also expresses preferences for certain kinds of donor activity through tax policy. Special tax exemptions are available under Section 10(23C) of the Indian Income Tax Act for organizations "considered to be of national or regional importance, or that are involved in . . . public services related to education or health." Higher tax deductions for donors are available for donations to specific projects "selected by the government" (100 percent deduction under Section 35AC of the Income Tax Act) and for donations to scientific, social science, or statistical research institutions (125 percent deduction under Section 35(1) of the Act). In India, such donations would generally be channeled through domestic individuals unless the overseas donor pays Indian income taxes and is eligible for deductions (Agarwal and Dadrawala 2004).

The New Supportive Substates

In recent years a range of subnational actors—provinces, states, and municipalities prominent among them—have become increasingly active in supporting diaspora engagement, including diaspora philanthropy, further complicating the spectrum of the supportive state. Subnational actors such as provinces and cities may formally or informally establish their own preferential policies, competing with each other (as in India, China, and elsewhere) for diaspora investment. Their activities force national governments—themselves seeking to work out their own supportive policies—to confront subnational differentiation and to determine whether to seek to control provincial and municipal activities to attract diaspora funding. "The real action is at the state [subnational] level," noted a participant in the 2006 diaspora philanthropy and global equity conference. But with the exception of some work for Mexico (Merz 2005) there is very little sophisticated understanding of subnational policies and dynamics in this area and the relationship between national and subnational policies.

RENT-SEEKING STATES AND INQUISITIVE STATES

Some states do more than offer varying degrees and types of support for compatriot giving. They act in ways that directly benefit the state itself, and that may reflect support for diaspora philanthropy, caution about it, or a sense of ambivalence. Two such forms of government activity are the *rent-seeking state* and the *inquisitive state*.

The *rent-seeking state* strives to encourage diaspora giving but also to direct a part of that giving into the state's coffers. State rent-seeking in the diaspora giving process can be accomplished in multiple ways. Some governments impose a direct tax on diaspora giving transactions, often as part of a wide range of remittance, investment, and other diaspora transactions. As one example, for many years Vietnam sought to deduct a tariff on some kinds of diaspora giving from abroad, directed to Ministry of Finance accounts.

There is, of course, a certain conflict between policies supportive of diaspora donations and rent-seeking by the state. These conflicts often reflect the differing missions of government agencies tasked with encouraging diaspora engagement, increasing tax revenues, maintaining internal security, and other overlapping priorities. A number of states that employed formal rent-seeking from diaspora givers have recognized those tensions in recent years and have sought to prioritize their various concerns. State rent-seeking can discourage overseas giving, or it can drive it "underground," beyond both the knowledge and the rent-seeking reach of the state.

In some states, balancing the increasing priority of facilitating an environment for diaspora engagement that reduces fiscal, regulatory, and other barriers against the need for fiscal revenues has resulted in a reduction of governmental rent-seeking in favor of an easier and less burdened environment for diaspora investment. In Vietnam, for example, the government has gradually decided that the twin priorities of continuing to increase overseas Vietnamese engagement, and maintaining some ability to track those activities and flows, trump revenue collection—and so, over time, by regulation and by conduct, the tariff on overseas giving has subsided.

Government rent-seeking in the overseas giving process can take other interesting forms as well. Through the establishment of preferred domestic philanthropic intermediaries, for example, the state can channel overseas giving to preferred projects or to government initiatives—a form of *non-tariff rent-seeking* at the retail level (through programs) rather than at the level of tax or tariff collection. Preferred domestic intermediaries can include national or local foundations set up as conduits for diaspora giving, or preferential arrangements with certain nongovernmental organizations.

The *inquisitive state* can be supportive or suspicious of diaspora philanthropy, and more generally of other forms of remittances. But it demands information, and collecting that data may contribute to the formulation of state policy and the channeling of diaspora contributions, or it might even discourage giving. The inquisitive state may require diaspora donors, domestic intermediaries such as banks or nonprofits, or direct recipients to report on their transfers. It may pressure local and subnational (state, provincial, regional) officials and governments for data on diaspora philanthropy and remittances, or gather data by other means. These requirements can both dampen diaspora initiative and serve to discourage innovative initiatives that might be viewed with more interest or caution by national or local authorities. If generalization in this area is possible, recent practice may be indicating a lessening of the reach of the inquisitive state as governments seek ever more actively to encourage various forms of diaspora investment, including philanthropy.

THE CONTROLLING OR RESTRICTIVE STATE

Further along the spectrum from supportive to suspicious come states that are more controlling or restrictive of diaspora giving. Here too there are many nuanced forms of government policy and action, some of which overlap with the "channeling" function noted in the earlier discussion of supportive states. States that seek to control or restrict certain forms of diaspora philanthropy are not necessarily suspicious of or opposed to such giving; they may have other, entirely understandable reasons for undertaking these policies—such as the prevention of religious strife, political conflict, or support for terrorism (see Kapur chapter in this volume). There may even be an equity component. Governments may seek to prevent inequitable allocations of philanthropic resources by overseas donors, though we see few examples of the use of controls and restrictions to effect equitable outcomes.

Some of the most common tools include controls or restrictions on diaspora giving for some or all *religious organizations, political parties or groups,* or *terrorist organizations.* Governments may seek to prevent religious or political tension by controlling or restricting donations to religious or civil society groups that promote religious or political conflict. They may undertake terrorism screening, either in a well-meaning attempt to prevent charitable funding from reaching terrorist organizations, or as a broader attempt to control diaspora giving. Controls or restrictions may be applied with a fine aim or quite broadly. They may be used to target specific and widely agreed upon dangers (such as real dangers of terrorism), or they may mask more general suspicion about diaspora giving and be used for broader control and restriction.

The specific methods vary. They include *bans* on particular areas of donor work or on particular organizational recipients, *licensing mechanisms* requiring permission for diaspora philanthropic investment in certain fields or with certain organizations (requirements that may be imposed on recipients, intermediaries, or donors), *currency requirements* that function to limit donations in certain forms or to certain recipients, and other forms of regulatory control and restriction.

A few examples suffice to illustrate the wide use of these controlling and restrictive mechanisms. *Bans* are common, but they are also sometimes easily circumvented. India, for example, bans a range of external giving for religious and political causes and groups, but still often turns a blind eye to religious giving (particularly to a range of popular temples and some extremist Hindu groups), and to giving to major political parties and their affiliates (Agarwal and Dadrawala 2004; Sidel 2004). The most famous use of *licensing mechanisms* for certain forms of overseas donations is also in India, where the Foreign Contribution Reg-

istration Act (FCRA) regulates certain forms of diaspora giving and, where applicable, requires recipients to receive either
long-term or one-time permission to receive foreign charitable
funds. The FCRA applies to giving by some Indians overseas,
but not to others (AccountAid India 2004; Sidel 2004; Agarwal
and Dadrawala 2005). *Currency requirements*—such as a rule that
donations be made in foreign currency or withdrawn in local
currency—are fading in importance but are still used by some
governments. As Devesh Kapur pointed out at the 2006 diaspora
philanthropy conference, exchange rates are a continuing barrier
to diaspora transfers.

DIASPORA ALLIANCES, WEAKENING STATES, AND THE ISSUE OF EQUITY

Governments may support diaspora giving (and broader remittances), they may seek a share of those funds, seek data, or seek
to control certain flows. But virtually all government barriers to
diaspora giving are weakening. Regulatory and political obstacles
of various kinds are gradually falling because of the need for
philanthropic funds and other remittances, the lack of political
popularity in many restrictions, the growing ease of transfers,
and, as several participants pointed out clearly at the 2006 diaspora philanthropy conference, the failures of many states to
effectively promote equitable development, resulting in the need
for diasporic intervention and increasingly agreeable states.

Some of the reasons for the weakening of state barriers,
controls, and restrictions relate directly to issues of equity in
diaspora contributions. Where, for example, states have failed in
their developmental duties, adopting favoring business investment while ignoring the needs of the poor, diaspora contributions
for public and social purposes may have a pro-equity bias given
the failures of the state. Or counter-equity diaspora giving—for
super-specialized tertiary care hospitals, for example, or business
schools that serve a narrow segment of a local elite—may go un-

challenged by a state that itself has failed in its equity duties. As Cynthia Sanborn and others point out, the developmental failure of the state has resulted in a lack of marked improvements in many countries, in Latin America and beyond, where new private wealth is spread highly unevenly and diaspora contributions are a form of private response to "state failure and state retreat."[1]

In recent years other dynamics have developed rapidly as well. In particular, new alliances have grown among diaspora givers; between diaspora donors and overseas intermediaries; and between diaspora donors and powerful local elites in receiving countries. All these give diaspora donors additional leverage in the giving process. These alliances can put sometimes intense pressure on recipient governments and can also raise concerns for equity in diaspora giving.

Alliances among Diaspora Givers

First, receiving states are faced with new alliances among diaspora donors. These groupings challenge receiving governments virtually as equals. Their demands for access to philanthropic recipients and projects are difficult to regulate or restrict. These alliances occur among the diaspora itself, and they mark a distinct change in the patterns and organization of diaspora giving.

As recently as five years ago the paradigm for diaspora giving was generally understood as individual taxi drivers, maids, nurses, and shopkeepers in overseas communities giving back as individuals or families to their homelands. This is a stereotyped image of a diaspora giver largely disconnected from peers in the country of emigration (Dugger 2000). But now diaspora givers—from taxi drivers and shopkeepers to professional, business, and other elites—are banding together on their giving, gradually creating alliances among themselves and challenges for even supportive recipient governments.

---

[1] My thanks in particular to Cynthia Sanborn and Katrina Burgess for raising these issues forcefully at the Global Equity Initiative 2006 diaspora philanthropy conference.

There are numerous examples of the potential of such alliances, in which thousands of Indian motel owners or Indian doctors in the United States have begun to pool their contributions and engage in dialogue with the Indian government through their powerful *national associations* in the United States. For the motel owners, the Asian American Hotel Owners Association (AAHOA) is the key group; for doctors, it is the American Association of Physicians of Indian Origin (AAPI), representing 41,000 Indian doctors in the United States (Sidel 2004). These alliances are not limited to what are usually perceived to be elite physicians or middle-class motel owners. Taxi drivers from South Asia and beyond have organized into groups such as the New York Taxi Drivers Alliance and the Pak Brothers Taxi Drivers Union and may also come to have a role in diaspora giving. Where diaspora donations are pooled through such groups, diaspora givers acquire additional power in the giving relationship with the receiving state—an additional power that can be used in ways that build equity or that damage it.

Two other forms of alliance among overseas diaspora givers involve overseas *hometown associations* and *new diaspora foundations*. Mexican migrants are giving through hometown associations that amplify not only the amounts they give but their influence with the Mexican state in doing so (Merz 2005; Zamora 2005; Burgess 2005; Orozco and Welle 2005). But while hometown associations have been most well studied in the Mexican context, they are active in providing philanthropy in Central America, Africa, and elsewhere, and deserve further comparative study (see chapters by Okome and Orozco in this volume).

Diaspora givers from Brazil, Jamaica, Colombia, India, Ireland, and elsewhere are also building private foundations or other organizations in the United States to amass and deliver funds. Such organizations as the Brazil Foundation (Forman 2006), the Jamaica Foundation, and many others have become or have the potential to become important players in amassing diaspora funds for development. They are also beginning to face the recipient state on a more equal basis than all but the most elite members of the diaspora. Perhaps the most well-known of all these groups is the America India Foundation (AIF), which has grown from its beginnings in providing relief after the Gujarat earthquake into a powerful force in Indian diaspora giving from the United States. AIF can interface with Indian national and state governments on a footing that only the wealthiest and most powerful in the Indian diaspora can do on their own. Alliances like these are reducing diaspora "frustration" and, in the frank words of one diaspora observer, Pradeep Kashyap, "quality controlling what the state governments are doing" through collaboration on projects.

In short, governments may need and desire diaspora funding, but some governments are now encountering considerably more powerful organizational representatives of their diasporas abroad than in the past. In general terms, the emergence of these overseas alliances and increasingly powerful organizational representatives of the diaspora pushes governments toward where they already seek to move—toward support and freedom for diaspora giving.

ALLIANCES BETWEEN DIASPORAS AND NON-DIASPORA OVERSEAS INTERMEDIARIES

The growing power of alliance in diaspora giving goes considerably further than groupings of donors abroad. Diaspora givers are also increasingly allying with non-diaspora intermediary organizations to deal with recipient governments. The result is an alliance between diaspora givers and overseas organizations with which recipient governments must often dialogue cautiously.

Over the past decade—accelerating just in the last five years—diaspora donors from the United States have begun working more closely with specialized philanthropic intermediaries that seek to grow and channel both diasporic and foreign donations.

The non-diaspora intermediaries that are part of these alliances with diaspora donors include Give2Asia at the Asia Foundation, the Acumen Fund, and a number of other such organizations; a few community foundations (particularly active with diaspora communities giving back to Mexico, Central America, and India); and in a very few cases large, traditional public charities such as Oxfam, Save the Children, Catholic Relief Services, and others.

The traditional public charities, which raise funds from hundreds of thousands or millions of donors, have come relatively late to the process of focusing on diaspora and capitalizing on the power of diaspora giving. This is despite the fact that the traditional public charities, such as Oxfam or Save the Children, often have by far the most well-developed existing programs. They have knowledge of and contacts in recipient countries, a deep and nuanced understanding of how to operate in a number of countries, an abiding concern for equitable development, and significant name recognition and trust in diaspora communities. Nor have American community foundations been as active in alliance with diaspora communities to channel funds home as they could be. The newer philanthropic intermediaries, as well as groupings of diaspora donors mentioned above, have stepped into a gap unfilled by the traditional public charities and community foundations that were initially best positioned through programs, knowledge, name recognition, and trust to serve the diaspora giving market. Yet, with diaspora giving growing rapidly in communities across the United States, there is room for public charities and community foundations to catch up—not only in order to contribute effectively to equitable development overseas, but also to engage with new donors in the United States whose generosity is, over time, likely to be shown in their American home communities as well as their original homelands.

This engagement by sophisticated donor organizations such as major public charities and community foundations can also significantly enhance the equitable nature of diaspora giving.

Groups such as Oxfam, Save the Children, and community foundations at all levels are explicitly concerned with ensuring access to the opportunities that philanthropy brings communities and measuring the impact of giving on equitable development. In many cases diaspora giving could benefit significantly from this commitment to equity, skill in program development, project planning, and impact evaluation. And those benefits could well extend to the state, as public charities and community foundations begin to serve as far more effective bridges between governments and diaspora givers than in the past, while bringing principles and tools to that engagement that may promote equitable development in state-run programs as well.

Non-diaspora intermediary organizations aligned with diaspora givers add weight to the discussions with recipient governments. Also, channeling contributions through them often changes the legal process of undertaking philanthropy back home into a well-honed and familiar procedure of relatively easy approval for gifts and grants by overseas public charities. Alliances with and giving through overseas non-diaspora intermediaries also strengthens the hand of diaspora givers by allowing them a wider range of options in their giving, such as donor-advised fund mechanisms, as well as easier access to tax deductions.

Alliances between Diasporic and Domestic Elites and Other Actors

Finally, diaspora elites abroad are now working closely with wealthy philanthropists and investors at home. They often work together on large-scale projects that relieve the state of significant service and investment responsibilities and make any potential government resistance to certain forms of diaspora giving considerably more difficult. But these projects may also have negative implications for equity in diaspora giving. In the Indian and Chinese diasporas, for example, substantial effort has been made in recent years to build major diaspora-funded educational and medical institutions at home, such as elite, tertiary specialized hospitals or business schools. These are initiatives that bring together wealthy Indians or Chinese overseas with wealthy professionals and investors at home along with investment or approval by state or national government institutions. The Indian School of Business in Hyderabad is one such initiative, and there are a number of others.

Many such initiatives—higher education open only to a very few, or super-specialized medical care available only to top payers—can only be described as satisfying the interests of elites at home and abroad. But even if recipient governments viewed them as counter-equitable in intention or result, they would be hard pressed to oppose the extraordinarily powerful alliances between diaspora and domestic elites that are making such institutions rise in India and elsewhere.

These three overlapping sets of alliances—between diaspora givers; between donors and overseas non-diaspora intermediaries; and between diaspora and domestic elites—help to put recipient governments at a disadvantage in dealing with giving from abroad. In doing so governments are in weaker positions to affect, mold, or provide input into diaspora donor decisions, or to seek—if they would wish—to counter the effects of donation decisions that are inequitable in nature. In this process, elite interests at home and among the diaspora may trump interests of equity in the diaspora giving process.

Of course, in many cases governments that have failed in the development process were never truly actors for equity in diaspora philanthropy. But the increasing power of diaspora alliances makes it even less likely that equity can play a role in government policy. In such situations the equitable aspirations of domestic donors—particularly large and well-known domestic donors with which members of the diaspora wish to engage—may prove to have more pro-equity potential than any actions by the state. In India, for example, the Azim Premji Foundation, funded and run by one of India's leading businesspeople, pushes for support for child development and local education at the K–12 level as part of its commitment "to significantly contribute to quality universal education as a foundation to a just, humane and equitable society." Its activities may have a greater role to play in encouraging giving for equity by the diaspora than anything the government may be willing or able to do.

Another recent example also shows that these alliances need not be counter-equitable in their priorities and developmental effects. The new Public Health Foundation of India seeks to mobilize diaspora, government, and domestic resources to counter the crisis of public and primary health care in India, a core equity issue there. The Foundation is the result of a partnership involving elite diaspora givers, the Indian state (in particular the Prime Minister's Office, the Planning Commission, and the Union Health Minister), and educational institutions in India and the United States. Already this alliance is growing to include powerful domestic donors as well as foreign non-diaspora donors (*Economic Times* 2006). The public health initiative may come to illustrate how the engagement of elite diasporas in domestic giving can have an assertively pro-equity bias (Public Health Foundation of India 2005; Gupta, Kumra, and Maitra 2006; Prime Minister 2006; *Harvard University Gazette* 2006).

Another seemingly pro-equity example of these alliances at work, with government support, is in the Philippines. The Ayala Foundation (US) has mobilized significant support from the Philippine community in the United States for a partnership with a "multisectoral social consortium" in the Philippines called Gearing Up Literacy and Access for Students (GILAS), which seeks to "put computer labs with internet access in all the 5,789 public high schools throughout the 7,100 islands in the next five years." This alliance between government, local corporations, local donors, and the diaspora has raised considerable resources, not least because "the Filipino diaspora . . . can choose to direct their donation[s] to a public high school in their own hometown" (Garchitorena 2006). As of June 2006, 810 Filipino schools had been supplied with Internet access through foreign and domestic donations of nearly $1.6 million (Ayala Foundation 2006).

WORKING WITH GOVERNMENTS FOR EQUITY IN DIASPORA GIVING

In light of this discussion of the role of receiving states, is it possible to find flexible but still equitable policies by national and local governments that widen the door for overseas philanthropic investment while maintaining some priority for equity in the process? Such policies are possible, but they are politically difficult to promulgate and enforce.

For example, governments can continue to provide incentives for diaspora giving while reducing regulatory obstacles of various kinds, and at the same time add specific preferences for certain kinds of giving that serve broad-based, equitable developmental goals. Government matching funds for certain kinds of diaspora giving (such as for primary education, primary health care, and other equitable development goals) could be made available, or the private or bilateral foreign donor community could seek to promote equity in diaspora giving by matching certain kinds of pro-equity diaspora giving. Domestic intermediaries could enjoy even more preferential treatment, including tax advantages, for similar sorts of pro-equity projects. Subnational authorities could be discouraged, though perhaps not effectively forbidden, from engaging in bidding wars with overseas diaspora groups and their domestic partners for certain kinds of elite-supportive projects. Governments could take additional steps to prevent diasporic giving with unabashedly counter-equity goals, such as support for extremist religious or political organizations, or for terrorist groups.

There are, of course, potential dangers and disadvantages to "bringing the state back in." A resurgent state in the arena of diaspora giving that is ineffective in its policies may repel rather than attract donors. The potential dangers include widespread corruption and the fear among diasporas that state engagement with overseas giving will inevitably increase corruption in program decisions and implementation. It is useful to remember that many overseas donors give through nongovernmental entities precisely because they are concerned with the corruption that can come with significant state engagement. Just as corruption is a cancer that saps at foreign investment—diasporic or otherwise—it can sap at philanthropic investment as well if governments are not careful to fight corruption as well as to promote equity.

A second and real danger is that states, seeing increasing flows of diaspora giving, will decide that the diaspora can fund certain basic social services that have traditionally been the province of the state, such as basic public education or public health. If the state's response to surging diaspora giving is to "outsource" governmental responsibilities to the diaspora and to local communities to seek diaspora funds, effectively treating overseas giving as a budgetary supplement for basic services, the state is abdicating its responsibilities and diasporas should resist that evasion of government roles. These are complex issues in many countries, with substantial local variation in policy and implementation, often requiring a detailed understanding of state budgetary processes and governmental responsibilities for funding basic services in an era of widespread administrative and governmental reforms in many countries. All of this argues for strengthening diaspora or other intermediaries that can, for donors who are willing, provide policy and program expertise to diaspora donors, including expertise on particular countries and even particular subnational governments and their policies.

Those governments that actively promote equity in overseas giving may encounter substantial difficulties as well. In an era of weakening state controls over a wide range of diasporic transfers—ranging from investment funds to remittances to diaspora philanthropy—there may be only so much the state can do to influence diaspora flows. Diaspora philanthropy affects recipient states, potentially improving and strengthening transparency and accountability, while reflecting loss of state influence as well. Government flexibility to allow diaspora funds in may correlate all too well with a narrowing set of policy options to support pro-equity donations, though even weakened and more flexible states should still seek to promote equity through diaspora giving where they can. As the state cedes ground to diaspora donors, it may also be ceding the capacity to promote pro-equity giving, leaving considerations of equity primarily to diaspora givers, and to the domestic organizations and individuals with which they work.

References

AccountAid. 2004. AccountAble Handbook FCRA. New Delhi: Account-Aid India (http://www.accountaid.net/).

Agarwal, Sanjay and Noshir Dadrawala. 2004. "Philanthropy and Law in India." Pp. 115–181 in *Philanthropy and Law in South Asia*, edited by M. Sidel and I. Zaman. Manila: Asia Pacific Philanthropy Consortium.

Barry, Kim. 2006. "Home and Away: The Construction of Citizenship in an Emigration Context." 81 *New York University Law Review* 11.

Bouquet, Emmanuelle. 2005. "Remittances and Financial Services." Pp. 62–67 in *New Patterns for Mexico: Observations on Remittances, Philanthropic Giving, and Equitable Development*, edited by B. Merz. Cambridge, MA: Global Equity Initiative, Asia Center, Harvard University: Distributed by Harvard University Press.

Burgess, Katrina. 2005. "Migrant Philanthropy and Local Governance." Pp. 99–154 in *New Patterns for Mexico: Observations on Remittances, Philanthropic Giving, and Equitable Development*, edited by B. Merz. Cambridge, MA: Global Equity Initiative, Asia Center, Harvard University: Distributed by Harvard University Press.

Chander, Anupam. 2001. "Diaspora Bonds." 76 *New York University Law Review* 1005.

———. 2006. "Homeward Bound." 81 *New York University Law Review* 60.

Department of Foreign Affairs [Philippines]. 2006. "Property Development Roadshow in U.S. Starts in May, Aims to Increase Fil-Am Investments, Remittances." May 12 (http://www.dfa.gov/ph/news/pr/pr2006/may/pr352.htm).

Dugger, Celia. 2000. "Return Passage to India: Émigrés Pay Back." *The New York Times*, February 29.

Economic Times. 2006. "Gates Charity to Help Set Up Health Schools." *The Economic Times*, May 31 (http://economictimes.indiatimes. com/articleshow/1598335.cms).

ERCOF. 2006. Economic Resource Center for Overseas Filipinos, Overseas Filipinos and Hometown Development: A Four-Country Roadshow. Quezon City: ERCOF Philippines, December 2005 (http://www.ercof.org).

Forman, Leona S. 2006. "BrazilFoundation: Transnational Bridging for Social Change." Presented at the Columbia University Brazil Seminar, March 23.

Garchitorena, Victoria P. 2006. "Diaspora Philanthropy in a Future of Increasing Global Migration." Presented at the Global Equity Initiative Conference on Diaspora Philanthropy and Global Equity, May 10–12, Harvard University, Cambridge.

Ghanaweb. 2003. "Harnessing Remittances for Economic Development: A Case for Remittance Policy in Ghana." September 12 (http://www. ghanaweb.com).

Gupta, Rajat, Gautam Kumra, and Barnik C. Maitra. 2006. "A Foundation for Public Health in India." *The McKinsey Quarterly*, June 30 (http://www.mckinseyquarterly.com).

Harvard University Gazette. 2006. "Enhancing India's Public Health." *Harvard University Gazette*, May 18.

Joint Conference on Remittances. 2005. "Remittances and Poverty Reduction: Learning from Regional Experiences and Perspectives." Conference co-sponsored by the Asian Development Bank, Inter-American Development Bank, Multilateral Investment Fund, and United Nations Development Programme (proceedings at http://www.adb.org/Documents/Events/2005/ADB-IADB-MIF-UNDP/program.asp).

Kapur, Devesh, Ajay S. Mehta, and R. Moon Dutt. 2004. "Indian Diaspora Philanthropy." Pp. 177–213 in *Diaspora Philanthropy and Equitable Development in China and India*, edited by P.F. Geithner, P. Johnson, and L. Chen. Cambridge, MA: Global Equity Initiative, Asia Center, Harvard University: Distributed by Harvard University Press.

Merz, Barbara. 2005. "New Patterns for Mexico." Pp. 1–18 in *New Patterns for Mexico: Observations on Remittances, Philanthropic Giving, and Equitable Development*, edited by B. Merz. Cambridge, MA: Global Equity Initiative, Asia Center, Harvard University: Distributed by Harvard University Press.

Najam, Adil. 2006. "Portrait of a Giving Community: Philanthropy as a Tool for Managing Diaspora Identity." Presented at the Global Equity Initiative Conference on Diaspora Philanthropy and Global Equity, May 10–12, Harvard University, Cambridge.

Opiniano, Jeremiah M. 2005. "Finance Experts Mull Overseas Filipinos' Investment Fund." OFW Journalism Consortium, December 15 (http://www.ofwjournalism.net/previousweb/vol4no10&11/prevstories4101.php).

Orozco, Manuel. 2000. *Remittances and Markets: New Players and Practice*. Washington, DC: Inter-American Dialogue and Tomás Rivera Policy Institute.

———. 2004. *The Remittance Marketplace: Prices, Policy, and Financial Institutions*. Washington, DC: Pew Hispanic Center.

Orozco, Manuel and Katherine Welle. 2005. "Hometown Associations and Development: Ownership, Correspondence, Sustainability, and Replicability." Pp. 157–210 in *New Patterns for Mexico: Observations on Remittances, Philanthropic Giving, and Equitable Development*, edited by B. Merz. Cambridge, MA: Global Equity Initiative, Asia Center, Harvard University: Distributed by Harvard University Press.

Prime Minister of India. 2006. "PM Launches Public Health Foundation of India." New Delhi: Prime Minister's Office (http://pmindia.nic.in/speech/content.asp?id=304).

Public Health Foundation of India. 2005. "Public Health Foundation of India—Executive Summary." Cambridge, MA: Public Health Foundation of India and Harvard School of Public Health, November (http://www.hsph.harvard.edu/pgda/Gupta%20EXECUTIVE%20SUMMARY%20of%20PHFI.pdf).

Sidel, Mark. 1997. "Diaspora Giving from the United States as a Funding Source for Indigenous Philanthropic and Nonprofit Institutions." Presented at the Ford Foundation Worldwide Philanthropy Meeting, October 14–17, London.

———. 2004. "Diaspora Philanthropy to India: A Perspective from the United States." Pp. 215–258 in *Diaspora Philanthropy and Equitable Development in China and India*, edited by P.F. Geithner, P. Johnson, and L. Chen. Cambridge, MA: Global Equity Initiative, Asia Center, Harvard University: Distributed by Harvard University Press.

———. 2004. "Courts, States, Markets and the Nonprofit Sector: Judiciaries and the Struggle for Capital in Comparative Perspective." 78 *Tulane Law Review* 1611.

Viswanath, Priya and Noshir Dadrawala. 2004. "Philanthropic Investment and Equitable Development: The Case of India." Pp. 259–290 in *Diaspora Philanthropy and Equitable Development in China and India*, edited by P.F. Geithner, P. Johnson, and L. Chen. Cambridge, MA: Global Equity Initiative, Asia Center, Harvard University: Distributed by Harvard University Press.

Young, Nick and June Shih. 2004. "Philanthropic Links between the Chinese Diaspora and the People's Republic of China." Pp. 129–175 in *Diaspora Philanthropy and Equitable Development in China and India*, edited by P.F. Geithner, P. Johnson, and L. Chen. Cambridge, MA: Global Equity Initiative, Asia Center, Harvard University: Distributed by Harvard University Press.

Zamora, Rodolfo Garcia. 2005. "The Impact of Remittances in Jerez, Zacatecas." Pp. 19–48 in *New Patterns for Mexico: Observations on Remittances, Philanthropic Giving, and Equitable Development*, edited by B. Merz. Cambridge, MA: Global Equity Initiative, Asia Center, Harvard University: Distributed by Harvard University Press.

CHAPTER 3

What Can Remittances and Other Migrant Flows Do for Equitable Development?

David de Ferranti and Anthony J. Ody

This chapter seeks to complement the volume's focus on global diaspora philanthropy by providing an overview of some key questions about migrants' remittances and related transfers. The chapter first asks how important remittances are, both in absolute terms and relative to other flows. It next investigates the contribution of remittances to equitable development, including asking who typically receives remittances and how they make use of them. The chapter then poses the question of what difference is likely to be made by access to institutional financial services on the part of remittance senders and/or recipients. An exploration of innovative types of financial transfers from migrants that go beyond the traditional individual-to-individual transaction model follows. The chapter closes with a brief summary of key policy issues—with a particular emphasis on considerations for receiving states.[1]

HOW IMPORTANT ARE REMITTANCES?

Migrants' remittances now constitute one of the most important forms of financial transfer to developing countries. Even conservative estimates show aggregate remittances to be at least equal to overall foreign direct investment (FDI) and twice the size of official development assistance.

The key driving force behind the importance of remittances today has been the growth in the number of migrants, especially of workers born in developing countries who now work in more affluent countries (whether in OECD countries, especially in North America and Western Europe, or in resource-rich countries such as the Gulf oil producers). According to United Nations data, migrants account for some 3 percent of the world's population, or around 175 million people (an estimate that, due to probable census undercounting of undocumented migrants, is more likely to be too low than too high). Migrants as a share of the population of developed countries rose from just over 4 percent in 1970 to some 8 percent in 2000.[2]

MEASUREMENT ISSUES

Difficulties in obtaining reliable data complicate any discussion of remittances. Flows that travel through "formal" channels, such as banks and money transfer companies, are the main focus of national statistical reporting. Flows passing through "informal" channels are inherently hard to capture directly and must be approached more indirectly.

Formal Flows

Even measuring formal flows places significant demands on national authorities and financial institutions, given that most individual transactions are small in nature (Orozco finds, for example, that the representative Latin American migrant in the US remits around $200 a month, representing perhaps 15 percent of their income[3]). The seriousness of the statistical effort varies greatly between countries, and there are known to be significant gaps (and delays) in reporting.

An ambitious effort to assess the overall scale of remittances—both formal and informal—was made recently by a joint World Bank-IMF team.[4] To produce as comprehensive an estimate as feasible of remittances passing through formal channels, the analysts first collated the officially reported data from all countries that were up-to-date in their reporting to the IMF. This was then supplemented by "filling-in" informed estimates for countries that were not responsive or current in their reporting.

Based on this exercise, the World Bank, in its "Global Economic Prospects 2006" (GEP), puts "formal" remittance flows to developing countries at around $160 billion in 2004 (and an estimated $167 billion in 2005).

Informal Flows

Informal flows may travel through any number of channels—from the relative or friend who carries banknotes home on periodic visits, to the "organized informal" sector, such as the (reportedly highly efficient) *hawala* networks that operate across the Islamic world. Direct statistical capture is impractical, but a variety of indirect methods have been used to estimate such flows.

One crude indicator of the importance of informal channels (at least in the recent past) is the fact that, for some countries, recorded remittances through *formal* channels increased sharply between 2001 and 2003, in the aftermath of the 9/11 attacks. This surely has to be interpreted as largely a substitution of formal for informal channels, in view of the heightened scrutiny that followed the attacks (including the greater difficulty for individuals to travel between some countries on a regular basis).

An obvious approach to estimating informal flows is to use direct surveys of remittance senders and/or recipients. In some cases, special surveys have been conducted on migration and remittances, such as Orozco's surveys for a number of countries in Latin America and the Caribbean.[5] He found, for example, that 55.6 percent of Haitians in the Dominican Republic made use of "friends or family" to send remittances, while the balance divided their business between about ten formal institutions.

In some countries—though fewer than one might hope—questions on remittances have been included in the household budget surveys widely conducted for other purposes (estimation of poverty, etc.). Such surveys are the source of the estimates shown in Table 1.

Table 1: Shares of Formal and Informal Channels in Total Remittances (%)

Country (with date of survey)	Formal	Informal
Dominican Republic (2003)	96	4
Guatemala (2004)	95	5
El Salvador (1997)	85	15
Armenia (2004)	62	38
Moldova (2004)	62	38
Bangladesh (2001)	46	54
Uganda (n.d.)	20	80

Source: Household surveys as reported in Freund and Spatafora (2005).

The range of variation is striking. In specific cases, a high role for informal channels may reflect some combination of uncompetitive formal channels and/or better-than-average efficiency within the "informal" sector.

The World Bank-IMF team adopted an alternative (and somewhat innovative) approach to estimation in their recent study (above). They first constructed an econometric model to estimate the relationship of (recorded) remittances to such variables as stock of migrants, incomes in home and host country, and—crucially—the estimated costs of sending remittances from Country A to Country B. (Such transmission costs for *formal* flows can vary widely between different pairs of countries, depending on factors such as the efficiency of, and degree of competition between, financial institutions in specific locations—a point we will return to later.) Having built this explanatory equation, the analysts then tested the sensitivity of predicted flows between different country pairs by inserting into the equation hypothetical transmissions costs assumed to approximate the plausible cost of *informal* channels. The difference between observed (formal) flows and predicted overall flows was taken as an estimate of informal remittance flows.

Applying this approach, the World Bank's GEP estimates "informal" remittance flows to developing countries in aggregate as likely to be at least 50 percent as much again as formal transfers (the underlying working paper gives a range of 35 percent to 75 percent, depending on whether the level of typical informal transactions costs is assumed to be closer to 5 percent or 2 percent). The output from the model, incidentally, replicates the finding (noted earlier on the basis of household surveys) that the estimated share of informal flows varies substantially as between different countries and regions—driven, within this model, by the varying levels of formal transmission costs in different locations.[6] Using this model as a basis, the analysts estimate the share of informal flows to be especially high to areas such as Sub-Saharan Africa and Eastern Europe and Central Asia, but much lower for East Asia and the Pacific.

COMPARATIVE SIGNIFICANCE

Even without allowing for informal flows, remittances constitute a major channel for transfers to developing countries. Table 2 gives comparative data for remittances and other international flows.

Table 2: Financial Transfers to Developing Countries ($ billions)

	1995	*2004*
Workers' remittances (formal)	58	160
Foreign direct investment	107	166
Private debt and portfolio equity	170	136
Official development assistance	59	79

Source: GEP 2006.

The apparent rate of growth of remittances between 1995 and 2004, as shown in the table, must be assumed to incorporate a significant degree of substitution from unaccounted informal to formal flows, as discussed earlier.

Country Comparisons

The above data are aggregates, and the significance of remittances is subject to wide variation at the country level. In absolute terms, the largest recipients tend to be highly populous developing countries, including India (an estimated $21.7 billion, according to the World Bank-IMF estimates for *formal* flows, in 2004),[7] China ($21.3 billion), Mexico ($18.1 billion),[8] and the Philippines ($11.6 billion). In relative terms, however, the largest recipients are often small countries with high levels of outward migration: Tonga (with remittances representing 31.1 percent of GDP in 2004), Moldova (27.1 percent), Lesotho (25.8 percent), and Haiti (24.8 percent).

Haiti provides a striking example of a country whose extreme political and economic difficulties over the years have made remittances something of a lifeline for a society with few other currently viable economic resources. Other cases of countries that have experienced extreme political stress and that rely heavily on remittances include Bosnia and Herzegovina (with remittances equivalent to 22.5 percent of GDP), Serbia and Montenegro (17.2 percent), and Lebanon (12.4 percent).

This said, it would be misleading to imply that significant outward migration, a sizeable diaspora, and the resulting receipt of appreciable remittances are in every case symptoms of national failure or collapse (economic and/or political). When a country experiences sizeable net outward migration, it does suggest that appreciable numbers of citizens believe they can find better prospects in locations other than their home country. This belief may reflect some combination of perceived differences in absolute income levels, and/or in growth rates. These differences, in turn, may stem from varying combinations of a country's natural resource endowments (small, remote island economies are often important sources of outward migration, as with Tonga), historical legacies, social capital and institutions, recent economic policy, and other factors.

At the global level, meanwhile, it seems reasonable to attribute the existence of large diasporas and remittance flows to a significant degree to the marked inequalities between countries—which, it should be recalled, are often very long-standing in nature—combined with the improved opportunities that technology and policies (*de jure* or *de facto*) have opened for individuals to cross borders in recent years. Overall, by no means should every country that benefits from remittances today be dismissed as a failed state or "basket case." Over recent years, China and India, important remittance recipients in absolute terms, have experienced some of the most rapid growth in history, and a number of important recipient countries in Central America, Asia, and elsewhere have achieved respectable-to-strong growth.[9]

HOW FAR DO REMITTANCES CONTRIBUTE TO EQUITABLE DEVELOPMENT?

In this section, we try to provide a basis for discussing how much remittances contribute to equitable development. In this context, there are various questions that can be asked about remittances—or, more generally, about any other flows to developing countries:

- How stable are flows in the short term and how sustainable over the longer term?

- What is known about distributional aspects of remittances? Who benefits? Do these flows primarily go to the well-off, or to people who would generally be regarded as poor by absolute standards? What of recipients' status by the relative standards of their own societies?

- What is known about how recipients typically use their receipts? How much of their receipts, for example, are consumed
  immediately, and how much are invested in either physical
  or human capital?

STABILITY AND SUSTAINABILITY

Over the short-to-medium term, a large number of studies of remittance flows have found them to be more stable and less subject
to cyclical variation than the other major types of flow. Indeed, a
significant number of country case studies have found remittances
to exhibit a *counter-cyclical* response to economic downturns (or
natural disasters) within the recipient country.[10]

There continues to be some debate over the sustainability of
remittances over the long term, with several different trends in
play:

a. To the extent that some migrants become established in the
    host country, their ties with the country of origin—and hence
    their motivation to remit—can be expected to weaken. The
    second generation cannot generally be expected to retain the
    same commitment to family members in the old country.

b. Somewhat offsetting this trend, in the medium term at least,
    is the tendency for first-generation migrants to improve their
    own financial situation over time, and as such to be better
    placed to remit larger amounts.

c. Over the very long term, the sustainability of remittances is
    likely to depend primarily on the extent of future migration. To
    what extent will current stocks of first-generation immigrants
    continue to be replenished by fresh cohorts? This question
    goes beyond the scope of the present chapter, but clearly
    there are considerations weighing on both sides. On the one
    hand, young workers from abroad can make important posi-

tive contributions to the economies of first world countries whose native-born populations are aging and shrinking; on the other, increasing political concerns are being expressed in some host countries about the perceived cultural impact of large-scale immigration.

Distribution

Unlike aid payments, passing primarily to governments, or FDI, entering the domestic economy via investments in hardware and software, remittances are directed overwhelmingly to private individuals. Most pass between relatively close family members. In Orozco's 2003–2004 surveys of remittance recipients in eight Latin American countries, remittances originating from a spouse were 20 percent of the total; from one or both parents, 16 percent; from a child or children, 22 percent; from siblings, 22 percent; from grandparents, 1 percent; from other relatives, 14 percent; and from friends, 5 percent.[11]

Who receives remittances depends largely on who migrates. Knowing where migrants themselves typically fit into the economic and social structure of their societies of origin gives a strong clue to the position of those who benefit from their generosity. However, it would be a mistake to assume a direct one-to-one connection between the status of the migrant and that of those he or she leaves behind, who—aside from a spouse and/or children—may include elderly parents or grandparents, and/or other family members who, whether due to youth, age, illness, disability, or other reasons, are at least partially "dependent" on the migrant, and thus may well be more economically vulnerable than the migrant himself or herself.

As a first generalization, research findings do not support the popular stereotype that representative voluntary (or "economic") migrants are drawn from the "poorest of the poor" in their home country. A 2004–2005 survey by the Pew Hispanic Center of 4,836 Mexican applicants for a consular identity document (*matricula consular*) in the US found that most had given up another job at home to move, rather than emerging from the ranks of the jobless or destitute.[12] This is plausible given that migration requires access to resources that the poorest of the poor often lack. Such resources may be financial—to pay, for example, for the costs of the journey (possibly including "facilitation" of illicit border crossings), and to cover settling-in costs at the destination.[13] But they may also take the form of human and/or social capital: the ability to navigate the various transactions connected with moving, and to offer skills in demand in the destination country, and—crucially—contacts with prior migrants who can share know-how on where to settle, how to break into the labor market, and so on.

At the opposite extreme from the "poorest of the poor" stereotype, it can be equally misleading to portray the typical migrant as invariably drawn from his or her country's educational elite. The market for migrants is a segmented one. There is indeed an international market for the PhD, the MD, and the MBA. But there is also a large market for relatively unskilled migrants to work in agriculture or construction, or help with cleaning hospital wards. According to the Pew Hispanic Center survey of Mexican applicants for the *matricula consular* in the US, 72 percent had less than a high school education, and only 6 percent had "some college or more."

A few other generalizations seem persuasive. Proximity to important labor-importing countries clearly plays an important role in affecting who is likely to migrate, especially at the lower end of the skill continuum. All else equal, relatively poor people born far from the US, Western Europe, or the Gulf are less likely to participate in the process (whether as migrants or as recipients of remittances). At the upper end of the skill market, meanwhile, it seems reasonable to propose, given everything now known about the strong role of family status and income in determining access to the best schools and other channels for advancement (especially in developing countries), that the high-end migrants are predominantly drawn from among the children of relatively affluent parents.[14]

Additional perspective into the social roots of lower-skilled migrants is given by two studies in Mexico, which found that the distributional aspects of remittances varied as between communities with a strong history of outward migration and those with few prior migrants.[15] In the latter, less well-established communities of origin, those who left were mostly drawn from families with above-average means by local standards—as such, remittances in these communities tended to reinforce existing inequalities. In communities with a well-trodden path to the north, by contrast, remittances proved equalizing, with poorer-than-average youngsters heading out. We interpret these findings as reflecting the ability of less affluent would-be migrants to tap into the established community's stock of social capital, represented by the know-how of earlier migrants, thereby lowering their own private costs of migration.

Beyond the question of who migrates, a second issue involved in assessing the distributional impact of remittances concerns variations in migrants' propensity to remit. There is some evidence that differences in propensities to remit may have a somewhat equalizing effect. A range of studies have found a higher proportionate propensity to remit relative to income among lower skill migrants than their more affluent counterparts.[16] One explanation offered in the literature is that higher-skilled migrants are more likely to take the members of their nuclear family with them more or less immediately, compared to a lower skilled migrant, who may prefer to keep his or her spouse and children in the country of origin (at least until established in the destination country). A second possible factor may be that many high-skill migrants, coming from comparatively affluent family backgrounds (for the reasons discussed above), may neither expect nor be expected to provide financially for their (relatively well-heeled) parents to the same degree as a lower-skilled migrant, whose relatives are more likely to be economically vulnerable.

In overall terms, studies based on household budget data appear reasonably consistent in finding that remittances generally have a positive direct impact in reducing poverty.[17] The studies show greater variation in their findings on the impact of remittances on *inequality*. This is to be expected from our discussion above on the variations in "who migrates?" At the same time, it is as well to recall that even families with somewhat "above-average" incomes in a typical migrant-origin community are for the most part hardly plutocrats. It can be easy for the literature to make too much of the significance of small income differences among people who mostly live in modest circumstances compared to the average citizen of a developed country.

UTILIZATION

How are remittances typically used by their recipients, and how far do they contribute to their well-being and that of those around them? Are they mostly consumed or mostly invested? How far are they used, for example, for investment in human capital, including the education of younger family members?

A standard economist's answer, based on first principles, might start by emphasizing that, assuming the recipients to be rational, their own freely taken decisions on utilization can be presumed to maximize their own expected (private) welfare. This insight should not be dismissed lightly. Whatever preconceptions outsiders might have—in favor, say, of investment over immediate consumption, or "necessities" over "luxuries"—remittances are privately owned resources, and there is no obvious reason recipients should not make at least comparably rational allocation decisions as they do with any other source of income. When the preferences of the remittance sender are added into the equation, to the extent that he or she may be able to make binding stipulations over the utilization of the funds, some recipients may feel they could have made more welfare-enhancing choices if uncon-strained. However, it is also arguable that the migrant may bring broader worldly knowledge to some of these choices than the stay-at-home. In any case, the overall impact must be assumed to be welfare-enhancing, or the recipient could presumably decline to accept the funds in view of the conditions attached.

Turning to evidence on the use of remittances, we find that in this area, as in some others discussed earlier, there are significant problems in the ability to answer the question of how remittances are used—problems both of methodology and of data availability. It might seem that the most obvious approach would be to ask recipient households how they use their remittance receipts. But caution is needed in taking literally the answers to questions of the kind "How did you spend X?" If the typical individual is asked, for example, how he or she spent his last raise at work, he may not necessarily give a meaningful answer. If the money went into the general family pot, how easy is it to answer the implicit counter-factual: what would *not* have been purchased if there had been no raise?

A better approach in principle is to derive answers on the use of remittances as a by-product from suitably designed gen-eral household budget surveys. If it were found, for example, that out of several thousand households, those with remittance income tended to spend more on school fees and textbooks than households otherwise comparable to them, it might inspire more confidence that marginal resource use out of remittances had been accurately identified than if the recipients had been asked directly. Unfortunately, as seen earlier in the chapter, relatively few household surveys thus far have been well designed for obtaining data on remittance income.

At this stage, the evidence on how remittances are used in overall terms appears problematic. One can point, for example, to studies that find the great majority of receipts being used for investment (e.g., 88 percent in Egypt, and high rates also in

Pakistan and Guatemala).[18] One can also point to work on Latin America finding the majority used for consumption (78 percent in Mexico, 77 percent in Central America, and 61 percent in Ecuador)—though this Latin American study has been criticized methodologically for being of the type "How did you spend X?"

To put both ends of this range in context, a marginal propensity to save out of *any* income as high as 88 percent would be exceptional; even if the marginal propensity to invest were "only" between 22–39 percent, this would be far from insignificant. Beyond this, there is certainly no reason to expect that an accurate answer to this question will be the same in every setting. It has been argued, for example, that migrants who expect to return relatively soon may be interested in investing in assets such as housing or a small enterprise to prepare the ground for their return (though investment in a business, specifically, *prior* to return implies the ability to trust a relative or other proxy to handle matters effectively and reliably on one's behalf), while those planning to stay away may be more concerned with supporting the level of consumption of family members at home.

Beyond this, there is a significant amount of evidence (for example, from studies of the Philippines, Mexico, and El Salvador) that remittances are often associated with higher investments in children's education, no doubt often with the direct encouragement of the migrant. Studies have also found that remittances can make an important contribution to helping ease credit constraints to the establishment of new small enterprises (Mexico, the Philippines). Finally, at the household and community level, just as at the national level, remittances appear to play a significant counter-cyclical role of helping to offset fluctuations in incomes, thus providing a degree of protection against extreme ups and downs. In some settings, though, the need is such that remittances are regularly providing only the most basic life-support or subsistence income.

Pulling It Together

To make rigorous overall judgments regarding the impact of remittances on incomes, poverty, and distribution within any particular society requires considering indirect variables beyond the direct impacts discussed so far: macro-economic variables, such as the possibility of "multiplier" effects, either positive (for real incomes) or negative (via inflation); the possibility that a high degree of dependence on remittances at the national level might induce appreciation of the exchange rate; and the possible impact of remittances on hours worked by recipients. To try to pull together not only the direct impacts (with the uncertainty that attaches even to them), but also these different indirect impacts, two possible approaches suggest themselves, either (i) large cross-country econometric studies to see whether remittance flows seem empirically to be associated with either positive or negative impacts on growth, poverty, or other key variables, or (ii) the use of economic models that might be able to simulate the interaction between different impacts.

Again, we find that, at this stage, the evidence is less than conclusive. Some cross-country studies detect positive impacts on growth and/or investment. However, a large study (of 101 countries), recently undertaken at the IMF, was inconclusive—possibly, the authors suggest, because the time frame over which some of the impacts play out is both long and variable.[19] Taking the alternative approach, simulations run on a rather simple "poverty change" model at the World Bank find remittances to have a positive impact in reducing overall poverty across countries, but it should be reiterated that the model is a basic one that does not handle all the interactions that might be significant.[20]

WHAT DIFFERENCE DO FINANCIAL SYSTEMS MAKE?

Does Finance Matter?

In this section, we seek to develop the argument that access (or lack of it) to broad, diversified, and reasonably efficient financial systems is likely to be an important contributing factor to the effectiveness with which remittances contribute to equitable development.

We start from a general proposition on the significance of financial systems for the "real" economy. Until not long ago, economists were far from consensus over whether the scope and efficiency of a society's financial sector made much of a difference to how well its economy performed in terms of such indicators as the rate of growth. However, recent empirical work has made all-out skepticism over the influence of finance on development a harder sell. Much-quoted work by King and Levine during the 1990s found a "statistically significant and economically large empirical relationship" between a country's level of financial development in 1960 and its rate of growth over subsequent decades (as well as its investment and productivity growth), even after controlling for income, education, political stability, and key policy variables. A range of subsequent empirical work has reinforced the conclusion that "finance matters" for overall growth and development.[21]

In their recent study, *Saving Capitalism from the Capitalists*, Rajan and Zingales argue that it is not just the size of the financial sector that matters, but—critically—the degree to which financial institutions are exposed to vigorous competition. Bankers who are not under much competitive pressure, they argue, settle for the easy life of working with existing types of depositors and safe (established) borrowers, rather than aggressively seeking new clients to serve, or contributing to innovation by backing the outsider with the radically new idea.

Among the evidence they cite is the "natural experiment" of state-level banking deregulation in the US. During the 1970s and 1980s, different states adopted different approaches to removing or retaining traditional barriers in the way of competition for established local bankers (for example, prohibitions to branch banking or the entry of out-of-state banks). The states that removed the barriers experienced increases in their economic growth of between 0.51 and 1.19 percent a year; those that resisted financial competition saw their annual growth rate *decline* by an average 0.6 percent. In a different context, studies of countries where foreign banks were allowed to enter the domestic market found that the access of the less affluent sections of the population improved as a result of the enhanced competition facing the local banks.[22]

Remittances and Financial Institutions

A significant amount of work has been done on the relationship between remittance senders and financial institutions in the specific context of the costs of effecting international transfers from the sender to the ultimate beneficiary. These costs have themselves attracted attention not only from analysts, but also from policy-makers (in both origin and destination countries) concerned at the steep unit costs faced by some migrants needing to send money home.

Sending remittances home can indeed be a costly business for some migrants. This is especially true for small amounts, reflecting the fact that most of the costs involved in making a transfer (such as staff time) are more-or-less invariant to the size of the sum involved. Examples cited in the World Bank's "Global Economic Prospects 2006" include an estimated cost of 21 percent of the total sum to send 40 euros between Belgium and West Africa (falling to under 4 percent as the size of the transfer reaches 900 euros), and over 10 percent to send $100 from the US to Mexico via the major money transfer companies (falling to less than 3 percent for a transfer of $500).[23]

The evidence seems clear that the transfer fees charged are highly responsive to the extent of competition among different service providers between any two end-points, as well as—more broadly—the quality of institutional (and physical) infrastructure at either end. Initiatives to remove artificial barriers to competition in this field (and to encourage transparency in what are often highly opaque sets of fees and currency exchange margins) seem to have considerable potential to benefit migrants and their families, not only by saving them the "deadweight loss" of excessive fees, but also because empirical work shows the volume of remittances to be elastic with respect to the level of transfer costs. In some countries, recent efforts to promote competition and transparency have already produced results in the shape of significant reductions in prevailing charges.

A more specific finding, relevant especially for low-income migrants, and *a fortiori* for those who are undocumented, is that transfers effected through banks tend to bear significantly lower fees than those made through dedicated money transfer companies—not infrequently around half as much.[24] It is possible that, in return, the transfer companies sometimes offer superior physical convenience (longer hours, perhaps, or denser networks in neighborhoods with a large number of immigrants, or in regions with many remittance recipients). Even so, both migrants and their families are likely to benefit from efforts to make it easier for them to access banks' diversified services—including (but not limited to) their money transfer services.

A noted recent advance has been the successful effort to induce US banks to accept the Mexican government's consular identity document (*matricula consular*) as a basis for allowing holders to establish bank accounts in the US. This program may very well hold lessons for other countries, and there are reports of some in Central America following in Mexico's footsteps.

Beyond these kinds of innovations at the policy level, increased competition for remittance business is generating a lot of commercially driven innovation. Various institutions now offer innovative card-based services—for example, joint accounts held by the remitter and a family member at home, who may be able to withdraw funds via ATMs. Numerous cross-national institutional alliances have been springing up to handle remittance transfers, involving various combinations of banks, credit unions, and microfinance institutions from different countries. Even businesses from outside the financial sector are getting involved: Philippine nationals working in Hong Kong, for example, can reportedly now use 7-Eleven convenience stores to send remittances home.[25] Businesses are even offering the possibility to send remittances in kind: in Mexico, the Philippines, and Senegal, for example, there are shops that will allow a migrant to order and pay for a television set or essential medicines to be released to a family member at home.

FINANCIAL SERVICES FOR REMITTANCE RECIPIENTS

Beyond improvements related to the act of transferring funds, there is good reason to believe that many remittance recipients, like many others in the developing world, could benefit considerably from increased access to a range of diversified and sustainable financial services. Benefits may include the ability to make better use of their remittance receipts.

Over recent years, a good deal has been learned about the difference that access to financial services can make to the quality of life of individuals and families. Muhammad Yunus of Grameen Bank, for example, realized that many poor village women in Bangladesh had opportunities to develop small-scale entrepreneurial activities, but few options to borrow the small amounts of capital required—other than from moneylenders who charged steep rates of interest. Grameen Bank and institutions like it were able to demonstrate the potential viability of microcredit—including the critical lesson that the poor did not need the subsidized interest rates that had contributed to the downfall of so many earlier government-run credit schemes.[26]

Without minimizing the importance of small loan programs, the fact remains that for most people—even among the poor—secure ways to *save* are a higher priority than access to credit. Natural entrepreneurs are a minority within most populations, yet almost everyone beyond the utterly destitute aspires to save at some point, whether on a short-term or seasonal basis, or for medium-to-longer-term purposes. A 2004 global survey by the Consultative Group to Assist the Poor (CGAP) found that, among existing microfinance institutions (accounting in total for some 750 million savings and/or loan accounts), the number of savings accounts outnumbered the number of loans by a factor of four to one.[27]

If almost everyone wants to save, all too many of those out of reach of banks or even microfinance alternatives have few good ways to do so. Savings in-kind—cows, gold jewelry—are illiquid (one cannot sell half a cow) and risky (the cow may die, the jewels may be stolen). Traditional savings clubs, known as merry-go-rounds in Kenya, *tandas* in Mexico, chit funds in India, *kibati* in Tanzania, and *esusu* in Nigeria, represent a triumph of ingenuity in coping with a dearth of institutional savings vehicles. But compared to a savings account, these clubs are inflexible, unresponsive to individual requirements, and vulnerable to moral hazard. In the absence of better alternatives, some villagers in India entrust their savings to itinerant deposit-collectors who, far from paying interest, charge safe-keeping fees of up to 30 percent on an annualized basis—a striking indicator of the cost of *not* having access to financial services.[28] Ugandans with access to savings accounts save three times as much as those without.[29]

Some of the obstacles to financial "access for all" are physical: distance, low population densities, and poor communications systems can make it hard to maintain traditional banking networks in remote regions. Some may be institutional: the typical, rather formal, bank office must appear a forbidding place to an illiterate villager who perhaps speaks only a local dialect.[30] Some can be policy-induced: "usury" laws that prevent microfinance providers from charging the interest rates needed to make their operations viable, or barriers to new competition that protect incumbent bankers. Data on access to financial services (as measured, for example, by possession of a bank or savings account of some kind) are subject to significant deficiencies, but they do show enormous variation between different countries. In some OECD countries coverage can be over 95 percent (average of 90 percent). In developing countries, by contrast, the average has been estimated to be only 26 percent, with significant variation around this mark.[31]

In countries with a reasonably competitive financial sector environment, the arrival of significant remittance flows can itself represent an important new business opportunity with potential to encourage financial institutions to improve recipients' access to banking services. More broadly, there are now signs, in countries where the policy environment is at least reasonably supportive, of an upsurge of innovation in financial services for the poor, including experimentation with new forms of institutional design and/or new technologies. To cite just a few examples:[32]

- In post-apartheid South Africa, the Postbank and the four main commercial banks launched low-cost bank accounts targeted at lower-income groups. Standard Bank launched an E-Bank program, with card-only access to savings accounts.

- India is discussing allowing different banks to offer competing services through the post office network. In Brazil, the government auctioned the right to offer banking services through the post offices. In South Africa, customers can use post office facilities to apply online for loans from any bank.

- An increasing number of developing countries now permit use of pre-paid cards, either as general substitutes for credit or debit cards, or for specific uses (e.g., phone cards). Inter alia, migrants may purchase pre-paid cards to send to family members, offering a relatively low-cost transfer mechanism, provided the home country allows for their use domestically.

- Use of cell phones for banking is now common in parts of Asia and is being explored, partially under a joint Vodafone-UN Foundation initiative, in several African countries.

- In Uganda, Hewlett-Packard is working on remote transaction systems with handheld devices.

- Grameen Bank continues to expand its product range, including introducing ten-year retirement savings accounts that pay 12 percent interest. Savers can take the proceeds as either a lump sum or an annuity.

- Banco Solidario, a microfinance bank from Ecuador, is targeting the large Ecuadorian diaspora in Spain and Italy with money transfer and contractual savings schemes marketed through locations in Europe.

- In the West African Economic and Monetary Union, a coalition of microfinance institutions and NGOs, supported by donors, successfully lobbied for reform of a "usury" law that had capped lending rates at double the Central Bank's discount rate (implying a maximum loan interest rate in 1997 of around 13 percent).

If governments provide a supportive policy environment—including, above all, policies and regulations that promote competition for the benefit of consumers, rather than protection of incumbent financial institutions—ingenuity and innovative technology can continue to extend the reach of organized financial services to many millions currently trying to manage their lives without these services.

BEYOND TRADITIONAL REMITTANCES

So far, we have focused on what might be described as the "traditional" pattern of migrant transfer: the remittance of funds between individual migrants, on the one side, and individual recipients, on the other. In this section we take a brief look at a variety of more or less innovative efforts to manage migration-related flows in a more systematic way—whether by voluntary collective groups, government bodies, or for-profit agencies—generally with the goal of maximizing the impact of such flows on development.

A recent study by Johnson and Sedaca of the relationship between migrant diasporas and home-country development provides the following useful taxonomy of different models of interaction:

1. remittances;

2. collective remittances for community development;

3. diaspora business and investment;

4. diaspora-based investment instruments; and

5. knowledge transfer/reverse brain drain.

With category (1) having provided the focus of the present chapter thus far, and category (5) raising issues that extend well beyond this chapter's mandate, the balance of the present section focuses on instruments fitting into categories (2), (3), and (4) above.[33]

Emigrants from Mexico, Central America, and the Caribbean, as well as from some African countries, have clubbed together to generate pools of resources to promote community development in their countries of origin. The most widely quoted examples are the US-based hometown associations (HTAs) of emigrants from Mexico, El Salvador, and other countries in Central America and the Caribbean. HTAs have sought to promote hometown development primarily through support for local infrastructure investments, in areas such as health, education, electrification, water and sewerage, and roads.

The aggregate of these resources represents only a small proportion of migrant-related flows—one estimate suggests that Mexican HTAs mobilized somewhat over $30 million in 2002,[34] which would have been well below 1 percent of total remittances to Mexico. Nonetheless, the potential of HTAs has attracted attention from both local governments and development agencies. In the state of Zacatecas, Mexico, the federal, state, and municipal governments each pledge to match migrants' resources dollar for dollar. The program reportedly generated some $10.9 million in HTA resources in 2002.[35] Development agencies working with HTAs include the Pan American Development Foundation (PADF) and the Inter-American Foundation (IAF).

The scale of typical HTA-supported projects is relatively small and localized in scope—in Mexico, a representative HTA may mobilize between $5,000 and $20,000. Qualitative assessments of the effectiveness of HTA efforts indicate that much depends on individual circumstances. With HTAs relying essentially on volunteers' time, effort, and know-how, the degree of commitment and expertise brought by different HTAs' memberships may vary widely. Knowledgeable sources interviewed by Johnson and

Sedaca pointed out that HTA-supported projects were in many ways similar to those funded by development agencies, and that the involvement of diaspora resources *per se* did not obviate the need to get basic issues of design and implementation right.

Significantly, the PADF and IAD programs both stress the importance of training and technical assistance to HTAs (and their local counterparts) in such areas as community needs assessment, program design and implementation, financial management, monitoring and evaluation, etc. This said, Johnson and Sedaca suggest that the most significant and distinctive contribution of the HTAs can sometimes be a cultural one: "[to] transform the political culture and local politics by energizing local activism and civic participation, as well as encouraging transparency and accountability within community and local government."[36]

Diaspora Business and Investment

The role of diasporas in helping to identify, create, and exploit new business opportunities goes far beyond the scope of the present chapter. As is widely known, after the People's Republic of China launched its economic reforms in the late 1970s, overseas Chinese communities who had already successfully developed extensive business opportunities in regions like Southeast Asia were also quite effective at spearheading massive new investment into mainland China, especially for the exploitation of new export markets. Although quantitatively on a smaller scale, the expertise of expatriate Indians is also credited as a key ingredient in the recent development of the Indian software industry. A number of other diasporas—and/or home-country governments—have taken deliberate steps to introduce greater organization and co-ordination into efforts to promote the commercial development of their homelands. Networks have been organized, for example, for overseas Lebanese, Armenians, South Africans, and citizens of the Caribbean islands.

Diaspora-Based Investment Instruments

In a number of countries, efforts have been made to develop investment vehicles specifically targeted to members of the diaspora, with the expectation that they may have a higher natural propensity to want to invest in assets identified with the "old country." The nature of these vehicles has varied quite widely. One model comprises a mutual fund ("country fund") that targets equity investments in the country of interest, and is managed by experienced investment managers (often drawn from within the specific diaspora community). The International Finance Corporation (IFC), the private sector development arm of the World Bank, has been active in helping to organize country funds in a variety of "emerging market" settings, including a number of the countries of Eastern Europe and the former Soviet Union. Even with the best management, individual country funds are by their nature "undiversified" with respect to country-specific risks, whether economic or political, and depend significantly for their success on the effectiveness of receiving state policy-makers in establishing a positive investment climate.

A different model for mobilizing diaspora resources for home-country development is the Sovereign Diaspora Bond. This instrument is issued by national governments, with the proceeds intended for the support of public programs such as infrastructure investments. Perhaps particularly when a country does not have a long track record with international bond issuance, governments may well hope that expatriate nationals, receptive to a patriotic appeal, may be less demanding as regards terms (and perhaps also less likely to bail out in trying times). Pioneered by the State of Israel in its early years of existence, this type of bond has by now been issued by such countries as Bangladesh, China, India, Lebanon, Pakistan, and the Philippines.[37] The sums involved can be substantial—India, for example, made issues of $4.2 billion in 1998 and another $5.4 billion in 2000. As yet another model again, financial institutions in a number of countries have begun to issue remittance-backed bonds, securitized by expected future inflows. Banco do Brasil, as well as banks in El Salvador, Mexico, Panama, and Turkey, are reported to have issued bonds of this kind.

KEY POLICY IMPLICATIONS

Governments both in host and origin countries have considerably increased their awareness of the importance of remittances and other migration-related flows over recent years. As this chapter has shown, remittances are by now among the largest financial flows to developing countries. Some nations, such as those under extreme political stress, could hardly manage without them. Whatever *caveats* may be raised, remittances appear, overall, to have a number of attractive features. They are generally stable, and often counter-cyclical. They put resources directly into the hands of people who are mostly poor or at least living on modest incomes. They frequently help to promote such equity-building goals as enhanced education for young people who might otherwise miss out on it.

Governments in both host and origin countries should be encouraged to continue and intensify efforts to help migrants access transfer channels that are cost-efficient and transparent. This means, in general terms, trying to eliminate any artificial regulatory barriers to wide competition among different financial institutions. It includes steps (like the Mexican *matricula consular*) to help migrants access formal financial services. Governments can also take direct action to promote transparency—for example, the British government now maintains a website that shows how much different institutions charge to send money from the UK to a wide range of overseas countries.[38]

More broadly, governments should aim to maintain financial sector policies and regulations that promote a high degree of effective competition in the provision of financial services. Barriers to entry should be viewed with suspicion, as should regulations such as "usury laws." Along with attacking regulatory distortions to the investment climate more broadly, a policy framework that allows competing suppliers to offer a wide range of financial choices is one of the most important contributions that governments can make.

Beyond this, governments and development agencies may usefully bear in mind that, both individually and collectively, migrants and their family members have their own expectations and priorities for the use of their own resources. In the wise words of a recent study, agencies that aspire to encourage migrants to make what the agencies perceive as an enhanced contribution to development need to remember and respect the migrants' and recipients' own priorities and to "meet them where they are."[39]

In a different vein, some have objected that, based on the historical record, remittances *per se* have not—in and of themselves—provided the basis for countries' achievement of "development" (itself, it may be noted, not a straightforward or unambiguous concept to define). Self-evidently, no source of financial resources can substitute for sound domestic policies, the development of capable institutions, essential public investments in infrastructure and human capital, and the other complementary measures needed to create a balanced and sustainable development process. This said, remittances do provide one important element (among others) within the overall set of resources available to support many developing countries in today's world, and directly help many millions of vulnerable people to live better lives than they would otherwise do. As demonstrated earlier, significant dependence on remittances at the country level is not inconsistent with solid overall economic performance.

The key challenge for recipient states, and for foundations and others who wish them well, will be to promote complementary measures and policies—including in the financial sector, as argued above—that will enable these important resources to be utilized as effectively and beneficially as possible. For countries that have experienced significant outward migration, remittances are no "silver bullet"—but with appropriate policies, they may at least provide a "silver lining."

Endnotes

1   The authors appreciate the assistance of Yamillet Fuentes in helping to prepare this chapter for publication.

2   World Bank 2006a: 26–27.

3   Orozco et al. 2005.

4   Freund and Spatafora 2005. The study is also summarized in World Bank 2006: Annex 4A.1.

5   Orozco et al., op. cit.

6   Note that if barriers to formality take forms not reflected in the estimated financial costs of transmission—e.g., heavy paperwork requirements—this particular model would tend to underestimate informality.

7   World Bank 2006a: 90.

8   Public discussion in Mexico typically works from a figure of around $20 billion a year for total remittances. We would re-emphasize that the figure in the text excludes allowance for informal flows.

9   The Dominican Republic, for example, which ranks twelfth globally for the share of remittances in GDP, sustained average growth of 6.0 percent over 1990–2002. In total, out of the eighteen countries in the "top twenty" with respect to remittance intensity (World Bank 2006a: 90) for which growth data are available, eight sustained average growth of above 4 percent over this extended period, and another three grew between 3 and 4 percent per annum. At the opposite end of the spectrum, three countries experienced negative growth (Moldova, Haiti, and Tajikistan).

10   World Bank 2006a: 99–100.

11   Orozco et al., op. cit.

12   Kocchar 2005.

13   According to Bouquet's analysis for Mexico, "a good *pollero* (smuggler) costs . . . as much as $2000." Bouquet 2005.

14   On the inter-generational transmission of status (and inequality) in developing countries, see World Bank 2006b; de Ferranti et al. 2004.

15　World Bank 2006a: 121–122.

16　World Bank 2006a: 92–93.

17　World Bank 2006a: 120–121.

18　For this and the subsequent paragraph, see World Bank 2006a: 127–128.

19　World Bank 2006a: 104–105.

20　World Bank 2006a: 119.

21　Useful surveys of recent work on the relationship between finance and overall development include: Levine 1997; Raghuram and Zingales 2004. For the related but distinct field of the significance of financial access to the individual, see, e.g., the survey article by Claessens 2005; Helms 2006.

22　Claessens, op. cit.

23　See World Bank 2006a: 135–157, which deals with remittance costs in considerable detail.

24　Claessens, op. cit.; World Bank 2006a: 137.

25　Hernandez-Coss 2005 provides information on a significant number of new partnerships. World Bank 2006a also has relevant examples.

26　Any good study of microfinance will cover the disastrous experience of subsidized government credit schemes (see Helms 2006, for example). Cheap credit nominally intended for the poor was almost invariably appropriated by the well connected, a culture of non-repayment typically developed, and the intermediary banks proved financially unsustainable and dependent on continuing inputs of public (and/or donor) funds.

27　Helms 2006: 24.

28　Helms 2006: 38.

29　Helms 2006: 25.

30　Several writers have produced classifications of the different dimensions of "access" to financial services—and the reasons why individuals might be excluded, or exclude themselves (see, e.g., Claessens, op. cit.).

31 From Claessens 2005, whose Table 1 pulls together data on access to banking services drawn from household budget surveys and other sources for over thirty developing countries.

32 Drawn primarily from the works by Claessens 2005 and Helms 2006 (above) supplemented for the mobile phone case by direct information from the UN Foundation. The case study of the West African "usury" law reform is from Ledgerwood 1999.

33 This section draws primarily on Johnson and Sedaca 2004.

34 The estimate, originating with an official of USAID, is quoted in Johnson and Sedaca, op. cit.: 21.

35 Orozco as quoted in Johnson and Sedaca 2004: 28.

36 Johnson and Sedaca 2004: 22.

37 Johnson and Sedaca 2004: 50.

38 http://www.sendmoneyhome.org managed by the Department for International Development (DFID).

39 Johnson and Sedaca 2004: vii.

References

Bouquet, Emmanuelle. 2005. "Remittances and Financial Service." In *New Patterns for Mexico: Observations on Remittances, Philanthropic Giving, and Equitable Development*, edited by B. Merz. Cambridge, MA: Global Equity Initiative, Asia Center, Harvard University: Distributed by Harvard University Press.

Claessens, Stijn. 2005. *Access to Financial Services: A Review of the Issues and Public Policy Objectives*. Accessible via the World Bank website.

de Ferranti, David, et al. 2004. *Inequality in Latin America: Breaking with History?* Washington, DC: The World Bank.

Freund, Caroline and Nikola Spatafora. 2005. *Remittances: Transaction Costs, Determinants, and Informal Flows*. Accessible via the World Bank website.

Helms, Brigit. 2006. *Access for All: Building Inclusive Financial Systems*. Washington, DC: Consultative Group to Assist the Poor.

Hernandez-Coss, Raul. 2005. "A Proposed Framework to Analyze Informal Funds Transfer Systems." *Remittances: Development Impact and Future Prospect,* edited by Samuel Munzele Maimbo and Dilip Ratha. Washington, DC: The World Bank.

Johnson, Brett and Santiago Sedaca. 2004. *Diasporas, Émigrés and Development*. Washington, DC: United States Agency for International Development.

Kocchar, Rakesh. 2005. *Survey of Mexican Migrants, Part Three: The Economic Transition to America*. Accessible via the Pew Hispanic Center website.

Ledgerwood, Joanna. 1999. *Microfinance Handbook*. Washington, DC: The World Bank.

Levine, Ross. 1997. "Financial Development and Economic Growth: Views and Agenda." *Journal of Economic Literature*, vol. 35, no. 2.

Orozco, Manuel, et al. 2005. *Transnational Engagement, Remittances and Their Relationship to Development in Latin America and the Caribbean*. Washington, DC: Institute for the Study of International Migration.

Rajan, Raghuram and Luigi Zingales. 2004. *Saving Capitalism from the Capitalists*. Princeton, NJ: Princeton University Press.

World Bank. 2006a. *Global Economic Prospects 2006: Economic Implications of Remittances and Migration*. Washington, DC: The World Bank.

World Bank. 2006b. *World Development Report: Equity and Development*. Washington, DC: The World Bank.

CHAPTER 4

The Janus Face of Diasporas

Devesh Kapur

While much has been written celebrating the role of diasporas, their darker aspects are becoming more apparent as well. Like Janus, the Roman god represented with two faces, each looking in opposite directions, diasporas have shown themselves to have dual natures, with sometimes conflicting identities and allegiances. Since diasporas reside outside their kin-state yet claim a legitimate stake in it, they challenge the traditional boundaries of nation states. And as actors that straddle national boundaries, diasporas have recourse to autonomous resources and values. Moreover, unlike most domestic actors, they can more easily interact with other actors across state boundaries. This chapter explores some of the negative effects of diasporas on the country of origin.

This chapter highlights three mechanisms whereby international migration and diasporas can have negative effects: economic impacts on institution building and equity, overseas networks and the flow of ideas, and long-distance nationalism. Negative economic effects can result from the absence of human capital critical for institution building. As institutions are critical for development, the long-term effects can be detrimental. And while remittances can have positive impacts on poverty, their effect on equity is more problematic. Negative effects also stem from overseas networks and the flow of ideas. The impact of the flow of ideas due to international migration might be greater than the flow of money. However, this is not necessarily positive—new skills could lie as much in the organization and techniques of violence as in new agricultural techniques. Diasporas are the key drivers of global criminal networks and contribute to increases in crime worldwide and in their countries of origin.

However, it is the related phenomenon of long-distance nationalism, specifically the greater possibility that diasporas finance and support extremist organizations (groups or parties more prone to using violence) that truly gives diasporas their Janus face, rendering their involvement in the country of origin's politics both more significant and more dangerous. This chapter will examine this issue in the most depth, looking at policies and conditions in origin states and host countries, as well as diaspora motivations, that may influence the likelihood, intensity, and types of long-distance nationalism. Finally, the chapter will explore long-distance nationalism through three case studies: the Indian diaspora, Sri Lankan Tamils, and Pan-Islamic diasporas.

DIASPORA CHANNELS OF INFLUENCE

An important question to ask before looking at the negative effects of international migration on the country of origin is how are these effects realized? One framework for analyzing these effects identifies four principal channels: *prospect, absence, diaspora,* and *return* (Kapur and McHale 2005). The *prospect* channel captures how the simple possibility of leaving the country can affect individuals' decisions, in particular their decisions to acquire human capital and invest in social capital, which may affect both the level and mix of human capital in the country. The *absence* channel measures the direct effects when some fraction of a country's population has emigrated. For instance, if these individuals have institution building abilities, their loss could have deeply inimical consequences on the country's institutions. This will be discussed in more detail below. The *diaspora* channel captures the role emigrants play from afar and is the one we are most concerned with in this chapter. The central idea is that an emigrant retains certain connections to the home country, and so should not be viewed as "just another foreigner" from the perspective of the home country. They may be more likely to transact with those in the country of origin, act as intermediaries, or send back remittances, both financial and social. The final channel through which emigration affects the country of origin is the *return* channel, when emigrants return with new skills, savings, connections, and ideas.

How are diaspora members participating in the politics of their countries of origin? In some cases they have the right to vote—whether as dual citizens or as citizens residing abroad. Perhaps more importantly, they influence the voting preferences of kin in the country of origin, an influence that is amplified if they send financial remittances (the diaspora channel). In other cases, they return and run as candidates themselves (the return channel). Where direct participation is ruled out, diasporas attempt to influence politics in the country of origin through financial contributions to political parties and candidates. The impact of these contributions will depend both on the relative magnitude of these contributions as well as the groups and parties to which they are made. The general claim is that diaspora members have greater average incomes than individuals in their country of origin—after all, why leave for a lower income? This increased wealth gives diaspora members greater potential for political influence.

Another channel through which a diaspora can affect the politics of its country of origin is through its influence on policy changes, particularly on issues where the diaspora has strong economic interests. Thus, a developing country's political economy might be affected not just by the usual sources of influence—be it the Bretton Woods Institutions, international financial markets, or the US Treasury—but also by its diaspora, in particular if the latter enjoys legitimacy and points of contact with decision-making elites in the country of origin.

NEGATIVE ECONOMIC IMPACTS ON INSTITUTION BUILDING AND EQUITY

It has become a virtual truism in recent thinking on economic development that institutions are the sine qua non of development (Acemoglu et al. 2005; Hall and Jones, 1998; Rodrik et al. 2004). But who is going to improve domestic institutions, and thus raise the development prospects of developing countries? Talented individuals—the ones with the most internationally marketable skills—are likely to be critical sources of both the supply of and demand for better institutions. International migration from developing countries is invariably positively selected; that is, the human capital of migrants is greater than those remaining behind. To the extent that this human capital is critical for institution building, and institutions are critical for development, the long-term effects of the absence of these migrants can be quite negative.

The loss of human capital can adversely affect a country's institutions in several ways. The option to emigrate could make younger people less willing to invest in skills that are most relevant to local institutions, preferring instead to invest in private sector skills that are more internationally marketable—becoming programmers, for example, rather than lawyers. Most critically, the absence of talented individuals affects the *supply* of institution builders. These are the professional classes with the managerial and technical capabilities to run schools, hospitals, banks, and government statistical systems, and to supervise road building and the like. As Fukuyama (2004:65) notes, "public agencies with poorly trained staff and inadequate infrastructure will have difficulty delivering services." The implications of the loss of scarce educated individuals may go beyond the loss of their narrowly defined human capital: it also undermines social capital, and with it the more informal parts of the country's institutional infrastructure.

In addition, absence can also impact the *demand* for better institutions. While by no means universal, historically the middle class—professionals and intellectuals—has played an important role in democratization (Kurzman and Leahey 2004). The more educated, and internationally marketable, are often better positioned to exercise "voice" and press for changes in the status quo—although it is certainly possible that highly talented individuals have a stake in the continuation of bad institutions that allow them to extract rents. Emigration can thus rob the country of influential voices for reform, especially those not in the business of rent extraction at home (Kapur and McHale 2006).

The effects of migration on equity are complex, depending critically on who leaves. Emigration with a given skill composition changes the size and composition of the domestic labor supply, and with it the distribution of incomes among those remaining behind. The absence of migrants with certain skills will have adverse impacts on income distribution due to an increase in the skill premium. Although there is now considerable evidence of the importance of remittances in reducing poverty (see World Bank survey, 2006, chapter 5), their effects on equity are more ambiguous. Indeed, remittances are more likely to amplify inter-household inequality, especially in the short run, although this may change over the medium and the long run both because of the spillover effects of remittance spending and the lower risks of migration for lower-income households. Another negative impact of migration on equity is its possible effects of amplifying regional and inter-ethnic inequality, since migrants are rarely randomly selected, but rather concentrated by towns and regions of the sending country.

NEGATIVE EFFECTS FROM THE FLOW OF IDEAS AND FROM NETWORKS

While the flow of financial remittances has received much attention, it is quite possible that it is the less visible, non-quantifiable, and intangible remittances, namely "social remittances" or the flow of ideas, that may have a more critical impact than their pecuniary counterpart. However, there is no reason that is always necessarily positive. The new skills may, for instance, focus on the organization and uses of violence. Pakistanis and Yemenis who migrated to Afghanistan to fight in the wars there, and then returned, have brought home a set of new ideas unlikely to be beneficial to their countries. Similarly, gang members of Central American origin in the United States who are deported back to their countries are much more adept in the use of guns. This has increased the levels of violence in their countries when they return.

A different way of thinking about the flow of ideas is the role of migration in changing preferences and expectations. If, for instance, migrants are drawn from elites, their policy recommendations may have a more elite bias. Most of the 40,000 physicians from India practicing in the United States are involved in lucrative high technology tertiary health care. Their skills and policy advice in India reflect these experiences, rather than address the massive primary health care lacuna in India. Low-income households in Mexico where a member is a migrant to the US appear to have more neoliberal leanings than those households that do not have any member in the US (Kapur and McHale 2005).

The network effects of diasporas are also not an unalloyed blessing. The growth of diasporas has strengthened transnational criminal networks. According to United Nations estimates, international crime is a $1–1.5 trillion annual industry, with drug trafficking, illegal arms trading, human trafficking and smuggling (especially of women and children for prostitution and servitude), and money laundering constituting the principal activities. While the impacts are large on both source and destination countries, the effects are understandably much greater on the former. These transnational links provide domestic criminal groups in source countries with substantial financial resources that are often large enough for them to emerge as significant political actors, with the power to destabilize weak states. The profits from drugs, often funneled through diasporic networks, have played important roles in the ongoing violence in Colombia, in warlordism in Afghanistan, and in Haiti's narco-coup in 2004. These activities bring in billions of dollars of revenue to source countries each year, but also increase their economic dependence on drug trafficking, prostitution, and other forms of illegal activity. Virtually all international criminal networks—whether Albanian, Italian, Colombian, or Chinese—rely upon their respective diaspora as a base for their activity.

There are several factors underlying the growing role of diasporas in international criminal activities. As with any business, international criminal activity requires enforcement mechanisms and trust, and diasporic networks can more easily internalize these mechanisms. Increased migration—much of which stems from states with weak economies and political instability—has created a large demand for both financial support and larger global networks. In many cases, the strength of such networks is compounded by diasporas' weak integration into host societies. Finally, forced repatriation of felons, such as from the US to Central America, has also strengthened international criminal networks.

Much like any international industry, many criminal networks rely upon expatriated populations to help facilitate their activities abroad. Probably the best-known organized crime group in the world is the Italian mafia, which has an extensive presence in expatriate Italian populations throughout Europe, Central and South America, the Caribbean, the US, and Canada. Other well-known examples include Russian organized crime; ethnic

Albanian criminal groups; mainland Chinese gangs and triads from Hong Kong, Macao, and Taiwan; Japanese *yakuza*; and Nigerian criminal organizations.

The Russian mafia is arguably the most educated international crime group and is particularly active in the oil and gas trading sectors and financial markets, as well as in the sale of arms overseas. With a presence in over sixty countries, it is especially influential in Eastern and Central Europe and in overseas resorts frequented by Russian speakers. Ethnic Albanian criminal groups originating from Albania or Kosovo are typically from tight-knit clans. Since the end of the Cold War they have expanded beyond their borders to become the most significant of smaller criminal groups active in trafficking drugs, arms, cigarettes, illegal aliens, and women for prostitution. Chinese organized crime has strong connections in Chinese enclaves around the world, particularly in the Netherlands, the UK, and Germany. Traditional triad groups from Hong Kong and Taiwan have been joined in recent years by mainland Chinese criminal gangs, which have expanded beyond traditional extortion, gambling, and trafficking in illegal aliens and drugs into more sophisticated areas such as credit card fraud, computer chip theft, and intellectual property rights violations. Though the Japanese organized crime syndicates known as *yakuza* mostly operate domestically, they have expanded into Asia, Australia, and the Western Hemisphere, acquiring guns, narcotics, and women for prostitution for the Japanese market. Nigerian criminals take advantage of large West African populations worldwide to operate global networks of drug trafficking as well as sophisticated, lucrative fraud schemes. Recent estimates suggest that 500 Nigerian criminal cells are operating in at least eighty countries. They are the world's most active traffickers of Asian heroin and are increasingly trafficking South American cocaine. In recent years, South American organized crime has increased as well, expanding into sectors such as money laundering and the production of counterfeit goods.

LONG-DISTANCE NATIONALISM

Most explanations of why diasporas engage in long-distance nationalism cite cognitive reasons centering on identity issues as the driving force. However, these theoretical explanations are of little help in understanding the intensity of a diaspora's nationalism relative to that in the country of origin, the intensity of one diaspora's nationalism relative to others, or what form this long-distance nationalism takes: whether ethnic or civic nationalism. Diasporas engage in the variegated forms of civic nationalism, ranging from lobbying the government of their adopted country on foreign policy to sending funds during a natural calamity. Yet they also support, to varying extents, ethnic nationalism, whose consequences can be deeply inimical but can also be easily exaggerated.

Diasporic identities range from the cosmopolitan to virulent ethnic nationalism. It should therefore not be surprising that the actions of a diaspora toward the country of origin manifest themselves in complex ways. The fact that diasporas are prone to long-distance nationalism is now well established, and indeed nationalism as a modern phenomenon of imagined communities is one that often grew in the minds of diasporic elites. The creation of Italy did not create Italians—and when they migrated in large numbers to the Americas in the late nineteenth and early twentieth centuries they did so as Sicilians, Neapolitans, and the like. Yet it was in the Americas that the narrower identities fused to form a nascent "Italian" identity (Gabaccia 2000). The act of migration and living abroad affects identities, attenuating some and amplifying others—but which ones, and why?

The role of diasporas in ethnic violence and civil wars in the country of origin has drawn particular attention given the serious implications (Shain and Sherman 1998). Historically, however, the long-distance nationalism of diasporas was portrayed in a more benign and positive light as the activity of "freedom fighters." Such was the case with Greek, Polish, Irish, and Slovak diasporas in the nineteenth and twentieth centuries, or the communities of Russian Socialists throughout Western Europe at the start of the twentieth century. Context makes an ideology appear threatening or not. While diasporas in the earlier period were fighting multinational nondemocratic empires, today they are battling democratic states and, hence, are perceived as more threatening.

The charge that a diaspora has supported a hard-line ul-tra-nationalist group in the country of origin is a familiar one. Diasporas have played a particularly important role in sustaining insurgencies. The cases of Palestinian, Irish, and Sri Lankan Tamil diasporas helping foster strong insurgencies are well-known. The sudden upsurge in strength of the Kosovo Liberation Army during the summer of 1998 at the expense of more compromise-oriented Kosovo elites may have been at least partially due to fundrais-ing efforts by the Albanian diaspora in the West. The Croatian diaspora was quite effective in helping swing the international community behind the Croats in their conflict with the Croatian Serbs in the mid-1990s. Armenian migrants in the United States fought hard in the 1990s to compel the US government to halt both its diplomatic overtures to the government of Azerbaijan and its efforts to help US oil companies secure exploration and drilling contracts in that petroleum-rich Caspian state. The ob-ject of these moves was to weaken the long-term potential of the future Azerbaijani military threat to landlocked, resource-poor Armenia.

Collier and Hoeffler (2000) find that, all other factors being equal, the risk of conflict starting after at least five years of peace is six times greater in nations with the largest diasporas as com-pared to those with the smallest. Moreover, "after peace has been restored, the legacy of conflict-induced grievance enables rebel movements to restart conflict by drawing on the support of their diasporas." Still, although their study also presents suggestive

Table 1: Diaspora Extremism since the 1990s

Conflict Country	Insurgent Group/Ultra-Nationalist/Extremist Groups	Diaspora Host Land
Afghanistan	Taliban	Pakistan
Kosovo	Kosovo Liberation Army	Albania
Algeria	Islamic Salvation Army (AIS); Armed Islamic Group (GIA)	France
Azerbaijan	Armenian separatists in Ngorno-Karabakh	Armenia, North America, EU
Croatia/Former Republic of Yugoslavia	Croatian nationalists	Croatia, Germany
Cuba	Cuban exiles	US
Egypt	Gamaat Islamiya (IG)	Middle East, UK
India (Kashmir)	Hizo al-Mujahideen, Harkat al-Ansar, Lashkar-e-Taiba	Pakistan
India	Vishwa Hindu Parishad	US, UK
Indonesia	Free Aceh Movement (GAM)	Libya, Malaysia
Israel (occupied territories)	PLO, Hamas	Middle East
Israel	Zionist Organization of America; Jewish Defense League	US
Lebanon	Hezbollah	Americas, Middle East
Russia	Chechen rebels	EU, Middle East
Rwanda	Forces Armees Rwandaises	Burundi
Sri Lanka	LTTE	Canada, EU
Turkey	Kurdish Workers Party (PKK)	EU (especially Germany)
United Kingdom	IRA, PIRA, Islamic groups	US, Pakistan

Source: Byman et al. (2001), Table A.1 and author's own additions.

evidence that diasporas are an important factor in civil wars, their importance relative to other factors continues to be disputed.

Why have diasporas emerged as important actors and supporters of civil insurgencies, militant movements, and terrorism around the world? Prior to the end of the Cold War, states were the crucial supporters providing direct military hardware, financial resources for manpower recruitment, and diplomatic support. Since then, state support for ideological movements has waned even as that given by diasporas has increased. In their survey of 74 active insurgencies between 1991 and 2000, Byman et al. (2001) found that 44 received state support of a magnitude critical to the survival and success of the movement; another 21 movements received significant support from refugees, 19 received significant support from diasporas, and 25 gained backing from other outside actors, such as Islamic organizations or relief agencies. Table 1 lists diaspora support for extremist causes (including insurgencies) in the "home country." Non-state actors including diasporas are playing a particularly important role in funding. Not only is their contribution substantial, but it is also more reliable, being less susceptible to the rapid changes that frequently characterize state support.

We will next turn to some factors that affect the likelihood and intensity of diasporic long-distance nationalism. Most studies that seek to explain why diasporas engage in long-distance nationalism point to characteristics of the diaspora, the countries of origin and settlement, and issues of identity that motivate individual action.

DIASPORA CHARACTERISTICS

It is a truism in migration studies that there is a strong selection bias among migrants, meaning that they do not reflect a randomly drawn sample from the general population pool of a country. The selection bias may refer to skills, education, age, occupation, risk averseness and dynamism, ethnic and religious selection, political beliefs, income, or regional and urban/rural selection. Often these characteristics are bundled in some groups, especially ethnic minorities, who are often more educated and entrepreneurial than dominant ethnic groups that hold the strings of political power. The expulsion of Jews from Morocco in the early 1950s and South Asians from East Africa and Myanmar in the 1960s resulted in a tremendous loss of entrepreneurial talent with all too apparent results. While migrants from Bangladesh and Pakistan to the Middle East are overwhelmingly male, the opposite is the case with those from the Philippines and Sri Lanka. Consequently, the effects on families and children are also very different. While internal migration in China has largely been from interior provinces, external migration has been from coastal provinces. It is therefore not surprising that overseas Chinese investment has been concentrated in the latter, contributing to widening regional inequality in China.

Another characteristic of diasporas that has important effects on their behavior is the time of leaving. How long a diasporic community has been out of its country of origin is important in that the greater the vintage of a diaspora the less intimate its links with the country of origin. Although this is changing due to technological advances, which have made it much easier to travel, maintain communication links, and keep abreast of various cultural media, it does emphasize the likelihood of generational differences within a diaspora.

POLICIES AND CONDITIONS IN THE COUNTRY OF ORIGIN

Conditions in the country of origin continue to mediate the nature of the interplay between the diaspora and its country of origin. Political turmoil spurs international migration and activates diasporic nationalism, which often makes an already bad situation worse. Global trends are weakening the cover of national sovereignty, and diasporic minorities in particular are playing a more activist role in their country of origin, especially where the community faces the threat of violence. One variable that repeatedly crops up is the "homeland" state's weaknesses, exemplified in so-called "failed states" such as Somalia. A recent United Nations Security Council task force warned of the presence of an "army" of jihadi fighters in Somalia, equipped with arms, "financed by remittances from Somalis abroad as well as Islamic 'charities,' smuggling, counterfeiting and even piracy off the Horn of Africa."

Where migration is a result of politics, its consequences are likely to be more inimical to the country of origin. Conflict-generated diasporas—with their identity linked to symbolically important territory, and their aspirations to return once the territory is liberated—often play critical roles with regard to homeland conflicts. Diaspora groups created by conflict and sustained by memories of trauma tend to be less willing to compromise, and therefore reinforce and exacerbate protracted conflicts. Diaspora groups may also be more confrontational than those in the homeland because members of the diaspora are less likely to pay the costs for continued fighting, while still benefiting from their sense of commitment to the cause.

In South Asia, conflicts within Punjab (in India) and Sri Lanka led the Sikh diaspora in the former and the Sri Lankan Tamil diaspora in the latter to actively support armed groups. Sikhs in Canada, the UK, and the US provided people and money for the Khalistan movement, particularly after Operation Bluestar and the massacres that followed the assassination of Mrs. Gandhi. While overseas support for the Khalistan movement has waned, overseas Sri Lankan Tamil communities continue to finance the LTTE (Liberation Tigers of Tamil Eelam, also known as the Tamil Tigers). Fair (2005) argues that an important factor in this divergence was differences in the geographical and political reach of their institutional arrangements. However, it could be argued that changes in the domestic context that gave rise to these movements in the first place were even more important. While

India succeeded in the restoration of democracy in Punjab and the elimination of militants there, Sri Lanka was unable to do so. Moreover, India critically improved the substantive and symbolic well-being of the Sikh community—by 2005 the country had a Sikh prime minister and the first Sikh chief of the Indian army, and in Punjab itself it was politics as usual. A similar case could be made of Northern Ireland, where concessions and agreements made by the British government, together with changes in the international context post–September 2001, led to a sharp decline in the Irish diaspora's support for militant groups there (see Adams 1986:131–155; Horgan and Taylor 1999 and 2003).

CHARACTERISTICS OF HOST STATES

The characteristics of the host state matter in several respects. First, Western countries are critical hosts of many sectarian diasporas for a number of reasons. They have been more open to asylum seekers and others fleeing conflicts and political persecution. As open societies, they are more prone to letting extreme ideologies alone, provided they do not promote violence in the country of settlement. Ironically, liberal policies to promote multiculturalism may have inadvertent negative effects by creating isolated and insulated immigrant communities. The very isolation of these diaspora communities renders them difficult to understand, allowing more militant groups to fundraise, prepare, and recruit with a freedom often unavailable in their countries of origin. These conditions also make it more possible for immigrants to be coerced into supporting insurgent groups in the "home" country. The PKK, or Kurdistan Workers' Party, provides a good example. Its penetration of European Kurdish communities has allowed it to exert considerable pressure on diaspora members to donate funds. As we will see later, the LTTE does the same with overseas Sri Lankan Tamil communities.

Second, host countries' foreign policies can amplify the effects of diasporas on the country of origin. Diasporas opportunistically find common ground with the host country's foreign policy goals, be it human rights, democracy, anti-communism, or more prosaic strategic goals. The actions of the Palestinian diaspora formed in the aftermath of the creation of Israel have been different if located in the US, which is very strongly aligned with Israel, or in an Arab country deeply hostile to Israel. The Iraqi diaspora in the US had little influence on the country of origin in the 1980s when the US was backing Saddam Hussein against Iran. However, once the US decided to reverse course, the diaspora became more influential. An important reason why the Haitian community in the US has much less influence than the Cuban community is the divergence (in the former) and convergence (in the latter) with US foreign policy goals.

Third, the possibility of dyadic conflict is much more likely where a host country shares an ethnic group with a neighboring country, and an ethnic majority exists in at least one of the states (Woodwell 2004). Increasingly, conflict diasporas have been pressing their claim to justice not in the country of origin but in the country of settlement. In turn this will adversely impact bilateral relations between the country of origin and the country of settlement. Pakistan's support for the Afghanistan Taliban or Kashmir stems in part from their common ethnic and religious characteristics. Conflict in the Great Lakes region of Africa (encompassing the Democratic Republic of Congo, Burundi, and Rwanda) and the Horn of Africa (including Eritrea, Ethiopia, Somalia, and Sudan) is partially related to ethnic groups straddling borders.

Fourth, host country size and wealth also matter in that they are more likely to result in a more successful diaspora, thereby increasing its effects on the country of origin. This is a function both of the success of the diasporic community within the destination country as well as the salience of the destination country. Although the Indian diaspora has been successful in East Africa and the US, the former has had little impact on India while the latter has leveraged that country's global significance.

DIASPORA MOTIVATIONS

What motivates diasporas to support long-distance nationalism? One view holds that diasporas seek to transcend the difficulties stemming from being perceived as "outsiders" in the society in which they have settled by inserting themselves even more forcefully in the troubled affairs of their places of origin. Violence is an instrument to draw attention to these conflicts, in general, and to the diaspora's positions, and demands, in particular. Thus the degree of assimilation or integration, on the one hand, and a diaspora's sense of distinctiveness, on the other, can provide the glue that binds the community together.

The conventional wisdom is that diasporic nationalism is a consequence of the failure of immigrants to identify with the host society: it fills their identity "needs" in the host society primarily because of low levels of assimilation. Thus Portes (1997) argues that the preoccupation with the country of origin is greatest among those immigrants who intend to return (such as political exiles and migrant laborers) and least among those immigrants who have made a long-term commitment to the host society (such as professionals and immigrant entrepreneurs). Others argue that ethnic identity will be salient even among professionals if they experience discrimination (Gellner 1983). Similarly, another view argues that loss of status is a driving force behind diasporic transnational political activity. Jones-Correa (1998), for instance, argues that Latino males face a greater loss of status upon migrating to the United States and consequently are more likely to participate in political activities in the country of origin.

While these theories argue that diasporic nationalism is linked to levels and aspirations regarding assimilation, Kenny (2001) argues that support for diasporic nationalism is strategically adopted by particular groups within the immigrant community as a means of generating support for their own local goals in the host society. This argument suggests that immigrants support homeland nationalism not because of their failure to assimilate, but because supporting nationalism in the homeland will advance their position in the host society. A related view holds that support for the country of origin is greatest among assimilating ethnics (Berkowitz 1997), since it is the "cheapest" way for them to maintain their membership status within the immigrant community while eschewing any commitments (especially cultural practices) that might impede their upward mobility.

Diaspora motivations differ considerably from those of state sponsors. While governments back insurgencies primarily for strategic reasons, diasporas, in contrast, are motivated largely by a desire to support a kinship group. Indeed, almost inherent to the idea of a diaspora is the notion of a homeland, whether real or perceived. Communities abroad often feel a genuine sympathy for the domestic struggles of their overseas kin and a sense of guilt because they are safe while their kin are involved in a violent struggle. As Canadian government executive Margaret Purdy has written: "Distance can make the heart grow fonder. Thousands of kilometers of separation and relative safety in a new homeland can generate romanticised notions and can obscure reality about the nature of homeland conflict." Moreover, "Diasporas do not suffer the consequences of violence, nor are they in day to day contact and accommodation with the enemy" (Purdy 2003). Insurgent groups play on both sympathy and guilt to gain financial and political support. In general, however, an insurgency's ideological bent is far less important to diaspora communities than its representation of a particular community's political and military aspirations.

Globalization and Religion

Ethnic diasporas have been empowered in recent years because of their growing size, visibility, and impact within the international system. Improvements in the accessibility and speed of long-range transportation have permitted larger migratory flows into industrialized countries, thus increasing the size of diasporas abroad. Diasporic communities now have more mechanisms to call attention to issues of interest in their home countries. The ongoing communications and information technology revolution, including the Internet, allows non-state actors to more easily fundraise, mount international public relations campaigns, or exert pressure upon governments in host countries. Global banking nets make it easier, faster, and cheaper to move money than ever before.

Although migration and diasporas are themselves a manifestation of globalization, other aspects of globalization may affect them by increasing their religiosity. There are several mechanisms that can create a positive connection between the two. For instance, Chua (2003) argues that market-dominant ethnic minorities benefit more from globalization, which breeds resentment and conflict. To the extent that ethnic and religious minorities overlap, this may increase religious conflict. Another possibility is that the secular anchor of citizenship is weaker with migrants, and hence they seek to anchor their identity with long-distance nationalism and greater religiosity. If so, would dual citizenship, by giving migrants stronger secular anchors, reshape their identity and weaken their attachment to more extremist causes? Alternatively, to the extent that there are strong selection effects in who migrates (by ethnicity and religion), remittance-induced differentials in income and consumption can rapidly reorient hierarchies in the country of origin. Note that since in poor countries even small amounts of overseas remittances can have large effects, this results in even more rapid hierarchical changes, which can drive conflict. Another variant stems from the fact that remittances are used more for consumption rather than investment. When the "conspicuous consumption of religion" occurs, through the building of new and lavish places of worship, the cognitive effects can increase inter-community conflict.

There is another possible mechanism at work among migrants. Like many people, when migrants are faced with uncertainty in their personal lives, even those who are otherwise secular can become somewhat more religious. The question is to what extent does globalization increase uncertainty and insecurity, and if it does so, is this a reason why the "secularization hypothesis"—that increases in economic development go hand in hand with increases in secularism—may be less valid today than in the past? If religion is a form of insurance, then we should see some substitution effects between secular forms of insurance and nonsecular forms of insurance (namely, religion). Therefore state weakening, or collapse, may cause religiosity to increase as the need for insurance in the midst of globalization grows.

Case Study One: Long-Distance Nationalism and the Indian Diaspora

The rise of Hindu nationalism in India in the 1980s and 1990s gave rise to charges that the Indian diaspora (particularly those based in Western countries) were supporting Hindu militant groups implicated in anti-Muslim violence within India. The anti-Muslim violence in the state of Gujarat in 2002 furthered the charge that diasporic donations had been financing the groups responsible for the violence.

That elements of the Indian diaspora are strong (indeed rabid) supporters of militant Hindu right-wing groups is not in doubt. But how widespread is the phenomenon? And how important is their support, both in propping up Hindu extremist groups and in promoting ethnic violence in India? The diaspora's role *is* important but, paradoxical and unappetizing as it may appear, its importance is not due to its principal focus, namely, its support for hard-line Hindu organizations. There have been many excellent analyses of the causes of Hindu-Muslim violence, be it a decline of social capital, electoral competition, or the (in)actions of state organs (see, for instance, Varshney 2002; Wilkinson 2004). Given the socio-economic base of Hindu nationalist groups in India, their access to domestic resources—both economic and political power—is extensive. And it would be hard to explain the rise and fall of Hindu nationalism in India by a constant, the Indian diaspora (variance in the dependent variable cannot be explained by a constant), unless we believe that there is variance in the latter as well (for a more detailed analysis see Kapur 2004).

It is *weaker groups* who want to challenge the Indian state (for whatever reason) that rely to a relatively greater extent on support from diasporas. While this argument depends on what constitutes "Indian," insofar as violence in India from overseas groups whose origins are within India's territorial boundaries is concerned, the ethno-nationalism of overseas Hindus is just one. An array of diaspora groups has been, and continues to be, involved in a range of insurgencies in India. In the northeast the United Liberation Front of Asom (ULFA), the National Democratic Front of Bodoland (NDFB), and the Kamtapur Liberation Organisation (KLO) have operated from Bhutan (until the government of that country mounted a major military operation in late 2003). The All Tripura Tiger Force (ATTF) and the National Liberation Front of Tripura (NLFT) operate out of Bangladesh, the Naga leadership has been based in Thailand, and sundry groups such as the Manipur People's Liberation Front have long operated out of Myanmar. Sikh groups in the 1980s, overseas Kashmiri groups, and even (very recently) Indian Muslims overseas have all been involved to varying degrees (Swami 2004).

The critical difference, of course, between overseas Hindus who are party to violence and many other groups is that the former are not directed against the Indian state, while the latter are. The reason is obvious. State oppression and egregious miscarriages of justice in India are not directed against the Hindu majority (the majority community may suffer from the infirmities of the Indian state but that is out of indifference and venality rather than active organized violence). The 1984 anti-Sikh and 2002 anti-Muslim riots are the most blatant examples of state connivance in organized violence and forced the communities to seek recourse from abroad. But once violence becomes a spiral, the direction of causality becomes blurred. Does the diaspora cause or react to events in India? Does communalism and violence in India make the diaspora more prone to directly or indirectly instigate violence in India? Are Hindus or ethnic minorities more militant in India or outside the country? While with all of these questions we can make informed guesses, in the absence of stronger empirical foundations, they will remain just that.

Case Study Two: The Sri Lankan Tamil Diaspora

The Sri Lankan Tamil diaspora formed during the civil war between the Tamil Tiger separatists (LTTE) and security forces in Sri Lanka, and over the past quarter-century it has played an integral role in the insurgency within Sri Lanka, with the aim of establishing an independent Tamil homeland (Tamil Eelam) in northern Sri Lanka. Overseas Tamil communities are estimated to provide around 80–90 percent of their annual income (estimated at nearly $100 million). These resources are raised across a vast global network that spans many countries but is concentrated especially in Switzerland, Canada, Australia, the United Kingdom, and the United States. In many cases people genuinely believe they are contributing to a charity, although many are also intimidated into contributing money, especially in Canada. Sri Lanka is Canada's leading source of refugees; there are more than 250,000 Tamils in Canada. The LTTE draws significant financial and political support from the Canadian Tamil community.

A recent report from Human Rights Watch found evidence of a new "aggressive and systematic fundraising drive" launched by the Tigers in Britain, Canada, and other Western countries in late 2005, coinciding with a sharp rise in violence in Sri Lanka. The report confirmed what others had been reporting for years—the culture of fear is so strong that even Tamils living overseas felt coerced and intimidated into giving the LTTE money (Becker 2006; La 2004). In London, the Tamil Tigers and groups linked to them have pressed individual families to pay them approximately US$3,000–$4,000 each. Business owners have been asked for amounts ranging from $15,000 to $150,000. Many are told that if they do not pay, they will face "trouble" when they return to Sri Lanka. Fear within the diaspora is also driven by intimidation and harassment of Tamil activists and journalists who criticize the Tamil Tigers publicly or are perceived to be anti-LTTE. Dissident Tamils are subjected to death threats and smear campaigns.

Overseas support includes propaganda to galvanize international support for the Tamil cause and fundraising from four main sources: direct contributions from migrant communities; funds siphoned off contributions given to NGOs, charities, and benevolent donor groups; people smuggling; and investments made in legitimate Tamil-run businesses. Overseas Tamil families are tapped for war taxes, whether small monthly payments from poorer families or larger ones from professionals and business owners. The system began in Britain in 1983 and has spread to other Western nations. In 1996, Toronto police estimated that nearly a million dollars a month was being raised in their city through the contribution system but the figure could easily have been double that. There is little doubt that without this economic backing, the group's ability to pursue the Tamil Eelam struggle would be significantly reduced (Becker 2006). This degree of organization and communication suggests that an effective international administration system exists among the diaspora community with many links back to Sri Lanka (Byman et al. 2001, chapter 3). In addition to fundraising for the LTTE's armed cadres in Sri Lanka, the Tamil diaspora—taking advantage of the liberal ethos of Western democracies—has been involved in sophisticated dissemination of propaganda using a variety of media forms.

In August 2006 the US government filed charges against alleged LTTE front organizations that it claimed were trying "to raise and launder money, acquire intelligence, purchase technology and military arms and equipment and improperly influence elected politicians." The weapons included shoulder-fired surface-to-air missiles and assault rifles; a $1 million bribe was allegedly offered to get the LTTE off the US government's list of terrorist organizations (Rashbaum 2006). The front organization was the Tamils Rehabilitation Organization (TRO), a global network of groups that had been on the front lines of fundraising and relief work following the tsunami that devastated Sri Lanka in December 2004.

CASE STUDY THREE: PAN-ISLAMIC DIASPORAS

In recent years the specter of terrorism has brought unwelcome attention to the role of diasporas from the Middle East and South Asia (especially Afghanistan and Pakistan). However, the difference from the previous two examples is their involvement in violence in the host country. In some cases, members of the most extreme groups might have grown up in a Western country, traveled to the country of origin, and become drawn to extremist ideology, receiving training as well. In many cases the same groups with committed cadres and ideological fervor provide charity and much needed relief work in the country of origin, supported by money raised from their diasporas. However, this work also serves as a veil of legitimacy for their less salubrious activities.

The protagonists charged with the alleged plot to bomb US-bound airliners from the UK in 2006 exemplify how diasporas have become implicated in one of the most pressing concerns in immigrant receiving countries. The prime suspect in the plot, Jaish-e-Mohammed's Rashid Rauf, was a British citizen whose parents had emigrated from Pakistan. He was also a son-in-law of Jaish founder Maulana Masood Azhar, who was released by India following the hijacking of an Indian Airlines plane in 1999. The Jaish-e-Mohammed group is linked with Al Qaeda and groups in Afghanistan and Somalia and has growing support from second- and third-generation Pakistani youth in Europe.

The charity involved in financing these plots, Jamaat ud Dawa ("Association of the Call to Righteousness"), is active in the mosques of Britain's largest cities. It played a significant role in carrying out relief efforts after the earthquake in Pakistani Kashmir in October 2005 and appears to have passed the earthquake donations raised in British mosques to the plotters (Filkins and Mekhennet 2006). On its website, Jamaat ud Dawa claimed that it has provided food to some 54,000 families who were struck by the earthquake as well as being "one of the most feared militant groups fighting in Kashmir." Jamaat ud Dawa is widely believed to be the successor organization to Lashkar-e-Taiba, which was banned in 2002 in Pakistan, under American pressure, after the attacks of September 11, 2001. It has called for holy war against the US, India, and Israel. The money raised in British mosques also went to the group's militant activities in Indian Kashmir.

Unlike other diasporas where support is mainly in the form of financial contributions, there is a disconcerting degree of direct involvement in this case. Young people going on charity work overseas are picked out by terrorist leaders to become terrorists themselves. Several of the suspects—mostly Britons of Pakistani descent—traveled to Pakistan last year, ostensibly to help with earthquake relief efforts. Although other organizations like Hamas, Hezbollah, and the Algerian Armed Islamic Group (GIA) differ in their goals, they share the close connection of significant social welfare activities with militant activities (Levitt 2006; Meehan 2004; Lia and Ashild 2001).

CONCLUSION

With the end of the Cold War and the decline of statist ideologies, there was a tendency to unreservedly valorize the role of civil society and the "third sector" in improving citizens' well-being and welfare. The role of diasporas, from diasporic philanthropy to the billions of dollars sent back as remittances, was celebrated in a similar vein. This chapter has sought to question some of the unbridled euphoria on the virtues of diasporas.

It must be remembered that citizens leave their country for a reason. And when they leave, the conditions that caused them to leave do not disappear—indeed, they often worsen. With global trends weakening the cover of national sovereignty, diasporic minorities will, in all likelihood, play a more activist role, especially where the community faces the threat of violence. To the extent that this activism is itself in the form of violence, the consequences can be deeply inimical. Ultimately, understanding the factors why people leave their country of origin is critical if we are to understand the varying behavior and effects of diasporas.

REFERENCES

Acemoglu, Daron, Simon Johnson, and James Robinson. 2005. "The Colonial Origins of Comparative Development: An Empirical Investigation." *American Economic Review* 91:1369–1401.

Adams, James. 1986. *The Financing of Terror*. New York: Simon & Schuster.

Becker, Jo. 2006. "Tiger at the Door." *Guardian Unlimited*. March 16 (http://hrw.org/english/docs/2006/03/16/slanka13011.htm).

Berkowitz, Michael. 1997. *Western Jewry and the Zionist Project, 1914–1933*. Cambridge: Cambridge University Press.

Byman, Daniel, Peter Chalk, Bruce Hoffman, William Rosenau, and David Brannan. 2001. *Trends in Outside Support for Insurgent Movements*. RAND Corporation Monograph Report MR-1405-OTI.

Chua, Amy. 2003. *World on Fire: How Exporting Free Market Democracy Breeds Ethnic Hatred and Global Instability*. New York: Doubleday.

Collier, Paul, and Anke Hoeffler. 2000. "Greed and Grievance in Civil War." *Policy Research Working Papers*. The World Bank, May.

Fair, C. Christine. 2005. "Diaspora Involvement in Insurgencies: Insights from the Khalistan and Tamil Eelam Movements." *Nationalism & Ethnic Politics*, spring.

Filkins, Dexter and Souad Mekhennet. 2006. "Pakistani Charity Under Scrutiny in Financing of Airline Bomb Plot." *New York Times*, August 14, p. 1.

Fukuyama, Francis. 2004. *State Building: Governance and World Order in the 21ˢᵗ Century*. Ithaca, NY: Cornell University Press.

Gabaccia, Donna R. 2000. *Italy's Many Diasporas.* Seattle: University of Washington Press.

Gellner, Ernst. 1983. *Nations and Nationalism.* Ithaca, NY: Cornell University Press.

Hall, Robert and Charles Jones. 1998. "Why Do Some Countries Produce So Much More Output Per Worker Than Others?" *Quarterly Journal of Economics* 114, no. 1:83–116.

Horgan, J. and M. Taylor. 1999. "Playing the Green Card: Financing the Provisional IRA: Part 1." *Terrorism and Political Violence* 11, no. 1:1–38.

———. 2003. "Playing the Green Card: Financing the Provisional IRA: Part 2." *Terrorism and Political Violence* 15, no. 2:1–60.

Jones-Correa, Michael. 1998. "Different Paths: Gender, Immigration and Political Participation." *International Migration Review* 32, summer, no. 2:326–349.

Kapur, Devesh. 2004. "Firm Opinions, Infirm Facts." *Seminar* 538, June: 32–35.

Kapur, Devesh and John McHale. 2005. *Give Us Your Best and Brightest: The Global Hunt for Talent and Its Impact on the Developing World.* Washington, DC: Center for Global Development and Brookings Institution.

———. 2006. "Cosmopolitanism and the 'Brain Drain.'" *Ethics & International Affairs* 20, fall, no. 3.

Kenny, John. 2001. "Mobilizing Diasporas in Nationalist Conflicts." Unpublished manuscript (http://yale.edu/ycias/ocvprogram/li-

cep/1/kenny/kenny.pdf#search=%22%22Kenny%22%20%22Mobi
lizing%20diasporas%20*%20nationalist%22%22).

Kurzman, Charles and Erin Leahey. 2004. "Intellectuals and Democratization, 1905–1912 and 1989–1996." *American Journal of Sociology*
109:937–986.

La, John. 2004. "Forced Remittances in Canada's Tamil Enclaves." *Peace
Review* 16, no. 3:379–385.

Levitt, Matthew. 2006. *Hamas: Politics, Charity, and Terror in the Service
of Jihad.* New Haven: Yale University Press.

Lia, Brynjar and Kjok Ashild. 2001. "Islamist Insurgencies, Diasporic
Support Networks, and Their Host States: The Case of the Alge-
rian GIA in Europe 1993–2000." FFI/Rapport 2001/03789. Kjellar,
Norway: Norwegian Defence Research Establishment.

Meehan, Howard V. 2004. "Terrorism, Diasporas, and Permissive Threat
Environments. A Study of Hizballah's Fundraising Operations
in Paraguay and Ecuador." Masters Thesis, Naval Postgraduate
School, Monterey, CA.

Portes, Alejandro. 1997. "Immigration Theory for a New Century:
Some Problems and Opportunities." *International Migration Review*
31:799–825.

Purdy, Margaret. 2003. "Targeting Diasporas: The Canadian Counter-
Terrorism Experience." Draft Working Paper, Centre of International
Relations, University of British Columbia, p. 5.

Rashbaum, William. 2006. "13 Tied to Sri Lankan Separatists Are
Charged by U.S. With Aiding Terrorists." *New York Times*, August
22, p. B1.

Rodrik, Dani, Arvind Subramanian, and Francesco Trebbi. 2004. "Institutions Rule: The Primacy of Institutions over Geography and Integration in Economic Development." *Journal of Economic Growth* 9:131–165.

Shain, Yossi and Martin Sherman. 1998. "Dynamics of Disintegration: Diaspora Secession and the Paradox of Nation-States." *Nations and Nationalism* 4, no. 3.

Swami, Praveen. 2004. "Lethal Remittance." *Frontline* 21, no. 01, January 3–16.

Varshney, Ashutosh. 2002. *Ethnic Conflict and Civic Life: Hindus and Muslims in India.* New Haven: Yale University Press.

Wilkinson, Steven. 2004. *Votes and Violence: Electoral Competition and Ethnic Riots in India.* New York: Cambridge University Press.

Woodwell, Douglas. 2004. "Unwelcome Neighbors: Shared Ethnicity and International Conflict During the Cold War." *International Studies Quarterly* 48:197–223.

World Bank. 2006. *Global Economic Prospects 2006: Economic Implications of Remittances and Migration.* Washington, DC: The World Bank.

CHAPTER 5

DIASPORA PHILANTHROPY TO ASIA

ADIL NAJAM

Asia is too large and too diverse a region to succumb to generalizations. Indeed, and especially in diaspora contexts, there is very little meaning to the term "Asian." For example, in much of the US—and especially on the West Coast—"Asian" when used in popular parlance nearly always implies a reference to people from East and Southeast Asia, e.g., China, Japan, and the Philippines. In the United Kingdom, on the other hand, the term is nearly exclusively used for diasporas hailing from South Asia, e.g., Bangladesh, India, and Pakistan. And hardly anyone ever refers to the Middle East as Asia, even though it very much is. Asians themselves tend to think of themselves and their experiences in the context of subregional, rather than continental, identities. More importantly, it is very difficult to conceive of a country—or even a small set of countries—that would be representative of the vastness and diversity of all of Asia.

Having said that—and precisely because the Asian canvas is so vast and diverse—one is tempted to draw equally broad and expansive conclusions in this review of philanthropy by Asian diasporas. In focusing on the experiences of Asian diasporas in the United States, we begin by broadly reviewing the long and diverse history of Asian diasporas and of diaspora philanthropy by them. We do this by looking at the key lessons that emerge from prior studies on three Asian American diasporas: Indian,

Filipino, and Chinese. We then move to a more focused review of the details of diaspora philanthropy by one Asian diaspora community—Pakistanis in America. Finally, in the conclusion section, we offer four lessons that are derived from the Asian experience, but which are generally and widely applicable to our overall understanding of diaspora philanthropy and its practice.

ASIANS IN AMERICA

As of 2005, according to the US Census Bureau, an estimated 13.5 million residents of the United States—around 5 percent of the total population—are of Asian descent (US Census Bureau 2005). Asians are also the fastest growing immigrant community in the United States, particularly with immigrants from China and India pouring in at unprecedented levels. As a RAND Corporation (2001) report points out:

> The Asian American population has also undergone dramatic changes in the last three decades. Since 1970 and the end of immigration limits originally imposed in 1924, the Asian American population has grown from 1.5 million to nearly 12 million in 2000 (including mixed race), and is projected to grow to 20 million by 2020. Once largely U.S.-born and consisting predominantly of Japanese Americans and Chinese Americans, the Asian American population is now predominantly foreign-born and spread across several different nationalities. As the sources of this immigration have diversified, this population has also become increasingly heterogeneous. The major sending countries include Vietnam, Korea, American Samoa, India, Thailand, the Philippines, and China. Asian Americans are only beginning to crystallize their presence as a force in America's political and cultural landscape.

Although census data can be unreliable for immigrant communities not directly mentioned on the census form, the largest Asian communities in the United States, according to the 2000 census, are the Chinese, Filipino, Indian, Korean, Vietnamese, Japanese, Cambodian, Pakistani, Laotian, Hmong, Thai, Taiwanese, Indonesian, and Bangladeshi communities, respectively. Of the largest Asian American communities, there are an estimated 3 million Chinese, around 2.5 million Filipinos, just under 2 million Indians, and around 1.25 million each of Koreans, Vietnamese, and Japanese. It should be noted that while Asians in America, as a group, are growing very fast, there is variation within this group. Quite clearly, and by a large margin, the largest growth over the last decade and a half has been in the number of South Asians (Indian, Pakistani, and Bangladeshi) and in more recent years the number of Chinese settling in the United States has also seen a steep rise (US Census 2000).

A key demographic trait of Asians in America is that they tend to be more educated and affluent than the population as a whole. Based on US Census data, Le (2006) estimates that about half of all Asians, age twenty-five and older, hold a college degree (Bachelor's or higher) and about 20 percent of this age group holds an advanced degree (e.g., Master's, PhD, MD, or JD). These numbers are higher than for any other ethnic group in the country. Asians are also more affluent than any other race group in the US, with a median household income of US$57,518. However, there is variance within Asian communities—for example, Asian Indians had reported a median income of US$68,771 per annum for 2004 while for Vietnamese Americans it was US$45,980. Le (2006) also estimates that about 46 percent of Asians sixteen years and older work in management, professional, and related occupations and that, in 2002, there were about 1.1 million businesses owned by Asian Americans, with economic receipts of around US$343.3 billion.

In short, the picture that emerges is that (a) Asians in America are a very large, highly educated, and affluent diaspora community, and that (b) national communities within this continental category are themselves significantly large and affluent. In terms of philanthropy, this would suggest that Asian American communities are likely to be institutionally well organized and economically well off. One would, therefore, expect a high level of philanthropic activity by Asian diasporas in the United States.

Indeed, there is ample evidence that the economic affluence of many of these Asian diasporas does, in fact, result in significant economic transfers to their countries of origin. The most notable exception is Japanese Americans, many of whom are now in their fifth generation in the United States and are assimilated enough to retain very minimal social or economic ties to their communities of origin in Japan (Zia 2001). For example, according to 2001 data from the International Monetary Fund (IMF 2003), India receives total foreign remittances of over US$9 billion, or around 2 percent of its GDP; for the Philippines the total amount is around US$6.4 billion but it constitutes as much as 9 percent of its national GDP; for Bangladesh the total amount is over US$2 billion, which constituted 4.5 percent of the country's GDP in 2001. Of course, as has been argued elsewhere in this book (see de Ferranti and Ody chapter), remittances should not be confused with philanthropic transfers and for none of these countries is the United States the principal source of remittances. However, these numbers do serve to suggest that (a) the diaspora communities of developing Asian countries retain and maintain deep economic linkages to their country of origin, and (b) diasporic contributions play an important, and sometimes central, role in the economic health of many Asian developing countries.

Because of the magnitude of these flows—both in terms of the net value and in terms of the proportion of national GDPs—much of the attention on diasporic contributions to the national development of home countries has been focused on remittances (see Maimbo and Ratha 2005; Terry and Wilson 2005). However, over the last few years a fledgling literature has emerged that has begun to look precisely at issues related to diaspora philanthropy by specific Asian American communities. This literature is still in its formative stages and utilizes multiple disciplinary and methodological frameworks that make robust comparative analysis—particularly in terms of comparing actual monetary flows—rather difficult. However, enough work has now been done on specific Asian American diaspora communities that we now have a fair idea of the contours of the giving patterns of these particular communities. In the next three sections we will highlight some of the interesting but nuanced findings from the available literature on diaspora philanthropy by three important Asian communities in America—Indians, Filipinos, and Chinese. In the last section we will delve deeper and in more detail into the giving patterns and motivations of another Asian American community—Pakistanis in America—before trying to synthesize key lessons for diaspora philanthropy in the concluding section.

The Indian Diaspora

Gopa Kumar's (2003) study on *Indian Diaspora and Giving Patterns of Indian Americans in the US* was one of the early attempts to empirically and systematically capture the giving patterns of Indians in America. Although it worked on a fairly restrictive sample size and some of its conclusions have since been superceded by later research, it recorded the evolution not only of the Indian diaspora in the US but also the evolution of its diaspora philanthropy. It demonstrated that this is and has been a highly organized and focused community that has systematically thought about and created institutional channels for philanthropic giving back to India. Importantly, the study highlighted two key aspects of diaspora giving by Indians in America, each of which has been validated by subsequent research (Manivannan 2006). First, that professional, regional (based on regions of origin), and religious organizations are the primary institutional formats for Indian Americans, particularly for philanthropic activities. Second, that there is a strong desire to direct philanthropic giving to development related causes in India, especially in fields such as health and education.

Various contributions in *Diaspora Philanthropy and Equitable Development in China and India* (Geithner et al. 2004) elaborated on the state of diaspora philanthropy in India and particularly on its relationship to the search for equitable development. For our purpose of understanding the broad thrust of diaspora philanthropy in the region, two particular findings from this book deserve to be highlighted. First, Mark Sidel looked much more deeply into the institutional arrangements that Indians in America had created for themselves and for this India-directed philanthropy—what he calls "Altruism's Structures." Like Gopa (2003) before him, he finds that the key mechanisms are professional associations (especially those of physicians and technology entrepreneurs), regional associations (these, however, are home region rather than hometown associations and are often based on linguistic and cultural affinities across large regions within India), and religious associations. None of this is surprising, but as we shall see later, other Asian communities do not necessarily follow the same patterns. Importantly, he alerts us to the fact that diaspora philanthropy can not only bring a large and diverse diaspora community together with a common sense of purpose and identity, but it can also highlight and exacerbate fractures within the diaspora and also within the "home" country:

> In particular, giving by and through Hindu religious groups to Hindu nationalist groups (Hindutva) in India has sparked ongoing struggle within the Indian community in the United States. And the importance of religious giving shows us just how political the issues of diaspora giving are, and how closely such philanthropy is tied to the key fissure points of contemporary India. (Sidel 2004:224)

This finding is relevant to more than just India; it is apparent in other cases that diaspora philanthropy can serve to not only maintain but also widen social, religious, and political rifts within the country of origin.

Kapur et al.'s (2004:206) survey-based research on NGOs in India highlights a different but equally relevant finding that is also applicable well beyond India: "More attention is being paid to the facilitation of raising and receiving funds and less to engaging the diaspora on the challenges that face efforts to bring about development." With all philanthropy in general, but with diaspora philanthropy in particular, we seem to constantly stumble upon a festering frustration where donors wish to be more "hands on" and involved, while the beneficiary institutions view them quite simply as "donors" and no more. Kapur et al. (2004) point out that diasporas have much more to offer than just their money and, as we find from other cases, it may well be that the bigger contribution they have to offer is their knowledge and experience rather than just their resources.

The leadership role of influential, high-profile Indians abroad is not only becoming a major theme of the diaspora philanthropy literature (Manivannan 2006) but is a—and possibly *the*—driving force behind a new generation of Indian American diaspora philanthropy. This is evident, for example, in the leadership role played by The Indus Entrepreneurs and other Silicon Valley entrepreneurs (Kumar 2003), and the American India Foundation and its co-chair Rajat Gupta (Mohan 2000).

The Filipino Diaspora

In *Good News for the Poor: Diaspora Philanthropy by Filipinos*, Jeremaiah Opiniano (2005) looks in depth at many of the same questions that confront diaspora philanthropy elsewhere in Asia and, not entirely surprisingly, often comes to similar conclusions. Of the many important points that emerge from this work, three are of relevance to us because they compare well with experiences elsewhere in Asia.

First, there is an instance where the Filipino finding is, in fact, quite different from some other places in the region. In the Filipino case, it seems that the context at both the collection and the distribution ends of diaspora philanthropy tend to be far more local. According to Opiniano (2005), hometown associations (based on the common hometowns that the donors hail from) as well as neighborhood associations (based on the neighborhoods that the donors live in within the host country) are both key to how the diaspora organizes itself for philanthropic giving. This seems like a much more local form of organization for philanthropic decision-making and much more akin to what we find in Latin America (Merz 2005) than, say, in South Asia (Najam 2006). It should be noted that the Filipino diaspora also organizes itself in other ways (alumni associations, foundations, professional associations), but in this case, unlike other cases in Asia, local institutional frameworks seem to be a primary vehicle of diasporic organization for philanthropic giving.

A second finding that should be highlighted from this case— one that *is* common to many other contexts—relates to *why* the diaspora gives. As Opiniano (2006:4) points out in a companion paper to the study already mentioned, "Filipinos' caring and philanthropic culture is brought abroad, and is then brought back here." In responding to the question of why diaspora Filipinos give back, he suggests five reasons, including: patriotism and urge to give back, sense of belonging and identity, loneliness abroad, desire to maintain ties with home country, and pride and competition within the diaspora community. This list is not unlike what the literature from elsewhere in Asia seems to suggest (Najam 2006). However, the key point to be made here is that this list can be boiled down to say that a sense of and a desire to maintain identity is a primary and overarching reason why diaspora communities give back. To view diaspora philanthropy as an "identity maintaining mechanism" leads us to a better understanding of not only why diaspora communities give, but also of what they give to, and how they wish to be involved in the giving process and in directing the use of their gifts.

A third and final point to be highlighted from the case of Filipino diaspora giving relates to what this community tends to give to. We find that there is a strong and clear preference for individual giving over institutional giving (Opiniano 2006). This, too, resonates with what we find elsewhere in Asia (Gopa 2003; Najam 2006). However, what is striking in the Filipino case, and different from the South Asian experience, is that it seems that even low-income diaspora Filipinos are more willing to form and/or give to foundations and neighborhood groups, which would then pass on their contributions to worthy causes. While the preference is for individual giving, it is not as strong a preference as this might be in South Asia. Put another way, it seems that there may be more institutional trust in voluntary groups within the Filipino diaspora than, say, the Pakistani diaspora (Najam 2006).

THE CHINESE DIASPORA

The Chinese are among the oldest Asian diasporas in the United States and have a long and distinguished tradition of giving back to their ancestral communities (Young 2004; Yin and Lan 2004). For this reason, the Chinese American experience also demonstrates better the impact that such giving can have in the long term.

> Records show that during the single fiscal year (July 1937–June 1938), overseas Chinese donations to disaster relief and social charities in China totaled more than 43.6 million yuan (around US$14.5 million). . . . Historically, the influx of money from overseas Chinese transformed *Qiaoxian* [hometowns of overseas Chinese] into remarkably 'modern' societies and made them quite different from other regions of the Chinese countryside in virtually every aspect. (Yin and Lan 2004:79)

One way in which the Chinese are very similar to the Filipino diaspora is the importance of the "home" region as the recipient of the direct assistance, both in terms of remittances and of philanthropic investments. However, in other ways the Chinese case is different from others—especially so in terms of the political context of giving. First, what we call the "Chinese American" diaspora has its ancestral roots in a variety of modern day jurisdictions—importantly, in the People's Republic, Hong Kong, and Taiwan (Young and Shih 2004). Second, the nature of the state and the economy in the People's Republic of China makes the government a far more important, even central, player in the "private" transfers of philanthropic resources (Yin and Lan 2004; Young and Shih 2004).

The state, it turns out, is very cognizant that "Chinese American philanthropic giving has played a significant role in China's progress towards modernization" (Yin and Lan 2004:109–110) and has responded by facilitating such giving. However, Young and Shih (2004:167) point out that while the state considers the diaspora "a constituency worth courting," it is worth noting that "much contemporary diasporan philanthropy appears to be bound up with . . . business relationships, although still significantly influenced by the cultural imperative of investing in and honoring the place of origin." While the Chinese political structure may be a special case, the trend toward Asian governments becoming more interested and active in encouraging and directing diaspora philanthropy is not unique to China (Opiniano 2005; Najam 2006; Manivannan 2006). This points to the importance of institutional channels for giving, as well as the level of trust that a diaspora might have in those institutional channels.

Another lesson that emerges from the Chinese American diaspora because of its longer history of diasporic giving, and which is very relevant to other Asian diasporas, relates to generational change. Young and Shih (2004:168) report that "donations came overwhelmingly from first-generation emigrants" and dwindled with second-generation Chinese Americans born and raised abroad. For many other Asian diasporas, the second generations are only just coming of age. It is likely that their experience will be the same as that of the Chinese Americans. However, in at least a few cases, it does seem that the second generation has a renewed enthusiasm for maintaining links to the country of origin; one example is the Pakistani American case, because of identity concerns heightened in a post-9/11 world (Najam 2006).

A final lesson from the literature on diaspora philanthropy by Chinese Americans concerns the evolution in the giving patterns of diasporas over time and the importance of how the diaspora itself is institutionally organized. Yin and Lan (2004:109) point out:

> New generations of Chinese Americans, of both recent immigrant and more established backgrounds, have demonstrated extraordinary abilities for networking. The channels of their giving have been expanded from personal contacts or clan and hometown organizations in traditional urban Chinatowns to broader and more professional networks based both in mainstream American society and transnational Chinese communities. . . . Donations made by Chinese Americans have moved from funding social charities and public welfare projects mainly in traditional *Qiaoxian* regions to benefiting a wide range of programs throughout China.

There are already indications that other Asian diasporas are going through similar transitions and the key question to keep track of is not simply whether the overall giving by diasporas goes down over time, but how the causes and issues that the giving is directed to change. The latter has a profound impact on equitable development and is likely to be as much a factor of how the diaspora itself is evolving as of the needs and demands from the "home" country.

To get a deeper flavor of many of these issues, let us now look at the diaspora philanthropy of a fourth Asian American community—Pakistani Americans—in much greater depth.

THE PAKISTANI DIASPORA

Pakistani Americans are certainly not *the* representative community for all of Asia. However, it may well be that some of their philanthropic impulses are representative of the philanthropic habits of other diaspora communities, especially Asian ones. In this section we will look at diaspora philanthropy by Pakistanis in America by way of examining the issues identified above in more detail. Moreover, and importantly, we want to understand not only what Pakistani Americans "return" to their country of origin, but also their non–Pakistan-related giving practices, including how they might focus part of their philanthropic energies on their adopted country.

The results presented here are mostly based on a large survey-based empirical analysis of the giving habits, attitudes, and preferences of the Pakistani American diaspora (Najam 2006). The research adopted a broad and inclusive definition of philanthropy that includes all giving and volunteering (in cash, in-kind, and in time) to and by institutions as well as individuals. Fifty-four focus groups (with a total of 631 participants) were conducted in various metropolitan centers across the United States as the primary source of contact with the Pakistani American community. A total of 461 survey forms also were analyzed.

We can divide the history of Pakistanis in America into five contiguous phases, each defined primarily by changes in US immigration regulations. The first phase is the pre-Pakistan period that began with the first wave of Punjabi men (invariably it was just men and they were predominantly from the Punjab) arriving in the mid-nineteenth century and lasted until the 1946 passage of the Luce-Celler Bill in the US Congress that paved the way for Indians—and soon-to-be Pakistanis—to acquire US citizenship through naturalization. The second phase continued from 1947 to 1965 and saw a trickle of Pakistanis coming to the US, with the beginnings of a distinct "Pakistani" community in America. This changed rather dramatically with the US Immigration and Naturalization Act of 1965, which marked the beginning of the third phase and triggered a steady and significant growth in immigrants from all over South Asia, including Pakistan. The fourth phase began in the late 1980s when favorable immigration laws and educational opportunities attracted large numbers of Pakistanis to the United States. This growth trend of the 1990s got a jolt, as did so much else in the world, with the tragic events of 9/11 and the tightening of immigration rules and practices in its immediate aftermath. The most current phase in the history of Pakistanis coming to the US is, therefore, best defined as the post-9/11 phase. (See Najam 2006 for details.)

There are an estimated 500,000 Pakistanis in America. The majority of them live along the East Coast of the US; New York City has by far the largest number of Pakistani Americans, while Houston, Washington, DC, Chicago, and Los Angeles also have very large concentrations of Pakistanis; and comparatively smaller but sizeable populations of Pakistanis are found in just about every major metropolitan city in the US. Pakistanis in America are a relatively new and relatively young community of immigrants. It is a community that has large numbers of highly trained professionals and is economically well off, with higher household incomes than the national average (Embassy of Pakistan 2003).

The analysis highlights two important characteristics of Pakistani Americans as an immigrant community in a country full of immigrant communities. First, Pakistani Americans have developed strong ties to America. Just under 75 percent of Pakistanis living in America already have US citizenship (through naturalization or birth) or permanent resident status. In short, Pakistani Americans are eager and active in maintaining their links to Pakistan, but this is a community that is also eager to make the US its permanent home. Second, Pakistani Americans are a fairly recent and still fledgling immigrant community. Three-fourths of Pakistani Americans (just over 75 percent) have themselves immigrated to the US ("first-generation immigrants") and only 25 percent are US-born citizens. Indeed, half of all Pakistanis who have immigrated between 1947 and 2004 did so during or after 1993, and one in every four (25 percent) has arrived in the last five years (1999–2004).

Giving Trends

The average giving—in terms of money and goods—for Pakistani households in America is around $2,500 per household per year, while the average Pakistani household in America contributes around 435 hours per year of volunteer time (Najam 2006). This suggests that Pakistanis in America donate approximately a total of $250 million in cash and in-kind and the equivalent of $750 million in volunteered time; or an estimated total of $1 billion in cash, in-kind, and in time volunteered.

It should be stressed that any gross numbers based on an opinion survey need to be interpreted with a measure of caution. Philanthropy studies in general are not suited to exactitude (Toppe et al. 2002). However, there are a number of features of the finding that are noteworthy.

Of the $250 million that we estimate as the total annual giving in cash and in-kind, about 80 percent ($200 million) is given as monetary contributions and the remaining 20 percent ($50 million) as an in-kind philanthropic contribution of goods. In terms of what motivates this giving, the total amount is split nearly evenly between faith-motivated and issue-motivated giving. Another way to cut the same pie is to note that around $100 million (40 percent) of this contribution goes directly to Pakistani causes in Pakistan. Another $50 million (20 percent) goes to Pakistani causes in the United States and the remaining 40 percent ($100 million) goes to causes unrelated to Pakistan.

Figure 1: Estimated Total Annual Giving by Pakistanis in America
(Giving in money, goods, and time)
Total ~ $1 billion

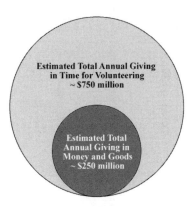

The monetary value of the estimated 435 hours of volunteered time per Pakistani household in America comes out to be around $750 million (Figure 1). This equals a total of 43.5 million hours per year volunteered by 100,000 Pakistani households, representing the equivalent of over 25,000 full-time employees. Much of this volunteered work may well be supplemental labor, and it is clear that volunteers fill in for work that would otherwise be done by paid workers. However, it is also clear that the vast network of Pakistan-related organizations could not operate without this massive investment of volunteered time by Pakistanis in America.

The overall findings suggest that Pakistanis in America are a generous and active community. Moreover, they suggest that while the community retains a deep commitment to "Pakistani" causes, their philanthropic interests are not confined to causes in Pakistan. Like the rest of America, faith is an important motivator of the giving habits of Pakistani Americans; but even more significantly, issue-motivated philanthropy constitutes an equally large proportion of their giving. Although this was not part of the research, every indication suggests that the trends for

Table 1: Issues That Pakistanis in America Consider Most Important

Percentage of respondents who considered this to be one of their three most important issues
(Totals add up to more than 100 because each respondent was allowed three choices)

Pakistani Causes Based in US	Pakistani Causes Based in Pakistan	Causes Unrelated to Pakistan	TOTAL (across causes)
#1. Community Development (36%)	#1. Poverty/Helping the Needy (62%)	#1. Religion (51%)	**#1. Poverty/Helping the Needy (29%)**
#2. Civil and Human Rights (34%)	#2. Education and Literacy (39%)	#2. Civil and Human Rights (39%)	**#2. Civil and Human Rights (25%)**
#3. Poverty/Helping the Needy (18%)	#3. Health (27%)	#3. Community Development (17%)	**#3. Religion (25%)**
#4. Political Mobilization (17%)	#4. Human Development (12%)	#4. Poverty/Helping the Needy (16%)	**#4. Education and Literacy (21%)**
#5. Arts, Culture, and Sports (14%)	#5. Religion (11%)	#5. Political Mobilization (15%)	**#5. Community Development (18%)**

other Asian diaspora communities—especially for South Asian diaspora communities—would be quite similar.

The survey also asked respondents to identify the three most important issues that they usually contribute to. An overwhelming result that emerges is that social issues—including poverty reduction and helping the needy, education, health, etcetera—are by far the most important issues for Pakistanis in America. Looking first at overall results for the entire sample, we find that the issue of poverty and helping the needy emerges as the top priority for Pakistanis in America, with 29 percent of respondents including it as one of their top three most important issues (Table 1). Each of two issues—civil and human rights and religion—is identified by about a quarter of respondents as among the most important issues that they contribute to. It should be noted that here they are referring to religion as an issue that they give to rather than as a motivation that inspires them to give. Following closely behind are the issues of education and literacy and of community development, which are identified by 21 and 18 percent, respectively, as being among their top three most important issues in terms of philanthropic giving. (See Najam 2006 for details.)

What is even more interesting, however, is how this list gets shuffled when we try to look at the most important issues by cause. For example, community development (meaning the development of the Pakistani community in the US) is identified by 36 percent of our respondents as among the most important issues in terms of their giving to Pakistani causes in the US. What is more interesting is that as much as 34 percent of respondents list civil and human rights as one of their most important issues in this category. This is quite obviously a result of the post-9/11 climate of fear that Muslim Americans find themselves in and the mounting threats that they perceive to their civil and human rights.

When one looks at the issues identified as being most important in terms of Pakistani causes based in Pakistan, the most striking finding is how strongly the Pakistani diaspora is focused on issues related to social development. Not only do 62 percent consider poverty reduction and helping the needy to be among their three most important issues for philanthropic giving, but the next three issues—education and literacy (39 percent), health (27 percent), and human development (12 percent)—are also all related to socio-economic development. Interesting, the issue of religion comes in at a rather distant fifth with only 11 percent of the respondents including it in their top three most important issues for giving to Pakistani causes in Pakistan.

The picture changes yet again when one looks at the issues that our respondents consider important for causes unrelated to Pakistan. The most often mentioned issue in this category is religion (51 percent). Based on the discussions we heard during the focus group meetings, it is clear that this refers primarily to giving related to the building, running, and maintenance of places of worship in the United States. Following rather close behind is the issue of civil and human rights, which is identified as important by 39 percent of respondents.

An interesting result related to the survey question that asked respondents to state whether their household's giving had decreased, increased, or stayed the same since September 2001, for each of the three types of causes (Pakistani causes in the US, Pakistani causes in Pakistan, and causes unrelated to Pakistan). In looking at the aggregate of all the responses received across the three cause types, we find that 62 percent of respondents report that their giving patterns have remained the same, 14 percent report a decrease in their giving, while 24 percent report an increase.

Trends from Pakistan

There are, of course, a whole host of findings from this study, but seven major trends are worth highlighting here because they are likely to be particularly relevant to other Asian diasporas.

First, as already noted, Pakistani Americans are a generous, giving, and active community. Although this is a relatively affluent community, we find that charitable instincts are spread across all income classes. On average, the Pakistani American household contributes 3.5 percent of its income to philanthropic giving, which compares very favorably with the giving habits of the average American household and with the average Pakistani household in Pakistan. Given these findings, it is both striking and surprising that the community suffers from a strong sense of "philanthropic inferiority," with many Pakistani Americans believing that they are not very philanthropically active and with most feeling that the community's giving is not strategically directed.

Second, there is a strong preference for giving directly to individuals in need. By a very clear margin, the single largest chunk of overall giving by Pakistanis in America goes directly to individuals in immediate need, rather than to institutions and organized charities. There is a very strongly held belief among Pakistani Americans that giving directly to the needy and the deserving is superior to institutional giving. This belief comes from (a) cultural and social habits that people have grown up with, (b) a rather deep sense of distrust in the honesty, efficiency, or effectiveness of organized charities and NGOs, (c) a sense that direct giving encourages greater accountability, and (d) a feeling that more of the contribution will reach and benefit the deserving. Kinship networks of friends and extended family (as opposed to organized charities) play a critical role in this direct giving to needy individuals. Importantly, however, although much of the charitable giving going to Pakistan goes directly to needy individuals, the vast majority of the contributions made in the US do not. This may simply be a case of the much greater availability of, and access to, deserving and needy individuals in Pakistan.

Third, people are motivated by faith, but mostly give to social issues. The desire to help individuals in need, including the needy within one's extended kinship networks, is by far the most important reason why Pakistani Americans give. In fact, this is cited as an even more important reason to give than the motivation of faith. Social issues—especially the issue of poverty and helping the needy but also including education, health, civil and human rights, and community development—are among the most cited issues that people contribute to and wish to contribute to. Like other communities in the US, Pakistani Americans have a strong sense of a moral duty to be charitable that is motivated by their faith. However, the responses received suggest that they channel far *less* of their contributions to religious organizations than Americans in general. Instead, more of their faith-motivated giving is channeled directly to poor and deserving individuals in dire need. Interestingly, linguistic and locational identities do not tend to play a significant role in philanthropic giving by Pakistani Americans, even though they seem to impact the giving of other Pakistani diasporas (for example, in the United Kingdom or in the Middle East). This may be because the number of Pakistanis in America is still small enough, dispersed enough across the US, and linguistically homogeneous enough that they do not divide into smaller subdiasporic communities. There are some exceptions to this—such as Pakistani Christians, Pakistani Zoroastrians, and Sindhis—but they are fairly small groups.

Fourth, the philanthropy of Pakistani Americans is not limited to Pakistan. Although the giving of the Pakistani diaspora is firmly rooted in its "Pakistani" identity, this is not the only identity that pulls at its philanthropic generosity. An estimated 40 percent of the monetary and in-kind giving by the Pakistani diaspora goes to Pakistani causes in Pakistan, another 20 percent to Pakistani causes in the US, and the remaining 40 percent to causes unrelated to Pakistan. Two important trends should be highlighted here. First, the longer someone has lived in the US, the more likely they are to give a larger proportion of their philanthropy to causes unrelated to Pakistan. However, they tend to do so by diverting additional philanthropic resources to non–Pakistan-related causes and without necessarily reducing their giving to causes in Pakistan. Second, largely as a result of post-9/11 effects, the Pakistani diaspora in America is becoming increasingly active in US-based philanthropy, including in mainstream US charitable organizations.

Fifth, 9/11 made the Pakistani diaspora more vigilant, but not less giving. There is grave and justifiable concern within the diaspora that the tragic events of September 11, 2001, have had a serious and debilitating impact on the Pakistani American community. There is unease about the potential impacts of post-9/11 government policies and how these might impact giving by all immigrant communities and especially Muslim communities in America. However, the unease comes not as much from what the policies are but from the uncertainty and lack of clarity about them. Despite this very strong sense of unease, there is no evidence—either in the survey results or in focus group discussions—that Pakistani Americans have actually stopped giving or decreased their giving. Instead, the clear and unambiguous finding is that people have become extremely careful and vigilant in terms of who they give to, how they give, and what they give for, but they have not actually become less giving.

Sixth, there is significant potential for more giving, including more giving to Pakistan. Overwhelming numbers of the respondents feel that, given the right conditions, their own Pakistan-related giving could increase significantly (83 percent); an even more overwhelming majority (93 percent) feels that there is great growth potential for overall giving by the Pakistani American diaspora. Our research also points toward a strong desire in the community to increase its giving to non–Pakistan-related issues, including involvement in mainstream US philanthropic causes. There is clearly a desire within the Pakistani diaspora in America to become ever more involved, both in philanthropy related to Pakistan and in civic life in the US. As in the Indian case, leadership by professionally successful Pakistani Americans is a central factor in establishing the credibility of philanthropic organizations. This is, for example, evident in the success of the Human Development Foundation, which was originally established by a group of prominent Pakistani American physicians and is the most successful Pakistani American charity running its own large-scale projects in Pakistan.

Finally, there are serious hurdles that make it difficult to give more to Pakistan. Although this community is ready to give significantly more than it does now, there are high barriers to accessing this additional giving. This is particularly true if one seeks to direct new or existing philanthropy to institutional giving in Pakistan. There are three major hurdles that need to be addressed before significant resources might be directed toward charitable institutions and NGOs in Pakistan. The first hurdle is the chronic lack of trust in the civic sector in Pakistan. Over 80 percent of our survey respondents believe that such organizations are inefficient as well as dishonest; over 70 percent feel that they are also ineffective and inattentive to the most pressing problems in Pakistan. The second important hurdle relates to the practical difficulties of giving to causes in Pakistan, including unclear US regulations about charitable giving abroad (especially after 9/11) and a lack of convenient mechanisms to transfer funds to Pakistan. There is also a dearth of reliable mechanisms to monitor the performance of organizations and a lack of opportunities to interact directly with organizations and their workers. The third barrier is that there is very little information available to Pakistani Americans about philanthropic organizations in Pakistan. This becomes particularly important because it feeds on, and exacerbates, both of the barriers mentioned earlier. In essence, most Pakistani Americans tend to have little trust in institutions in Pakistan, including in NGOs and philanthropic organizations; those who are willing to give face serious logistical difficulties in giving to causes in Pakistan, including difficulties related to transferring money; and finally, the Pakistani diaspora in America has fairly scant, often inaccurate, and generally negative information about the NGO and philanthropic sector in Pakistan, which keeps them from giving more.

FOUR LESSONS FOR DIASPORA PHILANTHROPY

How does all of the above help us to better understand and better respond to the challenges of diaspora philanthropy? One obvious conclusion would be that there is a very large amount of diaspora philanthropy already going on, it is happening in a lot of different ways, and diaspora communities—certainly Asian diasporas, but not just them—are quite adept at creating, maintaining, and nurturing multiple avenues and mechanisms for their philanthropic giving. Indeed, as the Pakistan case in the post-9/11 years suggests, philanthropic giving is an important *need* for diaspora communities, and they will invariably find a way to give even when the institutional mechanisms available to them become restricted.

Notwithstanding the above, the four cases presented here—diaspora philanthropy by Indians, Filipinos, Chinese, and Pakistanis in America—also point us toward a number of more nuanced lessons about why diasporas give, how they give, and what challenges they face in doing so. From the Asian experience discussed in this chapter, at least four such lessons seem to be of particular importance because our understanding of them could help us in better appreciating both the concept and the practice of diaspora philanthropy. First, there is a strong desire among developing country diasporas to give to individuals in need, rather than to institutional causes. Second, many developing country diasporas have fairly low institutional trust in either governmental or nongovernmental institutions in their country of origin. Third, for diaspora communities, philanthropic giving serves a crucial identity need. Fourth and finally, a key hurdle to greater diaspora giving is not simply the lack of resources to give, but severely constrained instruments for giving. By way of conclusions, each of these four I's—Individuals, Institutional Trust, Identity, and Instruments—is discussed below.

GIVING TO INDIVIDUALS

For entirely rational and reasonable reasons, many developing country diasporas prefer to give directly to individuals in need rather than to institutions working for structural change and reformation of society. We see, therefore, a greater proportion of diaspora philanthropy being directed toward alleviating private poverty and assisting in sustaining subsistence within one's kinship networks than toward institutional investments in such areas as education, health, and infrastructure. Arguably, institutional investments can often have a greater payoff from a development perspective because such investment, if done right, can trigger deeper and longer-term societal transformations.

However, as many in the Pakistani American diaspora insist (Najam 2006), if the resources now being directed toward private poverty were suddenly redirected toward institutional investments, the philanthropic safety nets would disappear from under those who barely subsist on such giving and "private poor" would turn into "public poor." In societies where the plight of the "public poor" is dismal, maybe directing diaspora philanthropy toward private poverty is not an entirely bad thing. Many diaspora givers also insist that they can control for quality as well as effectiveness if they give directly to individuals. The gratification that they themselves derive from the act of giving is more immediate and their control over the money being used properly is also more direct. On the other hand, it should also be noted that while giving directly to individuals can enhance the efficiency that comes from plugging any leaks, it does not allow for the efficiencies that come from economies of scale.

The challenge, then, is for diaspora philanthropists to find ways of giving that allow them to take advantage of economies of scale without losing the ability to supervise the use of their gifts and to retain personal contact with the beneficiary. The model of neighborhood associations at the giving end and hometown associations at the receiving end that the Filipino diaspora has gravitated toward (Opiniano 2006) tries to achieve exactly such a balance. The Chinese experience seems to have similarly created "community size" giving mechanisms that target individual needs in the *Qiaoxian* regions and utilize the natural concentrations of Chinese Americans in Chinatowns (Yin and Lan 2004). Indeed, in both the Pakistan (Najam 2006) and India (Sidel 2005) cases we see a similar trend made manifest through the creation of organizations here in the US that directly undertake projects in the country of origin and, thereby, seek to be close to both the donors and the recipients.

Lack of Institutional Trust

One more reason why many Asian diasporas choose to invest in giving to individuals rather than institutions is the chronic lack of trust in institutions, whether they are governmental or non-governmental. This was, for example, a resounding conclusion of the research on Pakistan (Najam 2006) and is also noted by those studying India (Manivannan 2006). This lack of institutional trust is likely to be prevalent in most developing countries, simply because most developing countries are characterized by weak institutional systems and, therefore, citizens of these countries tend to have (often, rightly) little trust in their institutions.

However, it is disturbing that in many countries the lack of trust is not restricted to government institutions and extends to nongovernmental organizations, whether they are domestic ones or international (Najam 2006). This does not bode well for development in general and certainly does not bode well for institutional governance in these countries. Here one is tempted to recall one of the findings from India (Kapur et al. 2005) that highlighted the need and opportunity for diaspora communities to invest not just their money but their knowledge and experience in the management of the institutions that they invest in. In both the Philippines (Opiniano 2006) and Pakistan (Najam 2006), nongovernmental organizations set up by diaspora communities themselves are doing exactly this by providing models as well as role models of good institutional governance. This, itself, is a significant form of knowledge philanthropy.

IDENTITY NEEDS

It is quite clear from all four cases in this chapter that for the diaspora community itself, philanthropy directed at their country of origin serves a significant identity need, whether it be in terms of national identity, regional or communal identity, or religious identity. That is what the diaspora "gets" out of diaspora philanthropy. One could hypothesize that the identity need that is being fulfilled is one of the prime determinants of what causes someone will give to.

This realization is not simply of academic value. It can have significant and serious implications for actual giving patterns. Because nations, like individuals, have multiple identities and because these multiple identities are often in real or construed conflict with each other, diaspora philanthropy can potentially become the fuel that fires the clash of identities within divided societies. This danger is particularly acute for diaspora communities who—because they are physically and temporally removed from the "home base"—often live in the "memory of the memory" that they left behind. There seems to be enough anecdotal and some empirical (see chapter by Devesh Kapur, this volume) evidence that diaspora giving can both fuel and fund identity conflicts.

The importance of identity needs also becomes evident as a second generation—born and/or raised abroad—comes of age. The philanthropic decisions of this and subsequent generations will depend on how they juggle their multiple hyphenated identities. Experience on this front seems to be mixed and it may be too early to conclude that future generations will necessarily reduce their giving to the country of origin.

Instruments of Giving

Probably the most surprising lesson that emerges from a review of these three cases, and of developing country diaspora philanthropy in general, is that the biggest hurdle to more and better directed diaspora giving is *not* a paucity of resources within the diaspora, it is a dearth of dependable instruments of giving that the diaspora communities have confidence in. Increasingly, the most important "instrument" of giving is a financial mechanism that would easily, reliably, and affordably transfer money (especially small amounts of money) from diaspora donor to homebase recipient. Especially in the aftermath of 9/11, and with the policy changes that have taken place as a result, the availability of such instruments has diminished while the cost of the limited instruments still available has escalated. One of the single most important things that could be done to change the quantum as well as nature of giving by developing country diasporas is to somehow provide easy, reliable, and affordable means of transferring small amounts of money.

However, money transfer is not the only "instrument" of giving that is in short supply. As stated earlier, reliable institutions—including reliable nongovernmental institutions—that the diaspora community has confidence in are also in short supply.

Very often it is also difficult to find useful and timely information on what needs to be done as well as what was done with the last batch of contributions that might have been made. The case of the Chinese American diaspora suggests that the confidence that the diaspora has in the available channels of giving is also important and having a multitude of channels available for giving to and by different groups is desirable.

The point to be made here is simply that for many developing country diaspora communities there is a significant amount of untapped "philanthropic potential" that is not being used because the instruments of giving are either not there or are deficient. The way to tap into this potential is to find means and ways that will make it easier to give, offer sufficient choice and options to diaspora donors, and make it possible to track the impact of what is given.

REFERENCES

Embassy of Pakistan. 2003. *Pakistani American Demographics.* Washington, DC: Embassy of Pakistan.

Geithner, Peter F., Paula D. Johnson, and Lincoln C. Chen, eds. 2004. *Diaspora Philanthropy and Equitable Development in China and India.* Cambridge, MA: Global Equity Initiative, Asia Center, Harvard University: Distributed by Harvard University Press.

IMF. 2003. *Balance of Payments Statistics Yearbook 2002.* Washington, DC: IMF Publications Services.

Kapur, Devesh, Ajay S. Mehta, and R. Moon Dutt. 2004. "Indian Diaspora Philanthropy." Pp. 177–213 in *Diaspora Philanthropy and Equitable Development in China and India,* edited by P.F. Geithner, P. Johnson, and L. Chen. Cambridge, MA: Global Equity Initiative, Asia Center, Harvard University: Distributed by Harvard University Press.

Kumar, Gopa, ed. 2003. *Indian Diaspora and Giving Patterns of Indian Americans in the US.* New Delhi: Charities Aid Foundation India.

Le, C.N. 2006. "14 Important Statistics about Asian Americans." Asian-Nation. Accessed August 8, 2006 (http://www.asian-nation.org/14-statistics.shtml).

Maimbo, Samuel M. and Dilip Ratha, eds. 2005. *Remittances: Development Impact and Future Prospects.* Washington, DC: World Bank.

Manivannan, Jayaram K. 2006. *Virtual Leadership: The Next Phase of Diaspora Philanthropy.* New York: Center on Philanthropy and Civil Society, The City University of New York.

Merz, Barbara J., ed. 2005. *New Patterns for Mexico: Observations on Remittances, Philanthropic Giving, and Equitable Development.* Cambridge,

MA: Global Equity Initiative, Asia Center, Harvard University: Distributed by Harvard University Press.

Mohan, Kalpana. 2000. "On Philanthropy" (part of cover story "Homeward Bound"). *SiliconIndia*, June 2000 issue.

Najam, Adil. 2006. *Portrait of a Giving Community: Philanthropy by the Pakistani-American Diaspora*. Cambridge, MA: Global Equity Initiative, Asia Center, Harvard University: Distributed by Harvard University Press.

Opiniano, Jeremaiah. 2005. *Good News for the Poor: Diaspora Philanthropy by Filipinos*. Quezon City: Association of Foundations.

———. 2006. "Filipinos Abroad as Social Development Partners." Presented at "Tapping Diaspora Philanthropy for Philippine Social Development" workshop, April 25–26, 2006, Mandaluyong City, Philippines. Association of Foundations, Ayala Foundation, and Peace and Equity Foundation.

RAND Corporation. 2001. America Becoming: The Growing Complexity of America's Racial Mosaic. Policy Brief RB-5050(2001) (http://www.rand.org/pubs/research_briefs/RB5050/index1.html).

Sidel, Mark. 2004. "Diaspora Philanthropy to India: A Perspective from the United States." Pp. 215–257 in *Diaspora Philanthropy and Equitable Development in China and India*, edited by P.F. Geithner, P. Johnson, and L. Chen. Cambridge, MA: Global Equity Initiative, Asia Center, Harvard University: Distributed by Harvard University Press.

Terry, Donald F. and Steve R. Wilson, eds. 2005. *Beyond Small Change: Making Migrant Remittances Count*. Washington, DC: Inter-American Development Bank.

Toppe, Christopher M., Arthur D. Krisch, and Jacobel Michel. 2002. *Giving and Volunteering in the United States—Findings from a National Survey.* Washington, DC: Independent Sector.

US Census Bureau. 2000. *United States Census, 2000: Data Sets.* Washington, DC: US Census Bureau (http://factfinder.census.gov).

———. 2005. Asian/Pacific American Heritage Month. Document CB05-FF.06-2. Washington, DC: US Census Bureau (http://www.census.gov/Press-Release/www/releases/archives/facts_for_features_special_editions/004522.html).

Yin, Xiao-huang and Zhiyong Lan. 2004. "Why Do They Give? Chinese American Transnational Philanthropy since the 1970s." Pp. 79–127 in *Diaspora Philanthropy and Equitable Development in China and India,* edited by P.F. Geithner, P. Johnson, and L. Chen. Cambridge, MA: Global Equity Initiative, Asia Center, Harvard University: Distributed by Harvard University Press.

Young, Nick. 2004. "Richesse Oblige, and So Does the State: Philanthropy and Equity in China." Pp. 29–77 in *Diaspora Philanthropy and Equitable Development in China and India,* edited by P.F. Geithner, P. Johnson, and L. Chen. Cambridge, MA: Global Equity Initiative, Asia Center, Harvard University: Distributed by Harvard University Press.

Young, Nick and June Shih. 2004. "Philanthropic Links between the Chinese Diaspora and the People's Republic of China." Pp. 129–175 in *Diaspora Philanthropy and Equitable Development in China and India,* edited by P.F. Geithner, P. Johnson, and L. Chen. Cambridge, MA: Global Equity Initiative, Asia Center, Harvard University: Distributed by Harvard University Press.

Zia, Helen. 2001. *Asian American Dreams: The Emergence of an American People.* New York: Farrar, Straus and Giroux.

WEBSITE SOURCES

The American India Foundation (http://www.aifoundation.org)

The Human Development Foundation (http://www.yespakistan.
   com)

The Indus Entrepreneurs (http://www.tie.org)

CHAPTER 6

AFRICAN DIASPORAS

Mojúbàolú Olúfúnké Okome

Wealth is not what you own, but what you give away.
—Ibo proverb

This chapter examines African diasporas, diaspora giving trends to Africa, and the equity ramifications of these phenomena on African socio-economic relations. As is well established, many of the presumed advances of globalization remain out of reach for most Africans (World Bank GEP 2006:9). Many Africans have come to associate the gains of globalization with locales abroad, driving an enduring desire to migrate in search of better opportunities. More Africans than ever before are migrating today, part of the 125 million people estimated to be on the move worldwide. Foreign consulates in African countries are swamped with Africans seeking immediate and permanent exit from their respective countries. Migration has become a survival strategy for many Africans, giving rise to diaspora communities throughout the world.

These communities are concerned with issues of well-being that transcend mere concern for kith and kin. While the scholarly focus has predominantly been on non-philanthropic transfers by migrants, preliminary findings reveal that there is substantially more philanthropy than is evident in the literature. Although such efforts remain modest, they are significant to the equity issue as

Epigraph from Chinua Achebe, quoting an Ibo proverb in an interview by Georgina Beier in *They Keep Their Fires Burning*. Bayreuth African Studies 185, pp. 141–152, 2005.

instances of commitment to addressing perceived problems of poverty, want, and inequality (Okome 2005a).

AFRICA'S DIASPORAS

There are many African diasporas that may overlap and intersect to forge new and ever-changing African identities. Just two of the numerous ways of looking at the continent's diasporas are by time period of emigration and by geography—including both external and internal African diasporas. Another way to glimpse the big picture of African migration is to survey a few of its causes.

The new, post–World War II African diaspora is still evolving, and African migration immediately after the war and today already differs qualitatively and quantitatively (Okome 2002a). Following the war, during Africa's anti-colonial struggle for independence, Africans went abroad seeking education, or engaging in travel for business or leisure. But these migrants generally returned to their home countries once their objectives were accomplished. The contemporary diaspora's most rapid growth coincides with more recent economic crises, unsustainable debt, the use of policies of structural adjustment to "reform" African economies, and political turmoil.

According to estimates by the International Labor Organization, more than 16 million Africans were migrants in 2000. Of these, 5.4 million were migrant workers. More women are migrating, accounting for approximately 47 percent of migrants in Africa. Contrary to the expectation that women migrants follow their spouses, these female migrants often make autonomous decisions to migrate (ILO 2005:21). The population movements also include refugees, mostly from Western Sudan, West and Central Africa (Baruah 2006:6), and the Horn of Africa.

The vast majority of African migration occurs within the continent, as people move from areas of socio-economic and political crises to areas of relative prosperity and stability. For example, South Africa and other thriving regional economies attract labor migrants from other African countries. An internal African diaspora exists that is as much a result of forced migration for some as the diasporas created outside Africa (with exceptions, such as diasporas that have resulted from trading relations) (Alpers 2001).

Recent African migrants to the US are small in number compared with the total US migrant population. The 2002 census reports that there are more than one million African foreign-born in America: 3 percent of the foreign-born population and 0.3 percent of total US population (US Bureau of the Census 2002). The reported number of African foreign-born in America reflects significant undercount because it does not include North Africans, who are counted as part of the Middle East. Also, only one in every four recent African immigrants in the US is counted in the census (Roberts 2005). The African foreign-born population is 6 percent of those who acquired permanent legal immigrant status in 2002.

Table 1: African Migrants by Region

35% Western Africa
26% Eastern Africa
20% Northern Africa
7% Southern Africa
<3% Middle Africa

Source: US Census 2002 American Community Survey.

Factors that encourage migration from Africa include "wage differentials and crisis pressures in less developed countries, established inter-country networks based on family, culture and history" (Baruah 2006:6), and "the antinomies of globalization" (Okome 2002a)—which implies that globalization has both negative and positive consequences that vary by national and international region, nationality, gender, race, and class.

While recent African immigrants are not subjected to the inhumanity of being ripped away from Africa by those termed by Everett as "European body snatchers" (2002:126–127) and do not endure the middle passage, Jayne Ifekwunigwe (2004) contends that recent African migrants are diasporan because they are fleeing unrelenting impoverishment on the continent.

African labor was, and still is, extracted from the continent into the "new world" as a result of what Okpewho, Boyce Davies, and Mazrui describe as the "Labor Imperative" and the "Territorial Imperative" (1999). While both imperatives drove the creation of the old diasporas before World War II, the "Labor Imperative" created the new African diaspora. Today's imperialism does not require the physical presence of imperialists within their empire. Instead, neo-colonial relations of power maintain imperialistic domination by extracting economic and financial resources and labor, using them in new ways in the peripheries of the empire. Today's imperialism is driven by transnational capital, especially multinational corporations in the global north. It is supported by state policies in both the north and the newly liberalized global south, which is compelled to integrate into the global economy.

Differing levels of privation and compulsion drive exit from Africa today. Some who take desperate measures to leave are long-term unemployed youth. Others are older professionals who may be either underemployed or unemployed (and considered unemployable) in their home countries. They are the *dramatis personae* in the tragic media reports: trafficked persons, stowaways, deaths in the Sahara, drownings in capsized boats in the Mediterranean, and those living on the margins in stronger economies. This is due to an "oversupply" of labor in sending countries and a demand for workers in the receiving countries where "formal and informal networks . . . link supply with demand" (Martin, Martin, and Weil 2002).

Some migrants flee political persecution and become exiles, yet others flee devastating famines, natural disasters, political conflict, and war—Somalis, Liberians, Sierra-Leoneans, Congolese, Rwandans, Eritreans, and Burundians are just a few. Some Africans flee religious persecution—the Egyptian Coptic Christians and some Southern Sudanese are among these recent migrants (Okome 2002a; Drumtra 2003; Schlecht 2003; Dryden-Peterson 2004). Lack of coordinated management of migrant flows may increase African migration (Martin et al. 2002). While many destination countries have policies to provide refuge for exiles, these policies are unevenly applied and subject to politicization particularly when there is insufficient documentation to prove refugee status.

Created by the old and new imperialisms, African diasporas maintain ideological and social connectedness with the continent (Patterson and Kelley 2000). Consequently, African migrant workers, refugees, and exiles are very much in touch with their homelands. This is seen in both diasporas' social practices, aesthetics, religious ritual, and the literary and scholarly imagination.

The new transnationalization of the African diaspora both strengthens and creates links between the old and new African diasporas. The most vibrant of these linkages depends on the ideologically driven construction of an African identity. But the process also creates intra-racial ethnic tensions, meaning that groups may be seen by those outside them as belonging to the same race, but within the group, there are fine distinctions made based on differences in ethnicity and national origin. These divisions prevent unity, collaboration, and coalition building to solve common problems (Watkins Owens 1996). Nationality, rather than the embrace of a Pan-African identity, still drives and substantively divides the various African diasporas. These tensions subvert the Pan-Africanist promise that the continent is an indivisible whole, whose progress can only be achieved with united effort to ensure that the governance and creation of wealth in Africa is taken over by Africans for Africans. African migrants must consciously collaborate to live up to the promise of being "productive and progressive for Africa" (Zeleza n.d.).

The linkages among African diaspora networks produce succeeding flows of migrants by dispersing information on how to navigate the tough economic and political realities and broad structural forces they confront. The networks contribute by supporting generational chain migration (Light, Bhachu, and Karageorgis n.d.).

The ability to form or join a community also substantially reduces the harshness of a new, often hostile environment. An informal, sometimes illegal economy forces some undocumented migrants into menial, low-wage labor and sex work for survival (Zeleza n.d.:18). Increased migration causes a proliferation of institutions, including religious, humanitarian, nongovernmental, and governmental organizations that serve documented and undocumented migrants. The World Wide Web provides another avenue to community. However, the poorest and technologically challenged are often unable to take advantage of this innovation (USDOC and NTIA 1999; USDOC, ESA, and NTIA 2000).

Unskilled African migrants are reviled by unfriendly policies, which criminalize them as undocumented migrants subject to gross exploitation by employers. These workers often begin their labor force participation in the informal and/or underground economy, and when lucky, work their way up in the socio-economic ladder. For unskilled African migrants, there is a great risk of getting stuck in a vicious cycle of perpetual informality and under-remuneration. Skilled contemporary African migrants are courted for technical and professional jobs. But skilled workers may also migrate as undocumented workers, beginning in the informal economy as underpaid, underemployed, and sometimes exploited workers until they secure documentation.

Some diaspora members are able to play political roles in their countries of origin and settlement. Certain sending countries, such as Nigeria and South Africa, may extend dual citizenship to their diasporas. Some, like Jerry Rawlings's Ghana and Haile Selassie's Ethiopia, may also extend dual citizenship to Africans from the old diasporas (*Ghanaian Newsrunner* 1995). Active diasporas may campaign for an extension of these and other rights. For example, the Uganda-North American Convention demanded dual citizenship in 2000 (*New Vision* 2000), and Ghanaian and other migrants' campaign for voting rights for the diaspora led to the codification of voting rights for the diaspora into law in ten African countries. Transnational migrants seek such policies to extend their power vis-à-vis the state. They also agitate for increased participation in politics in their home countries through voting, contesting for office, critiquing government policies, and pushing for change, increasingly communicating via the Internet.

REMITTANCES AND PHILANTHROPY

Types of Giving

It is generally believed that most remittances to Africa are transferred to cover the cost of daily expenses and to fund the welfare and subsistence needs of family members (Sander and Maimbo 2003:17; Loup 2005; Puri and Ritzema n.d.; Baruah 2006:8). Migrants also send staples as well as desired luxury goods like electronics. Some migrants establish bank accounts to save money for children's education and fund future migration by children and other family members (Puri and Ritzema n.d.).

Remittances are primarily used for daily needs and expenses (70 to 90 percent of remittances), typically labeled as consumption or as improving the recipients' standard of living. Other uses include health-related expenses and education (often grouped with consumption when seen as improving the standard of living); consumer durables (stereos, televisions, washing machines); improvements or acquisition of housing, purchases of land or livestock; sociocultural investment (birth, marriage, pilgrimage, death); loan repayments (often to pay for cost of migration); savings; and income- or employment-generating activities (Sander and Maimbo 2003:17).

The results of a survey conducted in France among migrants from Senegal, Mali, Guinea-Bissau, and the Comoros indicate that family support is the primary purpose for remittances to the home countries. Subsequently, they fund home construction, business investment, and community development efforts, which involve the provision of infrastructure for health and school facilities. Another report shows migrants from Ghana sending up to 70 percent of their remittances for family support to fund consumption, paying for education, health, and emergency needs. Only 30 percent of remittances go toward investment in land, cattle, and construction. For Malian migrants, 80 to 90 percent of the remittances go toward family consumption needs, and immediate survival needs are prioritized over long-term investment (Loup 2005).

Relatively fewer African migrants report that they send remittances for loan payments and investments than other migrant groups (Loup 2005:12). Most migrants will not neglect the welfare needs of their family members in favor of income-generating ventures that are not guaranteed to succeed.

Few Malian migrants, for example, invest in small-scale businesses and trade back home since the migrant's presence is crucial to the proper supervision and success of such business activities. With investments, livestock and petty trade sectors are preferred over transport or import/export businesses. Where non-family consumption needs are funded, house construction tends to dominate, and the government of Mali reportedly established a matching fund to finance housing. Mali and Burundi both match funds remitted by the diaspora for local development projects (Baruah 2006:19–21).

In a study of remittances to the Least Developed Countries, Uganda was cited as the only African country where treasury bills and bonds are made available to migrants, who are encouraged to invest in these vehicles. The Ugandan government also gives information on investment prospects and partnerships in development projects to its citizens in the diaspora.

In-kind donations include clothing; books; equipment; dissemination of free information; and radio, television, and Internet infrastructure. For example, the Kudirat Initiative for Democracy began as part of the Nigerian pro-democracy and human rights coalitional efforts to unseat General Sani Abacha. It worked with its coalition partners to beam Radio Kudirat broadcasts into Nigeria from abroad during Abacha's reign of terror and plans to develop and disseminate programs in five of Nigeria's numerous languages. Hafsat Abiola, the organization's founder, received international grants to support its projects (Sykes 1999:6–7). Arms and ammunitions supplied to ethnic militia and nationalist liberation efforts are yet another type of in-kind donation.

Some transfers are made as services: religious ceremonies, pro bono medical care, and education (Sander and Maimbo 2003:20). Many hometown associations (HTAs), migrant ethnic associations, and professional organizations provide pro bono medical care and other skilled services.

One of the most remarkable examples of other philanthropic giving is the establishment of six universities in Somalia, including four in Somaliland, a self-declared independent state that is not recognized by any other states. The Somaliland Forum, a group of Somali intellectuals in the diaspora, along with Californian Friends of Hargeisa University, spearheaded the establishment of the University of Hargeisa in 2000. They were assisted by the UN and its affiliated agencies, particularly the UNDP, as well as by Somali businesspeople and local communities (University of

Hargeisa). The University now has traditional educational structures as well as an online distance learning program funded by a
partnership between the World Bank, UNDP, and African Virtual
University (World Bank Institute 2005). University of Burao was
established in 2004 as a result of a public-private partnership,
again involving the Somaliland Forum, Somaliland Welfare Organisation in Oslo, and other Somali in the diaspora (University
of Burao). Graduates of the Technical Institute of Burao, which had
been established with German grants but was destroyed during
the wars in the 1980s and 1990s, played a key part in fundraising
for the project (*afrol News* 2004).

Record-Keeping
Official records on remittances, particularly for Africa, reveal
significant inaccuracies and gaps. Fully two-thirds of sub-Saharan African countries lack data or underestimate or overinflate
remittances (Baruah 2006:7). The exact amount and value of these
remittances are hard to determine, but some scholars have provided estimates of transfers. Many studies contend that the value
of informal remittances is greater than the formal. The estimated
value of unrecorded remittances by Egyptian migrants was as
much as 33 percent of all remittances between 1985 and 1986,
and those by Sudanese migrants in 1984, up to 85 percent (Puri
and Ritzema n.d.). For Sudan, a 1992 study by Brown estimates
that for 1983–1984, unrecorded remittances are responsible for
39 percent of adjusted GNP and they enhance net factor incomes
from 7 to 17 percent of adjusted GNP (Puri and Ritzema n.d.).

Volume and Frequency
The degree of attachment to family back home influences volume
and frequency of remittances. First-generation migrants tend to
give more and to remit more frequently, although subsequent
generations may be able to remit more substantial funds. Those
remitting money to Africa are predominantly low-income migrants (Puri and Ritzema n.d.). Table 2 shows figures of remit-

Table 2: Remittances in 2003 (in millions of US$)

Country (year if not in 2003)	Inflow	Outflow	Net
Angola (2002)	0	223	–223
Benin (2001)	83	10	73
Burkina Faso (2001)	50	44	6
Burundi	3	0	3
Cape Verde	92	1	91
Democratic Republic of the Congo	0	3	–3
Eritrea (2000)	3	1	2
Ethiopia	46	18	28
Guinea	111	46	65
Guinea-Bissau (2002)	17	5	12
Lesotho (2002)	184	21	163
Madagascar	16	8	8
Malawi (2002)	1	0	1
Mali (2002)	137	30	107
Mauritania (1998)	2	10	–8
Mozambique	70	29	41
Rwanda (2002)	7	32	–25
São Tomé and Príncipe (2002)	1	0	0
Senegal (2002)	297	39	258
Sierra Leone	26	3	23
Sudan	1,223	1	1,222
Togo (2002)	104	17	87
Uganda	295	264	31
United Republic of Tanzania (2002)	7	21	–14
Zambia (2000)	0	24	–24

Source: IMF Balance of Payments Statistics. Remittances defined as workers' remittances and compensation of employees (Baruah 2006:5). These figures do not provide US-specific data.

tances for Least Developed African Countries from 1998 to 2003 (Baruah 2006).

Only 5 percent of remittances are estimated to go to Sub-Saharan Africa (although the under-reporting and lack of data in this region should be taken into account). The Middle East and North Africa constitute 18 percent of remittance flows, and two African countries, Egypt and Morocco, feature among the top five countries to which remittances are sent (Sander 2003:4–6). The size of remittances is even more significant because its growth has outpaced the number of migrants and should increase over time. Migrants send an average of $200 per international transaction (Sander 2003:6). It is estimated that African migrants remit between 15 and 50 percent of their income, and in some instances, keep their entire income in their home countries as arranged in their employment contracts (Sander 2003:8).

According to President Issaias Afewerki of Eritrea in 2000, $100 to $150 million annually is remitted by Eritrean immigrants in the US to their country of origin as gifts and investments (Mufson 2000:A14). The 2002 IMF Balance of Payments Yearbook shows that among the top twenty developing country recipients of remittances in 2001, 8.5 percent of Uganda's GDP, 9.7 percent of Morocco's, 13.6 of Cape Verde's, and 26.5 of Lesotho's were sent by their migrant workers. Somalia received an estimated $800 million to $1 billion in 2000, ranking thirteenth among developing country recipients in per capita receipt of remittances. Mali derived as much as 17 percent of its financing for public aid in 1991 from remittances. Since the 1980s, Lesotho received three times as much from remittances as is disbursed as official aid, and Cape Verde received four times as much from remittances than from international aid for the last ten years (Pérouse de Montclos 2005:2).

MOTIVATIONS FOR GIVING

As the Ibo proverb in the epigraph suggests, philanthropy is a central ideal to being a good person within the context of African traditional mores. Most African migrants give back as much as they can, often at great personal sacrifice. They expect no returns other than the gratitude of recipients, and regional cultural mores may even dictate anonymous giving. Most African migrants are constantly preoccupied with how they can give back, what to give back, and how to foster optimal benefits from giving.

Much philanthropy exists as mutual aid for friends, extended family, lineage, and fictive kin, including, but not limited to those from an individual's ethnic group. As the Yorùbá say, *ilé l'a ti nkó èsó r'òde* (charity begins at home). Thus, the rationale is that wealth in people should be nurtured and fostered, and family (including the extended family) should be helped first, and then others.

Other social expectations also influence giving. Diaspora members give to friends and acquaintances who sometimes contact them for assistance. Such gifts may be to reciprocate old favors, to build goodwill, or are construed as benevolence by the giver. The perception that a migrant is "living the good life" generates demands for such handouts, and giving in response may be to show that this is true, even where such "good life" is fictitious or tenuous. There is also giving for rehabilitation and reconstruction after wars and natural disasters.

Other key features of migrant African philanthropy include its many small-scale efforts by numerous groups. These groups form along ethnic, kinship, and national lines. There is a tendency for these groups to seem invisible to external observers and non-members of in-groups. Professional associations tend to be national rather than continent-wide. Institutional cultures emphasize trust, loose organization, volunteerism, and male dominated decision-making.

The efforts of African migrants closely resemble patterns established by newly urbanized Africans in the continent during the colonial era. Many studies of African urbanization indicate the ubiquity of newly urbanized Africans' formation of HTAs and home improvement unions that give assistance, including philanthropy, to the towns of origin.

Older African diasporas in the US have the same philanthropic ethics and mores as urbanized Africans and migrants from the continent (Copeland-Carson 2005:77–87). Voluntary efforts "to redistribute financial and other resources for the purposes of promoting collective good" are found in the old diaspora, where African institutional mechanisms and social obligations adapted by African Americans in the past continue today (Copeland-Carson 2005:78).

MECHANISMS AND INSTITUTIONS

MECHANISMS

Formal financial service providers to Africa include banks, credit unions, post offices, traditional money transfer operators (MTOs) like Western Union and MoneyGram, and Internet-based MTOs. The mechanisms used differ by country and sometimes by region: for instance, Malian migrants in France use informal mechanisms to a greater degree, and Senegalese migrants use Western Union and banks, the latter when sending savings and investments (Loup 2005:15). Relatively fewer African migrants use formal mechanisms, either because banks do not offer the services, or the banks available in the host country may not have branches in the home country. Thus far, money transfer operators and ethnic businesses have been more proactive than banks in offering targeted financial services to African migrants.

Banks offer four basic kinds of services: SWIFT (Society for Worldwide Interbank Financial Telecommunication) transfers, credit to a recipient's bank account at the same institution, credit to a recipient at a different bank, and credit to an account for a cash pick up (Mutume 2005:8). In Kenya, the banks have a reputation for efficiency and availability, and migrants use them extensively. In Morocco banking services are provided by a state-owned bank, Groupe Banques Populaires (BP), with branches in several European countries. Immigrants can open joint checking accounts with relatives back home and do wire transfers that can be withdrawn at home or made to anyone at a fixed rate of 90 dirhams (approximately $9.00). The bank offers subsidized credit for real estate and entrepreneurial ventures in Morocco and several types of insurance, including for the repatriation of a body and airfare for emergency travel. It also sponsors a foundation that funds cultural events and special schools for the children of emigrants in Tangier and Agadir (Orozco 2003:9).

Some migrants have created banks specifically to serve their needs, as shown in Sylviane Diouf-Kamara's (1997) study of Senegalese migrants in New York City who remit significant transfers to Senegal through banks owned by members of their community and other networks.

After 9/11, Somalia lost the main mechanism for remittance transfers when Al Barakat Bank and MTOs in the country were closed down (UN Sec. Council 2001). It was not until September 2003 that the UNDP established the Somalia Financial Services Association with funds from the UK Department for International Development and technical assistance from KPMG Kenya. The association facilitates the transfer of approximately $750 million annually.

Post offices are reputed to be unduly slow and often unreliable, and tend to be used sparingly, with the exception of in the Southern African region. The US Postal Service introduced a money transfer system, Sure Money/Dinero Seguro, about eight years ago. People can send up to $2,000 per day from participating post offices to ten countries in Latin America. European postal services also have the Eurogiro system that facilitates international money transfers to over thirty countries (Orozco 2003:6).

Among MTOs, Western Union and MoneyGram have the most presence and name recognition; the former is reputed to control 25 percent of the entire market (Orozco 2003:6). Most migrants use them, especially in emergencies, but their high cost may curtail their ubiquitous use. The reliability and security of the services still make them more attractive compared with personal intermediaries who may misappropriate or be vulnerable to theft. Increased competition and more consumers in this sector could lower the cost, making these services more attractive.

Internet MTOs have less name recognition and serve more specialized or regional populations. Examples include Dahabshiil in Somalia (Baruah 2006:5) and Homelink in Zimbabwe, which was established by the foreign exchange–starved government after the IMF and World Bank sanctions that followed the 2000 elections. Some of the MTOs offer vouchers that are redeemable in shops at the home country, or deliver goods as well as money.

There is great dependence on informal methods of remitting resources to Africa. Most migrants take money and consumer goods themselves, or rely on trusted friends, family members and acquaintances to physically take money and goods back home. Informal arrangements are made with individuals, ethnic businesses, shipping companies, immigrant associations, and even through private homes (Mutume 2005). Increasingly, information technology tools are used to transfer knowledge, skills, and technology from migrant populations to their home countries (Okome 2002c).

Many migrants remit money through ethnic stores that are owned and operated by indigenes from their home countries (Orozco 2003:1). Some shipping companies and courier services provide services for immigrants or migrants who want to send goods and merchandise back home. There are also informal exchanges that arrange to have money available in the migrant's home country in exchange for the migrant providing the equivalent in their country of residence.

Hundi and *hawala* systems are used predominantly in East and North Africa. They are derived from "traditional migrating and trading networks" that link Africa, the Middle East, and Asia (Loup 2005:15). One party pays hard currency to another, who advances the equivalent of the funds to another designated party or for a designated purpose abroad (Orozco 2003:5). The exchange may not be immediate or may be staggered and is often not recorded in any official documents. After 9/11, the US government cracked down on the *hawala* and *hundi* money transfer operations because of the suspicion that many were used by terrorist networks (*Taipei Times* 2002; *Guardian* 2002). This created considerable problems for people who relied on these transfers to make remittances to family members back home.

Institutions
Africans in the diaspora are increasingly establishing formal philanthropic institutions, especially religious, ethnic, alumni, and hometown associations. Groups accumulate resources to fund designated projects through membership dues, special levies, annual fundraising, social events, solicitation of donations from the diplomatic community, and US public resources. Some of these groups use their resources to support other organizations in countries of origin. They also combine their efforts with international foundations or NGOs.

Religious institutions of both the old and new diasporas engage in missionary efforts in Africa. They donate buildings, school supplies, and equipment to immigrants' home countries. Many send money to support their mother institutions; some African diaspora churches report sending at least a third of their collections to the mother church (Okome 2005b). Some old diaspora institutions like the African Methodist Episcopal Church are highly experienced fundraisers for social services and technical assistance in the US and Africa. They are sharing fundraising and operational skills with similarly inclined new African diaspora institutions (Copeland-Carson 2005:84).

Ethnic mutual aid efforts, such as Yorùbá and Ibo migrant associations, raise funds for philanthropy for their immediate communities in the US and Nigeria. Pan-ethnic African philanthropy is also growing alongside more conventional efforts (Copeland-Carson 2005).

Alumni associations also engage in fundraising to pay for projects back home. Many such efforts include the construction and renovation of libraries, classrooms, and dormitories. They also donate books, journals, educational materials, and computers, particularly during the celebration of important milestones such as the institution's golden, silver, and centenary celebrations.

After the crises of the 1970s through 1990s, four international philanthropic institutions—the Ford, MacArthur, and Rockefeller Foundations and the Carnegie Corporation—collaborated to build capacity and infrastructure in African universities. The African university grantees now also fundraise among their migrant alumni. The University of Ibadan, for instance, has the Fanton challenge, a $250,000 dollar-for-dollar match offered by the president of the MacArthur Foundation and the Nigeria Higher Education Foundation (founded with funding from the MacArthur Foundation and headquartered in Uniondale, New Jersey). The drive encourages overseas alumni to donate toward capacity building by Nigerian universities (Nigeria Higher Education Foundation n.d.).

Many HTAs and home improvement unions collect and donate funds for school, hospital, church, road, and other infrastructure construction. Many participate in public health outreach to their home communities. Nigerian and Ghanaian ethnic associations and HTAs fundraise for provision of potable water and building community centers (Sander 2003; Okome 2005a). The Eko Club of Atlanta, one of the HTAs formed by migrants from Lagos, Nigeria, provides "humanitarian assistance to the poor, the needy, and the underprivileged in our communities here in Atlanta and in Lagos, Nigeria" through "higher learning and our health care institutions in Lagos" (Ajayi 2006).

Associations of migrants in France who hail from the Kayes Region in Mali have provided remarkable amounts of support to their home community (Loup 2005:17). Sixty percent of Mali's infrastructure was constructed using remittances. The donations came from approximately forty HTAs in France, paralleling the same number of HTAs based in Mali (Loup 2005:14; Sander 2003:18; Mutume 2005:10). Over the course of ten years, these associations sent remittances worth 3 million euros to support 146 projects. Ninety-four percent of the funds came from the associations, and the balance from NGO donors. The success of such efforts depends on the ability to meet the needs of the recipients, and recipients' level of involvement in planning and execution (Sander 2003).

Some African migrant organizations establish 501(c)(3) non-profit institutions that engage in mutual support in the land of sojourn and fundraising for remittance to the home countries of the migrants. These include medical organizations providing pro bono medical care. During the apartheid era, several nonprofit organizations were established to raise funds to support anti-apartheid efforts in South Africa. Some of these organizations are still active.

Prominent individuals are also founding new organizations. Hakeem Olajuwon, the Houston Rockets star, founded the Hakeem Olajuwon Dream Foundation in Nigeria to undertake broad philanthropic outreach (Copeland-Carson 2005:83–84). However, in the post-9/11 period, Olajuwon has attracted more media attention for his alleged support of a mosque that made donations to Al Qaeda (Kelley 2005). Dikembe Mutombo, also of the Houston Rockets, started a foundation that gives health, educational, and poverty-alleviation assistance to the Democratic Republic of the Congo (DRC). He has also attracted media attention and has collaborated with many international NGOs and international governmental organizations in other African countries. He has worked on HIV/AIDS prevention campaigns among youth, given donations to struggling African athletes, and spearheaded the construction of the first new hospital to be built in the DRC in over forty years (Copeland-Carson 2005:84; Dikembe Mutombo Foundation 2005). Kase Lawal, a Nigerian migrant in the oil industry, also engages in philanthropy to African and African American communities, as well as to Nigeria (Chappell 2006; Hughes and Robinson 2006).

Informal savings efforts are used to accumulate and mobilize financial capacity for individual or communal purposes. Among the Yorùbá of Southwestern Nigeria, these savings efforts are described as èsúsú or àjo. A group of individuals contribute an agreed-upon amount of money according to an agreed-upon schedule, which may be weekly, bi-weekly, monthly, or otherwise. Members make an agreement or draw lots to decide when each member of the group takes the entire pot. One of the members could be designated the banker, or a trusted person outside the group plays the role of banker. The banker ensures that the money is collected from each member of the group and disbursed to the recipient according to the agreed schedule. Such funds are used for many purposes, including remittances abroad for capital projects, philanthropy, and family support. Immigrants also use this savings method to accumulate funds to establish businesses, pay children's or their own school fees, repay debts, and enhance savings and investments in formal banking and financial institutions. Resources raised through such informal group efforts are also donated to religious organizations, political parties, alma maters, and cultural groups (Sander and Maimbo 2003:17).

EQUITY EFFECTS OF GIVING

Scholars debate whether or not diaspora giving has an impact on social or economic equity. For some, remittances, as contributions to income, have equity implications for recipients as well as for the society around them (Sander and Maimbo 2003). At the most simplistic level, it can be assumed that poor people with migrant family members would benefit most directly from remittances transferred to fund their welfare needs. Besides poverty reduction, consumption is facilitated, there is increased liquidity, and mutual insurance grows (Sander and Maimbo 2003:17). Mutual insurance is responsive to social norms of reciprocity: assisting others often means that they will return the assistance at a future time. Malians resident in France who hailed from Kayes gave substantial support during the 1973 and 1984 droughts, and, "in Lesotho, where a state of famine was declared in April 2002, some analysts argue that the food crisis was caused, not by drought or bad harvests, but by a drop in remittances" (Pérouse de Montclos 2005:7). If this assertion is to be taken seriously, remittances play a significant role in fostering equity.

In Burkina Faso, about 15 percent of households received international remittances in the 1990s. Most were the poorest, and most of them female-headed rural families. In the same period, rural households are estimated to have reduced their poverty level by approximately 7 percent and urban households by 3 percent (Sander and Maimbo 2003:17). In rural western Kenya, where agriculture is made difficult by poor climatic conditions, remittances have sustained local demand for construction, education, and other non-farm activities and services, with a more significant effect on the local economy than is experienced in urban areas where more imports are consumed relative to the rural areas. Thus, rural households seem to benefit more from remittances than their urban counterparts, and welfare benefits derived go further for individuals, households, and the local economy in rural areas (Sander and Maimbo 2003:18).

Many families make economic decisions that entail collective investment in one family member's emigration in order to improve the family's prospects as a whole. In the colonial and post-colonial past, many African families invested in education in this manner. The expectation is that the migrant family member will assist others in establishing networks of chain migration, or otherwise enhance the family's welfare. This might include the reduction of physical labor, such as in Zimbabwe, where most households with migrants abroad farm less land than those without (Sander and Maimbo 2003:17). Information on Nigerian migrant Bini women from Edo State who are recruited into Italy's sex industry reveals that the entire family sometimes invests in raising the initial travel fare and the cost of acquiring metaphysical protection to smooth the way and guarantee success. Scholars are yet to reach a consensus on whether this is a strategy of the poor, middle class, or wealthy, or whether migrants from poor families would give more than the others or vice versa.

Debt servicing can also be facilitated by remittances, as can foreign currency reserves increases, trade balance, and national income in general. Remittances are only second to official and private Foreign Direct Investment (FDI) as a source of development finance in most developing countries, and actually exceed FDI in many poor countries. Many scholars argue that they have counter-cyclical effects of increasing income during periods of economic downturn in the recipient country (Ratha 2003:157). However, others point out the well-known fact that migration, being spurred by the desire for better economic opportunities, causes flows of people from poorer to richer countries, a process that is bound to have some positive equity benefits (Sriskanda-rajah 2005:3). If more remittances go toward investments, their effects on the national economic profile of migrants' countries of origin will ramify. However, the chances that investments will increase quickly are remote, due to the emphasis on prioritizing giving to support family members.

Remittances have negative as well as positive potential, as the donations of arms and ammunitions to ethnic militia and nationalist liberation efforts suggest. Remittances to Benin City and its environs have funded the construction of palatial houses dubbed "Italos" (Faris 2006): an acknowledgement of the Italian source of the remittances from migrant sex workers. Since some participants in the trade can guarantee family survival and support, accumulate resources, make visible displays of affluence, build self-sustaining and reproducible networks, and then gain autonomy as madams, those who have other avenues to upward mobility foreclosed to them join the bandwagon (Carling 2005). In this case, the desire to level the playing field between the haves and the have-nots has generated a response that entails the trafficking of very young women into the sex trade.

Internal migrations, such as to South Africa, can also cause problems, generating conflicts, tensions, and xenophobia. Migrant workers cause economic growth and the emergence of new transnational communities, but stymie prospects for genuine development by encouraging governments to fall back on migration as a way to vent pent-up frustrations with political and economic malaise. Migrants' family members may also strive less, work more sparingly, and consume more while saving less (Chami, Fullenkamp, and Jahjah 2003).

Many have rightly commented on remittances' propensity to contribute to development, particularly in the face of inadequate or inappropriate aid and the acceptance of philosophical opposition to welfarism that the adoption of structural adjustment policies indicate. However, such transfers also may create moral hazards in that they may discourage more vigorous efforts to enhance life chances through an increase in the capacity to meet welfare needs. Worse, they make it possible for the state to assume that there is no reason to attend to welfare needs, and no assistance is warranted, because needs are adequately met. Official development assistance can be similarly affected. Most significantly, market forces are allowed to take over what should be state responsibility: guaranteeing the basic welfare needs of citizens. This legitimizes a system that makes participation in human and drug trafficking seem legitimate survival mechanisms for those with few other options.

RECOMMENDATIONS AND PROSPECTS FOR FUTURE GIVING

Giving trends by diaspora African communities to their countries of origin are not easily discernable. Concerted and systematic data collection is needed in recipient countries and African immigrant communities. While preliminary findings have shown that there is more philanthropy occurring than is apparent in the literature, more study is needed. Other subjects for further study are African diaspora groups and organizations—they have neither been systematically mapped nor subjected to rigorous research.

While macroeconomic measures and policies that lower the cost of financial transfers may encourage African diaspora members to give more, exchange rate variations and better returns on investments do not appreciably affect officially recorded transfers, although there are noticeable increases in informal transfers (Puri and Ritzema n.d.). There will probably be more giving if there are more mechanisms that foster increased predictability, reliability, and affordability. The current formal market conditions tend to favor those who can afford to make larger transfers, but if the cost of transferring smaller amounts of money could be reduced, more people would be able and possibly willing to remit, increasing the volume and value of remittances, with consequent positive effects on social welfare and equity.

The ability of migrants to control and administer their investments and remittances in destination countries would also influence the desire to give, save, and invest more. If less money were lost in the currency exchange process, people would also be inclined to send more remittances. More and better banking services, particularly products that would encourage investment, such as credit facilities, mortgages, and good investment options are also needed (Puri and Ritzema n.d.).

Migrants often leave with the intent to return home after acquiring more and better skills or accumulating wealth or at least some material resources. These migrants may tend to maintain deeper connections than those uncertain or unwilling to return. They also will tend to remit more, for investments and projects like house building and family support. If they acquire improved skills and experience, their return can also be considered a brain gain. However, while some migrants consider themselves temporary, they end up remaining permanently in the country of sojourn. In the information age, there are many ways in which distance does not necessarily preclude deep and intense communication and relationships, even if these are virtual. Virtual transnational communities may also develop that facilitate collaborative scholarship, the exchange of ideas, and investment. These will become more important, particularly as more African countries bridge the information gap with improved access.

There is great need for increased institutionalization among African immigrant organizations. Many in the US have formed non-profit outfits whose formal existence is belied by the continued dominance of very powerful individuals and the lack of democratic governance. Despite some cross-fertilization, there can still be a standoffish relationship between old and new diaspora institutions, many of which hire employees from their in-group. Also, elders are traditionally privileged for positions of authority (Okome 2005a). These attitudes will probably dissipate over time as the new diaspora becomes more established, and as second and subsequent generations develop who are more likely to have accumulated social capital and to be able to relate to the older diaspora's institutions.

Due to the informality of the new diaspora's institutions, their frequent lack of engagement with the formal philanthropic regime, and the consequent lack of awareness of professional mechanisms and tools for prospecting for donors, the level of growth of philanthropic remittances may be slow. There is room for even more collaboration between established international philanthropic institutions and African migrants. More can be recruited as staff and consulted as experts, and more partnerships can be formed that bring each side's expertise to bear upon a common agenda.

Given that those with family members abroad able to remit funds have access to additional resources, and that there is rampant unemployment and underemployment, along with drastic limitations on upward mobility, survival may well depend on remittances (Sander and Maimbo 2003:17). However, the wholesale dependence on remittances to support the family members and home communities of migrants amounts to the privatization of essential development functions and responsibilities that should be undertaken by governments. It is crucial to prevent the development of a hands-off approach to development by the state.

Remittances should grow in value and volume as the new African diaspora becomes more established in the US and elsewhere, and as the numbers of migrants increase over time. Philanthropic transfers should grow as remittances do. Although this giving has touched and transformed many lives, philanthropy has not, and probably cannot, lift the continent out of poverty because of deep structural barriers to African economic development. Whatever good is engendered through remittances, it should only be an adjunct to significant state effort to combat the marginalization and poverty so many in Africa face.

REFERENCES

afrol News. 2004. "Somaliland Now Counts on Four Universities." Accessed July 23, 2006, 8:17 PM (http://www.afrol.com/articles/13763).

Ajayi, Femi. 2006. "Striving to Make a Difference." Presented at the Fifth Anniversary of Eko Club Atlanta, March 11, Hilton Gardens, Atlanta, Georgia.

Alpers, Edward A. 2001. "Defining the African Diaspora." Presented to the Center for Comparative Analysis Workshop, Conference on Comparative Black History, Michigan State University, October 25, East Lansing, Michigan.

Baruah, Nilim. 2006. "Remittances to Least Developed Countries (LDCs): Issues, Policies, Practices and Enhancing Development Impact." Presented at the Ministerial Conference of the Least Developed Countries on Enhancing the Development Impact of Remittances, International Office of Migration, February, Cotonou, Benin (http://www.iom.int/en/PDF_Files/benin/Remittances_to_LDCs_Background_Paper_English.pdf).

Carling, Jørgen. 2005. "Trafficking in Women from Nigeria to Europe." Migration Information Source, July 1. Accessed March 22, 2006, 6:47 PM (http://www.migrationinformation.org/Feature/display.cfm?id=318).

Chami, Ralph, Connel Fullenkamp, and Samir Jahjah. 2003. "Are Immigrant Remittance Flows a Source of Capital for Development?" IMF Working Paper, IMF Institute, September, Washington, DC.

Chappell, Kevin. 2006. "Kase Lawal: From Nigeria to Houston to History: When It Comes to Oil Exploration, Refining and Trading, the

Head of CAMAC Holdings Is in a Class by Himself." *Ebony* 61, No. 3, January:75–78.

Copeland-Carson, Jacqueline. 2005. "Promoting Diversity in Contemporary Black Philanthropy: Toward a New Conceptual Model." *New Directions for Philanthropic Fundraising* 48, summer:77–87.

Dikembe Mutombo Foundation Press Release. 2005. "Dikembe Mutombo Selected as One of 237 Exceptional Leaders Selected to Participate in New Major Global Undertaking to Shape the Future." January 11 (http://www.dmf.org/PDF/PRESSRELEASE.pdf).

Diouf-Kamara, Sylviane. 1997. "Senegalais de New York: Minorite Modele?" (The Senegalese in New York: A Model Minority?). Translated by Richard Philcox. *Black Renaissance/Renaissance Noir* 1.2:92–115.

Drumtra, Jeff. 2003. "West Africa's Refugee Crisis Spills Across Many Borders." Migration Information Source, Migration Policy Institute, August 1.

Dryden-Peterson, Sarah. 2004. "Educating Refugees in Countries of First Asylum: The Case of Uganda." May 1 (http://www.migrationinformation.org/feature/display.cfm?ID=220).

Everett, Anna. 2002. "The Revolution Will Be Digitized: Afrocentricity and the Digital Public Sphere." *Social Text* 70:2.

Faris, Stephan. 2006. "Italy's Sex Trade Pulls Teens Pushed by Poverty." *Women's e-News*, March 22. Retrieved March 22, 2006, 6:20 PM (http://www.womensenews.org/article.cfm/dyn/aid/1005).

Ghanaian Newsrunner. 1995. "President Praised in Harlem . . . Hints on Dual Citizenship for Americans of African Descent." October 21–25 (http://www.newsrunner.com/archive/NW241095.HTM).

Guardian. 2002. "Funds Continue to Flow Despite Drive to Freeze Network's Assets." September 5 (http://www.guardian.co.uk/ september11/oneyearon/story/0,12361,786123,00.html).

Hughes, Alan and Tennille Robinson. 2006. "Black Gold: Kase Lawal's Business Prowess, along with a Spike in Oil Prices, Is Fueling CAMAC International's Rise to the Nation's Second-Largest Black Business." *Black Enterprise* 36: 11, June 1:128–130, 132, 134.

Ifekwunigwe, Jayne. 2004. "An Inhospitable Port in the Storm: Recent Clandestine African Migrants and the Quest for Diasporic Recognition." Presented at the Conference on Imagining Diasporas: Space, Identity, and Social Change, May 14–16, University of Windsor, Ontario, Canada.

International Labor Organization. 2005. "Women's Employment: Global Trends and ILO Responses." ILO Contribution, 49th Session, Commission on the Status of Women, UN, New York, February 28 to March 11, 2005. Retrieved July 23, 2006, 7:37 PM (http://www.ilo. ru/gender/files/WomenEmploymentsEng.pdf).

Kelley, Matt. 2005. "Hakeem Olajuwon's Mosque Linked to Terror." Associated Press, February 9. Retrieved May 1, 2006 (http:// nm.onlinenigeria.com/templates/?a=760&z=12).

Light, Ivan, Parminder Bhachu, and Stavros Karageorgis. n.d. "Migration Networks and Immigrant Entrepreneurship." UCLA, Institute for Social Science Research Papers, 5:1, Los Angeles, California. (http://repositories.cdlib.org/issr/volume5/1/).

Loup, Jacques. 2005. "Economy of Solidarity: Expatriate Workers Remittances to Sub Saharan Africa." Fondation L'Innovation Politique, June, Paris, France. Retrieved July 15, 2006, 3:13 PM (http://www. fondapol.org/pdf/Fondapol-Loup-VA-210605.pdf).

Martin, Susan, Philip Martin, and Patrick Weil. 2002. "Fostering Cooperation Between Source and Destination Countries," October 1 (http://www.migrationinformation.org/feature/display.cfm?ID=60).

Mufson, Steven. 2000. "Eritrea Won't Block Food Aid for Ethiopia." *Washington Post*, April 8, p. A14–15.

Mutume, Gumisai. 2005. "Workers' Remittances: A Boon to Development. Money Sent Home by African Migrants Rivals Development Aid." *Africa Renewal* 19, no. 3, October (http://www.un.org/ecosocdev/geninfo/afrec/vol19no3/193remittance.html).

New Vision. 2000. "Dual Citizenship Beneficial." December 30, 2000, Kampala. Reproduced by AllAfrica.com on the web on January 2, 2001 (http://fr.allafrica.com/stories/200101020422.html).

Nigeria Higher Education Foundation. n.d. Retrieved March 15, 2006, 10:32 AM (http://www.thenhef.org/fanton.php).

Okome, Mojúbàolú Olúfúnké. 2002a. "The Antinomies of Globalization: Causes of Contemporary African Immigration to the United States of America." *Ìrìnkèrindò: A Journal of African Migration* 1:1, September (http://www.africamigration.com/m_okome_globalization_01.htm).

———. 2002b. "The Antinomies of Globalization: Some Consequences of Contemporary African Immigration to the United States of America." *Ìrìnkèrindò: A Journal of African Migration* 1:1, September (http://www.africamigration.com/m_okome_globalization_02.htm).

———. 2002c. "Immigrant Voices in Cyberspace: Spinning Continental and Diasporan Africans into the World Wide Web." Presented at "Gendering the Diaspora: Women, Culture, and Historical Change in the Caribbean and the Nigerian Hinterland," a conference at Dartmouth College, November 21–24, Hanover, NH.

———. 2005a. "Emergent African Immigrant Philanthropy in New York City." Chapter 8 in *Race and Ethnicity in New York City*, vol. 7, edited by Jerry Krase and Ray Hutchison. New York: Elsevier Press.

———. 2005b. Interviews of pastors of African immigrant churches in Brooklyn, New York.

Okpewho, Isidore, Carole Boyce Davies, and Ali A. Mazrui. 1999. *The African Diaspora: African Origins and New World Identities*. Bloomington: Indiana University Press.

Orozco, Manuel. 2003. "Worker Remittances in an International Scope." InterAmerican Dialogue Research Series Remittance Project, Washington, DC.

Patterson, Tiffany R. and Robin D.G. Kelley. 2000. "Unfinished Migrations: Reflections on the African Diaspora and the Making of the Modern World." *African Studies Review* 43:11–45.

Pérouse de Montclos, Marc-Antoine. 2005. *African Diasporas, Remittances, and Africa South of the Sahara: A Strategic Assessment*. ISS Monograph Series no. 112, March:2.

Puri, Shivani and Tineke Ritzema. n.d. "Migrant Worker Remittances, Micro-finance and the Informal Economy: Prospects and Issues." Working Paper No. 21, International Labor Organization (http://www.ilo.org/public/english/employment/finance/papers/wpap21.htm).

Ratha, Dilip. 2003. "Workers' Remittances: An Important and Stable Source of External Development Finance." Pp. 157–175 in *Global Development Finance*. Washington, DC: World Bank.

Roberts, Sam. 2005. "More Africans Enter US Than in Days of Slavery." *New York Times*, February 21.

Sander, Cerstin. 2003. "Migrant Remittances to Developing Countries—A Scoping Study: Overview and Introduction to Issues for Pro-poor Financial Services." Bannock Consulting, prepared for the UK Department of International Development, June.

Sander, Cerstin and Samuel Munzele Maimbo. 2003. "Migrant Labor Remittances in Africa: Reducing Obstacles to Developmental Contributions." World Bank Africa Region Working Paper Series No. 64, November.

Schlecht, Jennifer. 2003. "War in Liberia Highlights Health Threats to Refugees." Migration Information Source, Migration Policy Institute, August 1 (http://www.migrationinformation.org/feature/display.cfm?ID=151).

Sriskandarajah, Dhananjayan. 2005. "Towards Fairer Flows: Policies to Optimise the Impact of Migration on Economic Development." Paper Prepared for the Policy Analysis and Research Programme of the Global Commission on International Migration Institute for Public Policy Research, September (http://www.gcim.org/attachements/TP4.pdf).

Sykes, Rebecca. 1999. "Alumna Speaks Out for Freedom." *The Andover Bulletin* 92, spring, no. 3:6–7.

Taipei Times. 2002. "'Hawala' Makes Tracking Capital a Daunting Task," October 2, front page (http://www.taipeitimes.com/News/archives/2001/10/02/0000105464).

UN Security Council. 2001. "Security Council Committee Concerning Afghanistan Issues Further Addendum." Press Release AFG/163 SC/7206. Retrieved July 24, 2006, 11:30 AM (http://www.un.org/News/Press/docs/2001/afg163.doc.htm).

UNDP. 2004. "New UNDP/World Bank Survey." Retrieved July 23, 2006, 10:21 PM (http://www.so.undp.org/Quarterly%20Updates/UNDP%20Somalia%20Quarterly%20Update%20-%20April%202004.pdf).

US Bureau of the Census. 2002. American Community Survey Profile 2002: 2002 ACS Tabular Profile for United States—Table 2. (http://www.census.gov/acs/www/Products/Profiles/Single/2002/ACS/Tabular/010/01000US2.htm).

US Department of Commerce and National Telecommunications and Information Administration. 1999. "Falling Through the Net: Defining the Digital Divide," July (http://www.ntia.doc.gov/ntiahome/fttn99/contents.html).

US Department of Commerce; Economic and Statistics Administration and National Telecommunications and Information Administration. 2000. "Falling Through the Net: Toward Digital Inclusion—A Report on Americans' Access to Technology Tools," October (http://search.ntia.doc.gov/pdf/fttn00.pdf).

University of Burao. 2004. "Update: A Major Meeting in Oslo Discussed Ways to Contribute to Burao's Young University," November 21. Retrieved July 24, 2006, 10:57 AM (http://www.buraouniversity.com/news/archive/21Nov2004.htm).

University of Hargeisa. 2006. "About University of Hargeisa." Retrieved July 23, 2006, 8:01 PM (http://www.hargeisauniversity.net/AboutUS.htm).

Watkins Owens, Irma. 1996. *Blood Relations: Caribbean Immigrants and the Harlem Community, 1900–1930.* Bloomington: Indiana University Press.

World Bank. 2006. *Global Economic Prospects: Economic Implications for Remittances and Migration, 2006.* Washington, DC: The World Bank.

World Bank Institute. 2005. "Somali Universities Enter the World of Distance Learning." Retrieved July 23, 2006, 9:50 PM (http://web.worldbank.org/WBSITE/EXTERNAL/WBI/0,,contentMDK:20852653~pagePK:209023~piPK:207535~theSitePK:213799,00.html).

Zeleza, Paul Tiyambe. n.d. "African Labor and International Migrations to the North: Building New TransAtlantic Bridges." (http://www.afrst.uiuc.edu/SEMINAR/AfricanLabor.doc).

CHAPTER 7

DIASPORA ENGAGEMENT IN THE CARIBBEAN

BARBARA J. MERZ

Like most Caribbean nations, Guyana, Haiti, and Jamaica have significant diaspora populations. While they face different development challenges and have different diaspora policies, for all three countries the question of how to leverage diaspora engagement in development is a priority concern. This chapter will summarize research on these three nations in order to illuminate how diaspora groups engage in Caribbean development—and how the groups themselves view that engagement.

Much scholarship and policy dialogue has focused on remittances (see chapter by de Ferranti and Ody in this volume). However, less attention has been given to the other ways in which diasporas support their home country's development, such as contributions of time and professional expertise—"brain circulation" as opposed to "brain drain." This chapter on the Caribbean diaspora aims, in part, to draw attention to the potential benefit of these non-money contributions to the Caribbean, recogniz-

This chapter draws on research case studies prepared for the Canadian International Development Agency (CIDA) by Barbara Merz and Kathleen Dunn (December 2005). Special thanks to Kathleen Dunn who co-authored the case studies; to Naresh Singh who continues to serve as part of the Caribbean's engaged diaspora; to Ellie Buteau and Kathleen McKenna for analysis of the survey data; and to Cynthia Chang, Bernard Parham, Ginger Tanton, and Alexandra Wood for their research assistance. In addition, I am grateful to participants in the May 2006 Global Equity Initiative's conference on diaspora giving and equitable development for their comments on and improvements to an earlier version of this chapter.

ing that there are negative effects on development stemming from the massive outpouring of migrants. The three case studies presented here analyze the views of both diaspora members and in-country leaders involved in Caribbean development in order to explore current and future opportunities for diasporas to enhance development in their countries of origin.

The scale of Caribbean out-migration is staggering. Thus, in proportion to their local populations, Caribbean nations have some of the largest diaspora communities in the world (Nurse 2004). However, similar to other regions, these diaspora communities are far from monolithic and reflect the diversity of their origin countries—even within national groups. Caribbean nations have multiple colonial heritages and their national languages include Dutch, English, French, Haitian Creole, and Spanish. Therefore, it is unsurprising that diaspora engagement with the Caribbean is also diverse. The three countries selected as case studies—Guyana, Haiti, and Jamaica—are not meant to be representative for all of the Caribbean. However, deeper exploration of diaspora engagement within this limited set of countries reveals a range of opportunities and challenges that may provide insight for other Caribbean countries that wish to engage their diasporas to enhance development.

Development is a complex concept. The definition of "development" as used in this chapter is based upon work by Amartya Sen, Nobel Prize winner in economics and Senior Fellow with the Global Equity Initiative, who defined development as the effort to promote human capability through expanding the range of things that all people can choose to be or to do with their lives (Sen 1999). The human capability approach to development seeks to remove obstacles—such as illiteracy, ill health, lack of access to basic resources, or lack of civil and political freedoms—by expanding opportunity. (See Chapter 1 of this volume.) This approach to development is not rigid across cultures or over time. Sen deliberately left the capability approach to human development "incomplete" to ensure ongoing relevance to a variety of settings. Through participatory processes, communities set human development goals for themselves to reflect individual and cultural diversity (Alkire 2002).

To better understand how diaspora engagement may advance human development, it is important to consider whether or how diaspora contributions map onto local development agendas. To do so, it is necessary to compare diaspora contributions with stated development priorities of in-country leadership. This chapter reports on similarities and differences in these development priorities both among the three countries and in each case between the diaspora and in-country respondents—and suggests possible ways of increasing diaspora contributions to enhance development in the Caribbean.

Surveys and interviews conducted as part of the research were designed to gather original data on diaspora engagement and respondents' views on their contribution to development in their country of origin. Researchers collected survey data on the perspectives of a small sample of actively engaged diaspora members and interview responses from leaders within the countries of origin. Information and views about diaspora contributions were compared and contrasted among leaders both at home and abroad. The data portray a rich diversity in Caribbean diaspora activity in the three cases.

One hundred diaspora members from Guyana, Haiti, and Jamaica completed the Diaspora Engagement Survey. The survey elicited diaspora members to describe the methods and magnitude of their personal engagement with their country of origin. The diaspora sample includes members from over sixty diaspora organizations ranging from alumni groups and professional associations to diaspora umbrella associations. The diaspora survey findings were then complemented by interviews with leaders within the country of origin. Over fifty in-country leaders were interviewed, representing a cross-section of nonprofits, business, and government representatives.

The scope of this research is purposefully limited to diaspora leaders and a targeted set of leaders within Guyana, Haiti, and Jamaica. The data collection from both diaspora and in-country leaders provides a comparative lens on contemporary views regarding diaspora engagement in three Caribbean nations. Nevertheless, the small sample size and targeted focus may obscure reasonable explanatory factors on the question of what encourages or constrains diaspora engagement in Caribbean development. Diaspora engagement alone should not be viewed as a panacea for Caribbean development. In fact, the mere existence of such an enormous diaspora population from relatively small countries indicates a profound loss of human capital that each of these nations must face.

DIASPORA CHARACTERISTICS

There are several defined migration corridors from the Caribbean to major cities in Canada, the United States, and the United Kingdom. For example, French-speaking Montreal has long been a draw for Haitian migrants. It is also well-known that Cuban migrants have predominantly settled in Miami, Florida. In the United States the Caribbean population has largely settled in two eastern states: New York (36 percent) and Florida (36 percent) (Lapointe 2004). In Canada, the cities of Toronto and Ottawa have grown with both Afro-Caribbean and Indo-Caribbean immigrants. In the UK, there is a long history of Caribbean migration given the British colonial relationship with the region. Individuals from the Anglo-Caribbean islands landed in England as early as the seventeenth century, often arriving in the domestic service of planter families returning to Britain. More recent Caribbean migrants have settled in ethnic neighborhoods such as those found along Brixton Road in London. While this clustered migration has been the centerpiece of some political and social tensions in London, it has also created a rich local culture with Caribbean influences found in new restaurants, music, and art. Despite these patterns, migration corridors continually evolve and are dependent on migration policies in both sending and receiving countries.

It has also been suggested that global migration patterns are bringing new ideas and changing expectations in both sending and receiving countries. An important example is migration's influence on gender equity (see Chapter 1 of this volume). In the Caribbean, a recent study for the United Nations International Research and Training Institute for the Advancement of Women provides details on the predominately female migratory flow from the Dominican Republic. Dominican women have been migrating as the main economic providers for their households. The UN study reports that the money earned and sent by Dominican women migrant workers to Spain has empowered them as decision-makers within their households both at home and abroad. As breadwinners, they have influence over how their earnings are spent. In 90 percent of cases money was remitted directly to other women—often to a mother or a sister who was left in charge of the household back home. Despite rising economic power for these women, traditional gender roles persist in the Dominican Republic. Women's improved status as household provider has not yet led to changes in ideas and culture that promote gender equality. The study concludes that gender beliefs change at a slower pace in this Caribbean case study than would be expected by the autonomous decision-making demonstrated by these migrant women (García and Paiewonsky 2006). These results, it must be noted, are limited to the diaspora population studied: in this case, the female diaspora was characterized by higher levels of poverty and lower levels of education than the diaspora population in the US, where a large number of Caribbean migrants are from urban middle-class backgrounds.

As each of the regional chapters in this volume emphasize, diaspora engagement varies greatly by country, by history, and by socio-economic strata. Diaspora preferences are shaped by structural variables such as gender, class, and race. Contributions back to one's country of origin are often connected to identification with place and specific issue-based causes. Consequently, understanding diaspora engagement requires analysis at the national, regional, and local level. The following table summarizes key demographic and macro-economic facts on population, migration, and poverty rates by country to provide context for the summary of research findings that follows.

Table 1: Key Facts by Country

	Guyana	Haiti	Jamaica
Current In-Country Population[a] (millions)	0.7	8.3	2.6
Estimated Diaspora Population[b] (millions)	0.4–0.7	1–2	0.8–2
Net Annual Migration Rate[b] (migrants/1,000 population)	–7.49	–1.31	–6.27
Percentage of Population below National Poverty Line[c]	35%	80%	19%
Unemployment Rate	>9%	66%	12%
Annual Remittances[d] (millions USD)	100	810	1,400
Top Destination Countries for Migration	US, UK	Canada, US	Canada, US, UK

Sources: a) Figures from http://www.cia.gov/cia/publications/factbook. b) Figures from http://www.migrationinformation.com. c) Statistics based on national governments' definition of the poverty line. d) 2003 figures from http://www.worldbank.org/data/countrydata/countrydata.html.

SUMMARY OF RESEARCH FINDINGS

The sample of diaspora leaders is evenly distributed among the three countries studied. The gender balance in the sample is 56 percent male and 44 percent female. Respondents reside in the US, Canada, and the UK. They are well-educated (91 percent have a college degree), are mostly middle-aged and older (50 percent are over fifty years of age), and are by and large middle-class (over 80 percent earn more than US$50,000 per year). Basic demographic information about the overall sample of respondents is summarized in the graphs below.

Figures 1–4: Demographic Information
on Diaspora Engagement Survey Respondents

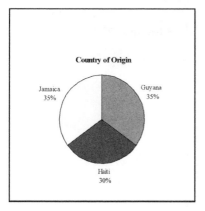

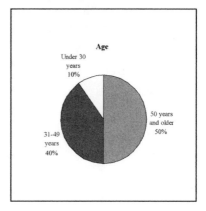

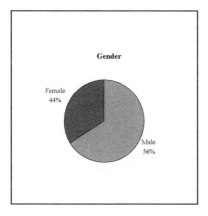

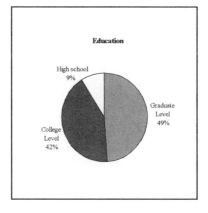

Diaspora members engage with their country of origin through a combination of time, in-kind, and philanthropic donations. Survey results show that the desire to support hometowns, educational institutions, national development, religious institutions, family and friends, and wider development all motivate diaspora engagement. The causes for which diaspora are most personally engaged are in the areas of education, community development, and youth.

Many respondents were motivated by national loyalty. "Helping with issues important to my country's development" received the highest number of "very high importance" responses. However, motivations to help family and home communities also ranked highly. This is consistent with a view of diaspora engagement as "long-distance nationalism" originating from reasons centering on identity, which is formed at multiple levels including family, community, and nation (see chapters by Kapur and Najam in this volume).

Table 2

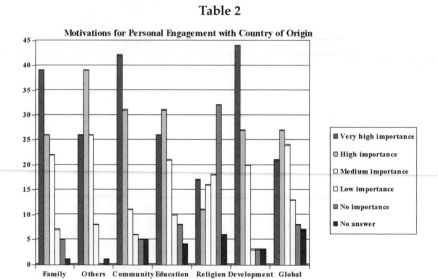

When offering a self-assessment of their future engagement, the majority of respondents reported that their engagement could be higher if they trusted that their contributions would be put to good use. Only a quarter reported that it is already as high as it could be. Three-quarters of the respondents believe that contributing skills and knowledge is the most effective way to impact the future development of their home country.

The responses point toward frequent returns to the country of origin: 59 percent report that they return at least once annually. The purpose of the visit is principally to see family and friends (85 percent), to participate in development-oriented activities (51 percent), and to conduct business (39 percent). Others reasons for return visits included interacting with government officials, vacationing, and attending conferences or cultural festivals.

Issues to which diaspora members contribute in their country of origin and their country of residence are substantively aligned. The top three issues that diaspora members contribute time and money to in their country of origin are education, community development, and youth concerns. These same three issues were the most frequently cited for contributions of time and money in their country of residence. Interestingly, in the country of residence, the next most important issue is arts and culture, whereas in contributions to the country of origin it is for economic growth. Providing for basic economic opportunities still dominates over arts and culture in the philanthropic landscape of all three country cases. However, there were exceptions to this general trend. For example, in Guyana, many diaspora members contributed to a June 2005 commemoration to mark the twenty-fifth anniversary of the assassination of Walter Rodney, a Guyanese historian-politician. The event included cultural and artistic events to highlight Guyana's shared African and Indian heritage and featured Dr. Rodney's writing. While rallying diaspora commitment to this cultural event, the organizers placed great emphasis on the return of the diaspora to Guyana to commemorate.

As might be expected, respondents on average spend almost twice as much time on resident country causes than on country of origin causes, but they spend almost twice as much money and in-kind donations on country of origin causes than on resident country causes. The time per month spent on causes in the country of residence averaged 40 hours while the time per month spent on causes in the country of origin averaged 23 hours.

Table 3
In-kind Donations versus Philanthropic Donations

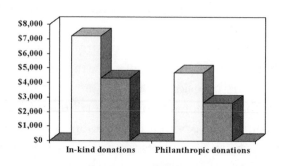

☐ Country of Origin Causes ■ Resident Country Causes

Table 4
Contributions of Time Reported by the Diaspora Respondents

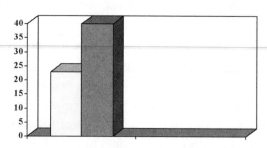

☐ Time to Country of Origin Causes ■ Time to Resident Country Causes

Issues to which diaspora respondents contribute in their countries of origin and what they consider to be the development priorities of the country were not as closely aligned. Across all three countries, respondents viewed the top development priorities as education (47 percent) and economic growth (33 percent). The categories listed are broad, so it is not possible to interpret whether education was singled out for greater access to education, for higher quality, or at what level, i.e., primary, tertiary, or graduate. Similarly, economic growth could identify a range of levels and approaches. Nevertheless, it is clear that diaspora members are concerned with the current status of education and economic growth in their countries of origin and that many individuals have chosen to migrate from the Caribbean because of the prospect of better schooling or jobs abroad. The next sections highlight diaspora survey findings by country for Guyana, Haiti, and Jamaica.

Guyana—Development Priorities and Obstacles

Guyana's high emigration rate has created a diaspora so extensive that nearly everyone in the country has either family or friends in the diaspora. The number of Guyanese living outside Guyana is as high as the current population within the country. A distinctive feature of the Guyanese diaspora is its split along ethnic lines. The Guyanese population is comprised of individuals who migrated from India, Africa, and in smaller numbers from China, in addition to a minority population of indigenous Amerindians. A majority of Guyanese retain an identity of "belonging to an imagined community of a distant ancestral nation" (Orozco 2004). Some Indo-Guyanese maintain traditional Indian dress and customs and practice Hindu religious ceremonies and a few consider themselves Non-Resident Indians even after their families have lived for generations in Guyana. Consequently, many Indo-Guyanese and the Afro-Guyanese consider themselves part of the Indian or African diasporas—creating a "double diaspora" identity for those who have moved away from Guyana. This dual identity of many Guyanese colors how the diaspora interacts abroad, how it gives back to Guyana, and how it perceives government action.

In terms of identified development priorities for Guyana, greater political stability, economic stability, and better education were the top three priorities for both surveyed diaspora leaders and in-country interviewees. However, there was a glaring disconnect in diaspora responses between what they identified as priorities in Guyana and what they identified as the Guyana-related causes to which they currently dedicate their time and money. Most respondents engage in social causes rather than in the political or economic causes they identified as the highest priorities for Guyana's development. The wide variety of reasons given for return visits to Guyana indicate a mix of personal and professional purposes, such as conducting medical tours and outreach programs, attending reunions for high schools, conducting research, sharing professional skills on a consultative basis, and attending a cultural festival.

When Guyanese diaspora leaders were asked if their personal engagement contributed to Guyana's development, they felt that they did contribute and listed concrete examples such as: working as a regional malaria advisor, conducting direct outreach through health clinics and schools, and interacting with NGOs in the country. Other contributions include in-kind donations such as shipments of educational materials to schools or ministries. For example, the UK Guyana Law Association collects law books and computers from the diaspora community and ships them to the chief justice in Guyana, who is responsible for distributing them to courts for use by judges and magistrates in Guyana. In an interview with Carl Singh, the chief justice of the High Court in Guyana, he noted that the diaspora of the UK makes a significant contribution to the law in Guyana: "[t]he library is filled with donated books and materials and these materials benefit the administration of justice in the country" (Singh 2005).

Guyana's racial divisions have contributed to a divisive political environment between Indo-Guyanese and Afro-Guyanese parties. Race-based divisions tend to replicate themselves in the organizations of diaspora groups. However, during recent emergency responses, the diaspora overcame race-based divisions in many cases. Guyana's diaspora was particularly active in the aftermath of major disasters such as the flooding in early 2005. Although the floods received very little international media attention, the diaspora became one of the key channels of support. Such diaspora groups as the Guyana Tri-State Alliance; Health & Educational Relief for Guyana, Inc.; the Guyanese-American Cultural Association of Central Florida; the Guyana Flood Relief Organization; and the Queen's College of Guyana Alumni Association galvanized flood aid by holding fundraisers (Phillips 2005). Although the activity was limited to temporary relief, there is interest in whether the experience may be extended to ongoing development efforts. Another promising development among the Guyana diaspora has been the creation of a group investment fund to build low-income homes near Georgetown, the capital. This is an example of diaspora engagement meeting market demand where the domestic economy alone does not serve.

Ongoing race-based divisions may contribute to the lack of trust evidenced by the diaspora. Seventy percent of Guyanese respondents agreed with the statement that their engagement could be significantly higher if they had more trust that their contributions would be put to good use. Even this targeted sample of highly engaged diaspora leaders spends both more time and more money on causes based in their country of residence than on causes based in Guyana. (For more analysis of the Guyana case, see Merz and Dunn 2005a.)

Haiti—Development Priorities and Obstacles

Every one of the surveyed Haitian diaspora leaders reported that the diaspora could and should play a greater role in Haiti's development. As the poorest nation in the Western Hemisphere, with 80 percent of its people living below the poverty line, Haiti's development priorities are vast and pressing. Haiti's population of over eight million people is the largest of any Caribbean country. Political violence, recurrent government turnover, and frequent natural disasters contribute to the inability of the country to meet the basic needs of many of its citizens. Corruption in Haiti complicates matters. In Transparency International's Annual Corruption Perceptions Index (CPI), Haiti ranks second to last of all 159 nations surveyed (Transparency International 2005). Corruption undermines economic growth and repels foreign investment. In light of the challenging environment, Haiti will need to engage a range of resources to make progress toward development priorities. Haiti's diverse diaspora may be one such resource.

Diaspora respondents already contribute to Haitian causes that relate to education, community, and economic development; however, the majority of respondents report that the Haitian government does not adequately seek to involve them in the country's development. The greatest obstacle reported for diaspora engagement with Haiti was lack of receptiveness on the part of the Haitian government (60 percent). However, Alix Baptiste, the Minister of Haitians Living Abroad, notes that the Haitian government has explicitly created a ministry to actively engage diaspora. Although many in the Haitian diaspora may not currently know about or appreciate it, the government is sponsoring diaspora outreach through this designated Ministry—one of the few such diaspora-specific posts in the Caribbean (Baptiste 2005).

Other obstacles to Haitian diaspora engagement in development noted in diaspora survey responses were: lack of dual citizenship with Haiti, lack of trust in policy-makers, lack of security, and lack of political stability. With regards to coordination by the Ministry of Haitians Living Abroad, diaspora respondents encouraged their government to adequately fund the current Ministry and create satellite bureaus outside of Haiti. The Ministry could publish current projects of Haitians in the diaspora through its website. Diaspora members would have a forum to present their ideas, rationales, and outcomes of projects sponsored by various Haitian diaspora groups. The respondents also noted that the Ministry should spread information on opportunities for the diaspora to invest in Haiti.

As it did in Guyana, the problem of distrust appeared in the case of Haiti, though in somewhat different form. Importantly, some in-country leaders expressed doubt about greater diaspora involvement in Haiti due to concerns of corruption and elitism in the country. They also noted that not all of those living in Haiti welcome diaspora involvement in domestic political affairs. (For more analysis of the Haiti case, see Merz and Dunn 2005c.)

Jamaica—Development Priorities and Obstacles

In the case of Jamaica, there was good alignment on development priorities between diaspora leaders and in-country interviewees. However, concerns about security loomed much more prominently for those living in Jamaica. From their perspective, crime is the central issue holding Jamaica back, and they noted that a precondition to development is the need to deal with growing crime rates. However, the Jamaican government has failed to get crime under control. In fact, violent crime indicators continue to escalate. Several interviewees noted that crime and insecurity are directly linked to economic development because they can drive away long-term investment, increase costs of production, decrease worker productivity, and raise insurance rates. An often overlooked cost of sustained crime rates is the loss of Jamaicans who choose to live in more secure locales abroad.

Circular movement between Jamaicans at home and abroad complicates attempts to define and quantify the diaspora. Jamaica, like other Caribbean countries, has seen significant numbers of its best-educated leave in pursuit of opportunities abroad. An estimated 76 percent of Jamaicans with a college education live in the United States (Lapoint 2004:5). Despite, or perhaps due to, high out-migration Jamaica faces an unemployment rate of 12 percent and about one-fifth of its citizens live below the poverty line. In addition to crime, poor infrastructure and low levels of education continue to plague the country. Nevertheless, great wealth exists on the island, giving rise to opportunities to court the diaspora to return and to invest in business ventures, particularly in safe-guarded tourist areas. While all in-country interviewees felt that the diaspora should play a role in Jamaica's development, many noted that diaspora contributions do not replace the significant costs to Jamaica of its brain drain.

All Jamaican diaspora survey respondents also indicated that the diaspora should contribute to Jamaica's development. Approximately half feel that involvement through diaspora organizations and networks based outside Jamaica is the most effective way to contribute. There was little attention paid to the essential role of human capital in development. As Devesh Kapur has pointed out, one must answer the question of "who" is going to improve domestic institutions, and thus raise the development prospects of the country. International migration is invariably positively selected (see Kapur chapter in this volume). One major obstacle to temporary or permanent return migration to Jamaica is the widespread concern for unacceptably high levels of crime discussed above. Thus, the Jamaican government must consider how to tap professional expertise in the diaspora through out-reach. Fortunately, the Jamaican government has begun to invest in programs to cultivate diaspora engagement. Unfortunately, many diaspora members view these state programs as largely inadequate.

The Jamaican government created a diaspora outreach initiative spearheaded by Senator Delano Franklin, the Minister of State in the Ministry of Foreign Affairs. At a Jamaican diaspora conference in 2004, diaspora members from the US, Canada, and the UK helped to create a centralized Jamaican diaspora website, supported the official designation of 16 June as National Diaspora Day, and backed the creation of a Diaspora Advisory Board to counsel state-led diaspora initiatives. One such state-led effort is the Jamaican Diaspora Foundation. The Foundation will function as a research institute at the University of the West Indies' Mona Business School. It will attempt to coordinate diaspora resources through a diaspora skills database, cataloguing skills of diaspora members interested in giving back to Jamaica. Despite these Herculean plans for diaspora outreach and coordination, only 11 percent of the diaspora respondents indicated that the government's outreach is sufficient. (For more analysis of the Jamaica case, see Merz and Dunn 2005b.)

In-Country Interviews: Relationships with the Diaspora
The diaspora is not a distant community for any of the three countries. Every interviewee reported some direct relationship with the diaspora, such as a parent, child, aunt, cousin, or friend who had moved abroad. Nevertheless, the interviewees acknowledge a lack of trust between those who had moved and the policy-makers who remained behind. This was identified as the most significant obstacle to greater diaspora engagement in the country of origin. Distrust was most pronounced in the Guyanese and Haitian diaspora responses. Another hindrance for Guyana's relationship with its diaspora was the lack of an explicit government diaspora policy. Guyanese officials expressed their desire for enhanced diaspora engagement and Guyanese diaspora leaders expressed receptivity to explicit government policies to guide their involvement. Yet, relations between the Guyanese diaspora and the state remain officially unconsummated.

In Haiti, some interviewees expressed doubt about greater diaspora impact, noting that not all of those living in Haiti welcome this involvement:

> The biggest obstacle for those in the diaspora who want to or who would want to become engaged in effective development for the country is above all the lack of infrastructure, the absence of incentive, and a certain rejection of the diaspora by an important fraction of nationals who stayed in the country. (Chavenet 2005)

Diaspora can be perceived as a threat to local leaders and entrenched social elites. Some diaspora respondents acknowledge feeling disconnected from modern Haitian perspectives and lifestyle. They note that real cultural barriers exist between the diaspora and those who have remained in Haiti. Socio-economic divisions that existed on the island perpetuate abroad within the diaspora. Any effort to promote diaspora engagement must consider these divisions. Better utilizing of the diaspora as an engine for economic and social opening is urgent, as one Haitian interviewee noted in his stark observation:

> The diaspora must help Haiti become a more open society since an island could never be a closed society and prosper. The diaspora could be a deciding factor in bringing about a positive opening of the economy, otherwise Haiti will remain isolated; eight million Blacks lost at sea. (LaTorture 2005)

Another interviewee, a former Commerce Minister of Haiti, offered a specific entry point for diaspora contributions to business development through joint ventures:

> The diaspora could enhance its contributions through the creation of a small business administration program that

would create joint ventures between Haitians in Haiti and those abroad. This is a very feasible and concrete option. (St. Lot 2005)

However, she also notes that diaspora members are hesitant to create businesses due to security problems and a lack of solid property rights in Haiti. This illustrates that effective diaspora engagement often depends on state stability and organization as precursors to meaningful participation.

From the outside Jamaica is viewed as a model Caribbean nation for its well-organized and high-profile official diaspora engagement. Diaspora members from Guyana and Haiti frequently cited Jamaica as a shining example of diaspora relations. However, those within Jamaica were not as glowing about their country's diaspora initiatives. Jamaican respondents questioned their government's political motivations in coordinating diaspora. They expressed skepticism of the government's efforts to cultivate wealthy diaspora members overseas to lobby on behalf of Jamaica. Senator Franklin's initiative was viewed as elitist. Many believed that the initiative accentuates ties between the government and wealthy Jamaicans—either at home or abroad. Respondents also expressed doubts about the universally positive benefits of remittance flows into Jamaica.

Remittances can be considered a double-edged sword for development. Jamaican diaspora members criticized the Jamaican government for using the over $1 billion remittance flow as an excuse to not undertake a more aggressive economic development policy at home. This criticism is not unique to Jamaica; it is common in other high-remitting migrant communities such as Mexican-Americans. The Jamaican diaspora survey respondents cited Mexico as a state with strong diaspora programs. The Mexican government has attempted to harness the development potential of remittances, particularly in rural Mexican towns where massive migration continues. Mexico's national social development program, the "Three-for-One" Program, matches every dollar donated by a hometown association with a dollar each from the local, state, and national governments. The program is meant to encourage Mexican hometown associations in the US and to donate pooled funds to community development projects throughout Mexico, though the results of such projects are highly variable (Merz 2005). Jamaicans, too, are exploring ways of increasing the development impact of remittances. For example, the leading Jamaican business group, Grace Kennedy, takes a portion of its remittance transfer fee and funds educational projects, as does Jamaica National Bank. However, others have pointed out that the Caribbean remittance market is dominated by both monopolies and oligopolies resulting in some of the highest transaction costs in the Western Hemisphere (Lapointe 2004). Additionally, remittances should not distract the state from cultivating increased economic opportunities at home.

ENGAGING THE CARIBBEAN DIASPORA: OPPORTUNITIES FOR STATES, AGENCIES, AND CARICOM

The survey results show a complex array of ways that diaspora are giving back to their countries of origin. However, some diaspora leaders believe that their potential to contribute to development is underestimated. One representative diaspora survey response states that "[t]he government must appreciate the value of the diaspora *beyond remittances* and open meaningful and effective ways to draw on their expertise, skills, and experiences for the well-being of the country's future." Therefore, for states and development agencies interested in increasing the impact of diaspora engagement with the Caribbean, three areas of opportunities arise from this research. First, trust-building measures between diaspora and the home-country governments are essential. This is true across all three case studies, but is particularly relevant for Guyana and Jamaica. Haiti's recently elected government will require time to build basic infrastructure and reestablish the legitimacy of the state before it can work on the trust-building it also needs. Second, Caribbean states need to clearly articulate their development priorities to signal areas for diaspora contributions of time, talent, and money. Third, greater coordination of ongoing diaspora engagement efforts is needed—both between diaspora groups and the state as well as among diaspora groups. Finally, there are compelling reasons to promote regional dialogue around strategies for diaspora involvement in Caribbean development.

In assessing future impact on development in the region, both the equity implications and the sustainability of diaspora ventures must be carefully considered. The findings reveal that diaspora contributions to development in their country of origin are often centered on personal preferences of place or issue-based causes. Promoting greater diaspora engagement without clarification of local priorities poses a risk of misalignment of diaspora efforts with locally defined development goals. However, better alignment will likely be an iterative process. When diaspora groups first begin there is a greater chance of a mismatch between their contribution and national development priorities but as diaspora groups get more experience and become more sophisticated in their interventions, alignment on development priorities should improve. Part of this process is to ensure that there is local accountability and assessment of the projects—not only by the state but also by the communities that the project is meant to serve.

The promotion of greater diaspora involvement in home country affairs should not be assumed to have only positive impacts. Diaspora survey results indicate that diaspora engage or plan to engage on issues they feel to be the priorities for their country of origin. However, there is insufficient engagement with local policy-makers to effectively align activities with local development priorities. Therefore, promoting greater diaspora engagement requires continued dialogue with in-country leadership to ensure that development efforts by the diaspora are informed by what local leaders consider to be top priorities.

Diaspora engagement is largely unaccountable to equity concerns. Therefore, divisions and inequalities inherent to socio-economic status within the country may be replicated within the diaspora and possibly perpetuated through diaspora contributions. These realities pose challenges for agencies that aim to promote equitable development and expand opportunities among the most vulnerable populations throughout the Caribbean.

The extensive web of connections between diaspora members and their countries of origin results, in the vast majority of cases, from individual initiative rather than government or programmatic structures. These findings reveal that the independent nature of diaspora engagement is a key factor in its success. Governments, aid agencies, and local civil society should seek opportunities to facilitate greater diaspora engagement while maintaining respect for its independence.

Remittances have dominated the discourse on Caribbean diaspora contributions to development (Lapointe 2004). However, remittances play both a positive and a negative role in equitable development of the region. On the one hand, remittances are clearly making an economic contribution in the form of consumption, savings, and sometimes investment. Additionally, out-migration—the source of remittances—reduces unemployment pressure in the region. Certainly the poverty level of these three nations would be higher but for the receipt of remittance transfers. On the other hand, there are also valid criticisms of remittances (Kapur 2004; see also the chapter by de Ferranti and Ody in this volume). First, the reliance on transfers from Caribbean workers overseas can undermine state responsibilities. Reliance on remittances shifts the burden for social services to personal and familial networks. Second, remittances may reinforce or augment economic inequity in the society. Government expenditures often redistribute wealth through social spending whereas private remittance streams do not. Some, but not all, members of society benefit from remittances streams. In order to receive transfers from abroad the family needs to have enough money or connections to have one of their members migrate, a difficult and costly endeavor. Inequitable distribution of remittances may lead to economic and social exclusion, further exacerbating inequity. Third, remittances often are used for immediate consumption rather than investments in human or business capital. These criticisms lodged against remittances are validated by anecdotes in each of the countries studied; however, it seems clear that if remittances to the region were to abruptly end, the Caribbean would see some tragic personal and public welfare consequences.

While the long-term consequences of financial remittances remain unclear, there are also important and potentially untapped non-monetary diaspora contributions. Peggy Levitt has coined the term "social remittances" to refer to "the ideas, behaviors, identities and social capital that flow from receiving country to sending country communities" (Levitt 1998:927). Less tangible than money, diaspora contributions of social remittances include new ideas, networks, and accepted norms. These remittances can affect attitudes toward women's rights in the country of origin, the value of education, or political processes to empower ethnic minorities within a democratic state. Though as the study of women migrants from the Dominican Republic cited above shows, shifting the culture paradigm within the country of origin to recognize gender equality will take time. These shifts may begin at the family level through the practice of greater women's empowerment in household decision-making and may ultimately shift perceptions at the national or regional level.

Notably, seventy-five of the one hundred diaspora leaders surveyed believe that contributing their skills and knowledge to their country of origin is the most effective way to impact development. The less studied and potentially more important contributions of the diaspora for development may lie in this engagement. While remittances are private resources, typically earmarked for family members and friends, non-remittance engagement includes contributions of time, goods, and professional services to social development, public policy, and economic growth through private investment. The discourse must, therefore, begin to consider the non-remittance contributions that are ongoing and show potential for strong growth.

For diaspora members in each of these countries, there is an imperative to work with in-country leadership to find opportunities for contributing diaspora time and talents to shared development goals. Establishing a diaspora forum that is independent from national governments would allow open debate on diaspora interests both in the countries of residence and in the countries of origin. The diaspora community should continue to seek opportunities for financial investment into the economies of their home countries. Additionally, diaspora investors may be uniquely suited to identify obstacles to greater investment and to work with local governments to unravel red tape. Finally, Caribbean diaspora groups have the option to explore other models formed in regions and countries that have a longer history of organized engagement with the state—such as India, Mexico, and the Philippines. Through an improved understanding of diaspora engagement in other regions, Caribbean countries may benefit from practices that have evolved over time to more effectively align diaspora members and states to reach shared goals.

A cautionary note must be sounded in the case of the Haitian diaspora. Unlike Guyana and Jamaica, Haiti is not yet positioned to take advantage of many kinds of diaspora engagement until greater political and social stability within Haiti is reached. Kathleen Newland and Erin Patrick have written on the role of diaspora from the poorest countries of the globe, including Haiti:

> What the poverty-stricken in Sierra Leone, Somalia, Liberia, Haiti, and Sudan (to name just a few) need, above all, is peace,

and then progress toward the construction of an economic climate that will encourage emigrants to make social and economic investments in their countries of origin. Diaspora groups may have a role to play in peace and reconstruction processes, and governments that host them should carefully consider encouraging the involvement of those who can be seen as honest brokers. (Newland and Patrick 2004:v)

Bearing this in mind, there is a pivotal role that development agencies can play in shaping the discourse related to suitable diaspora interventions. Development agencies sometimes catalyze and broker dialogue between diaspora leaders and government officials. Interaction between diaspora leaders and their countries of origin can be a mutually beneficial exchange. Development agencies that seek to magnify this potential require in-depth knowledge of the country-specific context where they operate. This contextual understanding includes knowledge of the dynamics of the diaspora population and the perceptions of those interactions within their countries of origin. As was stated at the beginning of this chapter, enhancing the prospects for human development requires a mapping of locally defined development priorities with the assistance that outside actors offer. Only with a substantial confluence of these aspirations with appropriate assistance may diaspora or other external development actors empower the lives and life choices of individuals within the country of origin.

Regional coordination of diaspora efforts should be raised at a multinational body such as The Caribbean Community and Common Market (CARICOM). CARICOM has a large membership of states including: Antigua and Barbuda, Belize, Grenada, Montserrat, St. Vincent and the Grenadines, Turks and Caicos Islands, The Bahamas, British Virgin Islands, Guyana, St. Kitts and Nevis, Suriname, Barbados, Dominica, Jamaica, Saint Lucia, and Trinidad and Tobago. CARICOM observers include: Anguilla,

The Cayman Islands, Haiti, Puerto Rico, Aruba, Colombia, Mexico, Venezuela, Bermuda, Dominican Republic, and the Netherlands Antilles. From its inception, CARICOM has concentrated on promoting integration of these numerous economies. It works to create a common Caribbean market and coordinate the foreign policies of the independent member states to achieve greater impact through a collective voice. Through CARICOM, individual countries could coordinate diaspora efforts to utilize economies of scale to conduct outreach and maintain updated regional information. Certainly using the means of a regional response rather than an individual country response could enhance the resources available. However, it may pose a challenge to achieve agreement on those means and the amount of resources each country could or should allocate to achieve desired outcomes.

As was stated at the outset of this chapter, the Caribbean region is highly diverse, and so although a regional effort may make sense for some of the members, there would be many issues that would still need to be established at the country level. Perhaps a more realistic collective effort would be a sustained forum for regional dialogue on the future role of the diaspora in the Caribbean. This forum could showcase various national models for diaspora engagement, as all countries have something to offer from their experience. Importantly, Caribbean governments are not the only actors supporting diaspora engagement in the region. Development agencies, philanthropic foundations, and civil society organizations are also seeking ways to augment the positive benefits of diaspora engagement. Sharing lessons and models can and should be part of the regional development dialogue.

CONCLUSION

Given that the Caribbean still confronts mounting out-migration, especially of skilled workers, the success of its regional development depends, in part, on meeting internal demands for good people in key positions, such as doctors, nurses, teachers, security officers, lawyers, and engineers. These talented individuals are also key to building strong institutions, which serve as the bedrock of development. The Caribbean needs to invest in talent and needs to offer opportunities for talented individuals to find meaningful work domestically. This is a profound challenge as the Caribbean faces competing employment opportunities in wealthier nations where diaspora communities are already established. CARICOM must deal with the problem of employment opportunity as it works to create a healthier region. For as much as diaspora individuals give back to their communities from abroad, the opportunity cost of their absence may never be replaced by their potential contributions from abroad.

Caribbean diasporas reveal the delicate dynamics of diasporas and development. As has been recorded elsewhere, many diaspora members have low institutional trust in the government institutions in their country of origin (see Najam chapter in this volume). This is true for the cases presented here. Guyana, Haiti, and Jamaica each have particular lessons for diaspora studies, although they collectively underscore the complexity of diaspora relations with their countries of origin. The simplistic notion—that diaspora engagement is a matter of resource transfer from wealthy nations to developing nations—falls quite short of encompassing the diversity of diaspora practices and aspirations reported in the findings. Additionally, these case studies have posed questions with relevance for other diasporas: Is the country of origin sufficiently stable to receive increased diaspora engagement? How might ethnic divisions or tensions be exacerbated by diaspora involvement? To what extent is there resistance by the local population to "outsiders" claiming a legitimate space in influencing or setting development agendas? Should countries prioritize stemming the tide of out-migration over celebrating diaspora contributions from abroad? These and other questions reveal the complexity we have yet to appreciate regarding the role of diasporas in development.

REFERENCES

Alkire, Sabina. 2002. "Valuing Freedoms: Sen's Capabilities Approach and Poverty Reduction." Queen Elizabeth House Series in Development Studies, Oxford University Press.

Baptiste, Alix. 2005. The Minister of Haitians Living Abroad, Port-au-Prince, Haiti. Telephone interview conducted by Barbara Merz, October 2005.

Central Intelligence Agency. 2006. *The World Factbook.* March 23 (http://www.cia.gov/cia/publications/factbook/).

Chavenet, Anaïse. 2005. President and Director-General of Communication Plus, Port-au-Prince, Haiti. Telephone interview conducted by Barbara Merz, October 2005.

García, Mar and Denise Paiewonsky. 2006. "Gender, Remittances and Development: The Case of Women Migrants from Vicente Noble, Dominican Republic." A Study for the United Nations International Research and Training Institute for the Advancement of Women (INSTRAW). September (http://www.un-instraw.org/en/docs/Remittances/Remittances_RD_Eng.pdf).

Idées de France. 2005. *Haitian Diaspora* (http://www.ideesdefrance.fr/Haitian-Diaspora.html).

Kapur, Devesh. 2004. "Remittances: The New Development Mantra?" G-24 Discussion Paper Series. United Nations Conference on Trade and Development (http://www.unctad.org/en/docs/gdsmdpbg2420045_en.pdf).

Lapointe, Michelle. 2004. "Diasporas in Caribbean Development." Report of the Inter-American Dialogue and the World Bank, August 2004.

LaTorture, Paul. 2005. Former Head of the Central Implementation Unit, Port-au-Prince, Haiti. Telephone interview conducted by Barbara Merz, October 2005.

Levitt, Peggy. 1998. "Social Remittances: Migration-driven, Local-Level Forms of Cultural Diffusion," *International Migration Review* 32, no. 4, winter 1998.

Merz, Barbara J., ed. 2005. *New Patterns for Mexico: Observations on Remittances, Philanthropic Giving, and Equitable Development.* Cambridge, MA: Global Equity Initiative, Asia Center, Harvard University: Distributed by Harvard University Press.

Merz, Barbara and Kathleen Dunn. 2005a. "Beyond Money: Diaspora Engagement in Development, Case Study 1 of 3, Guyana." Working Paper for the Canadian International Development Agency (http://www.fas.harvard.edu/~acgei/caribbean.htm).

———. 2005b. "Beyond Money: Diaspora Engagement in Development, Case Study 2 of 3, Jamaica." Working Paper for the Canadian International Development Agency (http://www.fas.harvard.edu/~acgei/caribbean.htm).

———. 2005c. "Beyond Money: Diaspora Engagement in Development, Case Study 3 of 3, Haiti." Working Paper for the Canadian International Development Agency (http://www.fas.harvard.edu/~acgei/caribbean.htm).

Migration Information Source. 2005. *Migration Statistics* (http://www.migrationinformation.org).

Newland, Kathleen and Erin Patrick. 2004. "Beyond Remittances: The Role of Diaspora in Poverty Reduction in their Countries of Origin." Migration Policy Institute (http://www.migrationpolicy.org/pubs/2004.php).

Nurse, Keith. 2004. "Diaspora, Migration and Development in the Caribbean." Focal Policy Paper (http://www.focal.ca/pdf/migration_caribbean.pdf).

Orozco, Manuel. 2004. "Distant but Close: Guyanese Transnational Communities and Their Remittances from the United States." Inter-American Dialogue. Commissioned by USAID, Washington, DC.

Phillips, Michael, ed. 2005. "Guyana Flood Relief." *Hot Calaloo.* (http://www.hotcalaloo.com/Guyana%20Flood%20Relief.htm).

St. Lot, Danielle. 2005. President of Women in Democracy, Port-au-Prince–based NGO aiming to increase the participation of women in the Haitian national dialogue; Former Haitian Minister of Commerce, Industry, and Tourism. Telephone interview conducted by Barbara Merz, October 2005.

Sen, Amartya. 1999. *Development as Freedom.* 1st ed. New York: Alfred A. Knopf.

Singh, Carl. 2005. Chief Justice of the Guyanese High Court, Georgetown, Guyana. In-person interview conducted by Barbara Merz, June 22, 2005.

Transparency International. 2005. "Corruption Perception Index Report." (http://www.transparency.org/policy_and_research/surveys_indices/cpi/2005).

World Bank. 2006. Data & Statistics (http://www.worldbank.org/data/countrydata/countrydata.html).

CHAPTER 8

CENTRAL AMERICAN DIASPORAS AND HOMETOWN ASSOCIATIONS

MANUEL OROZCO

The number of hometown associations (HTAs) has multiplied in recent years. HTAs are entities formed by immigrants who seek to support their places of origin, maintain relationships with local communities, and retain a sense of community as they adjust to life in their new country of residence (Orozco 2000, 2003a, 2005a). Among the Central American diaspora, local community development projects have spread through the visible activism of HTAs in the region, which includes Guatemala, El Salvador, Honduras, Nicaragua, Costa Rica, Panama, and Belize. This chapter surveys trends in the Central American diaspora and then looks closely at the work of HTAs in three countries: Guatemala, El Salvador, and Honduras. The experiences of these HTAs have implications for other diaspora groups and those who work with them. While membership in HTAs is not widespread, Central American HTAs leverage their efforts toward effective development and benefit their home communities in important ways. Their impact can be even more noticeable when they are organized, encouraged by the right government policies and programs, and can partner with local governments, companies, NGOs, and others in the development world. Drawing on interviews with more than thirty association leaders, this chapter details how these HTAs operate and how development players might best engage this active and organized slice of the Central American diaspora.

Research assistance and support for this chapter were provided by Rebecca Rouse and Douglas Pulse.

215

CENTRAL AMERICA: ECONOMIC AND POLITICAL TRENDS

Central America has experienced significant movement of people over the past forty years, particularly since the civil wars of the late 1970s. At least four trends, including the shared history of political violence and repression, slow economic growth and corresponding low wages, the demand for cheap labor from abroad, and repeated natural disasters have influenced migration and led to the rise of the Central American diaspora.

The repression and civil wars of the 1970s and 1980s led to mass migrations. Guatemala, El Salvador, Honduras, and Nicaragua experienced brutal forms of political repression directed by a ruling class formed by praetorian guards, conservative oligarchies, and conformist elites. The main agents of repression in Central America resorted to ideological tools such as anti-communism or anti-atheism as a way to justify or legitimize increased repression (Vilas 1994). In practical terms, a culture of violence persisted in the region, due in part to state attempts to retain political power (Galtung 1990). Death squads, corrupt police, repressive armies, and clandestine security apparatuses promoted the idea of containing any threat against "the established order," even if such order was historically and structurally rooted in inequality. The end results in each of these countries were civil wars that lasted more than ten years and mass movements of people migrating predominantly into Costa Rica, Mexico, and the United States (Dunkerley 1994).

Even during periods of relative stability, slow economic growth and low wages drive Central American migration. This is partly the result of persistent income disparities, as well as the negative effects of globalization. In addition, local currencies have remained weak. Overall these economies have not been able to grow above 3.5 percent a year, which is equal or near population growth. Compounding this situation is the fact that the region has a predominantly young population, with a productive force of less than 40 percent. Moreover, the way in which Central America responded to the demands of the global economy has not offered opportunities to increase productivity throughout the region, but rather has focused on enclave economies in tourism, non-traditional exports, or *maquila* exports. These sectors are highly vulnerable to external fluctuations that are usually out of the control of these economies and often exhibit lower distributive effects than other activities with greater value added components. These countries face additional difficulties in competing with global markets that are either subsidized in the industrialized economies, oversaturated with similar commodities, or have a demand for high-quality high-technology–oriented manufacturing. Thus, the region has been too dependent on a few commodities to stay integrated in the global economy. For example, the value of coffee exports declined in the late 1990s, which also resulted in the commodity's reduced share of total exports in almost every country in the region except Nicaragua. El Salvador was especially hard hit, with coffee exports declining from 40.4 percent of total exports in 1990 to 13.1 in 1998. Together, these factors have not been conducive to sustainable growth rates. Instead, the productive bases of Central American economies have struggled to cope with increasing costs of living, now more pronounced as energy prices exact a heavy toll on many of these societies.

Many Central American countries operate on low wages and precarious employment, making them unable to compete with domestic markets, much less with the global economy. Wages are often one third or one quarter of the cost of living. For example, a store clerk in Salcaja, Guatemala, or Suchitoto, El Salvador, earns US$200 or US$150 per month, respectively. At the same time, the cost of the basic monthly food basket in these countries ranges between US$150 and US$350. This reality makes it difficult for workers to maintain a decent standard of living through their own employment. The gap between earnings and cost of living has been a key factor in the decision to migrate for many Central Americans (see Table 1).

Table 1: Monthly Cost of Living (Excluding Housing), Income, and Remittances (USD)

	Suchitoto, El Salvador	Salcaja, Guatemala
Cost of living:		
Food	209	201
Services (utilities)	40	43
Education	29	56
Health	34	68
Entertainment	40	35
Income:		
Wages	125	162
Total earnings, remittances included	622	353
Monthly remittances amount received	515	181

Source: Survey of 60 remittance recipients and non-recipients.

In addition, natural disasters have historically devastated local populations and economies in many of these countries, particularly those in the Caribbean Basin. Natural disasters wreak more long-lasting havoc where poverty and vulnerability are the greatest. In Central America, extreme poverty and agricultural dependence increased vulnerability to these disasters. Hurricanes Joan and Mitch, for example, in 1988 and 1998, respectively, left a pattern of destruction that disturbed the delicate infrastructure of these economies.

In the last few years, a series of disasters struck the region, including drought, hurricanes, and earthquakes. Central America was hit with a drought in early 2000 that significantly affected four countries in particular: Guatemala, El Salvador, and, even more dramatically, Honduras and Nicaragua. According to the United Nations World Food Program, nearly 1.6 million Central Americans were affected, half of them from Honduras. Many

Central Americans faced starvation. In Guatemala, more than one hundred peasants died during the first six months of 2001 as a result of the drought. In other countries the death toll was even higher. Following the drought in 2001, two earthquakes in El Salvador affected the economic and housing infrastructure of more than one hundred thousand households. Five years later, the country is still recovering and rebuilding from that disaster. Between 2002 and 2006, the region has faced other natural disasters, which have added to the strains on the economy and increased the flow of migrants.

However, migration has also been shaped by demand for foreign labor by industrialized countries facing their own challenges in the competitive global economy. This migrant labor force works in service industries that are intrinsically connected to the global economy, which demands cheap labor and activities that other players in the economy are not prepared to carry out. This process of labor "integration" suffers relatively high levels of exclusion and marginalization due to the undocumented nature of many of its migrants who respond to economic push-pull and transnational networks and linkages (Andrade-Eekhoff 2003). This is a labor force that often lives under poor conditions and works in labor intensive industries such as agriculture, food-processing, hospitality, cleaning, construction, and retail. Migrants in the poultry industry in the US South working for Tyson Foods (Fink 2003:200; Striffer 2005) live under precarious circumstances, working long hours with a limited social safety net. Similar conditions can also be found among foreign part-time workers in the "logistics sector," such as FedEx package delivery (Smith 2005). Interestingly, this demand for this kind of foreign labor in the United States has not changed dramatically over the past seven years. For example, unemployment among Hispanics in the US has declined as the economy improved after the 2000–2002 economic recession.

TRANSNATIONALISM AND HOMETOWN ASSOCIATIONS

The trends and dynamics mentioned above have intertwined with the formation of transnational ties between a nascent diaspora and its homeland. These realities result from people's struggles to carve their own niches out of a "McDonaldized" life. While diasporas may find their "original" lifestyle or identity compromised, they often end up producing new hybrid cultures and transnational identities (Pieterse 2004). Their ties to their homelands produce transnational lifestyles and identities. For example, a Pan-Mayan ethnicity has emerged in the *Guatemalan* transnational community linking Santa Eulalia, Huehuetenango, Guatemala, and Los Angeles, California (Popkin 1999, 2005). Similarly, Honduran Garifuna ethnic group diasporas in New York and New Jersey maintain strong ties to their community on the Atlantic Coast of Honduras. Immigrants and diasporas are increasingly key protagonists of distant proximities: through their labor force, they integrate their home and host countries into the global economy in order to keep their families together. But their lives are also fragmented, however, by the experience of distance and separation from their families and nations.

In practical terms, a typical immigrant's economic ties with his or her home country extend to at least four practices that involve spending or investment: 1) family remittance transfers; 2) demand for services such as telecommunications, and consumer goods or travel; 3) capital investment; and 4) charitable donations to philanthropic organizations raising funds for the migrant's home community. The first of these, remittances, is the most widespread and important migrant economic activity (Orozco 2005b; Ratha and Maimbo 2005). While the determinants of sending do not vary between nationalities, the frequency and quantity of money sent fluctuate across groups. For example, Salvadorans and Guatemalans in the US send an average of US$300 a month, whereas Dominicans, Haitians, and Jamaicans send $200 (Orozco 2005b).

Second, migrants also maintain links with their home countries by staying in touch, calling, and visiting their homeland. They purchase and consume foodstuffs from their home countries such as tortillas, beef jerky, cheese, rum, and coffee and spend money on phone cards to call their families. The final two practices involve donations and investments. In the case of donations, migrants raise funds through HTAs to help their hometowns, an important activity that can provide substantial economic resources for the communities of origin. These donations may amount to US$100 to US$200 a year per individual, and in some countries, like Honduras, donations in aggregate may translate to more than three million dollars. Finally, migrants often also have a desire to invest in a property or a small business, devoting between US$5,000 and US$10,000 to such investments.

These threads weave together families, communities, and society. Table 2 shows the extent of the connections Central Americans maintain with their home countries. Overall, one in three Central Americans maintains strong links with their home country (Orozco 2005b).

Some diasporas use HTAs as a space in which to create their transnational identities. HTAs are a subset of minority-based migrant philanthropic organizations. Their activities exhibit at least four features (Orozco 2000). First, their activities range from charitable aid to investment. Second, the structure of these organizations varies, with more or less formal domestic structures and sporadic relationships with their hometown and governments abroad. Third, the organizations' decisions about defining their agenda or activities depend on an array of factors, such as availability of resources, relationship with their hometown, preferences of their members, and organizational structure. Fourth, like other Latino nonprofits, they have a small economic base.

To some extent, Central Americans participate in these associations as a way to validate their identity. One critical element that defines a person's identity is the ability to exercise his or

Table 2: Practices of Transnational Engagement among Central Americans (in percent)

Country	El Salvador	Guatemala	Honduras	Nicaragua	Latinos
Calls once a week	41	56	57	70	61
Sends over US$300/year	32	43	8	13	31
Buys goods from home	66	50	74	83	73
Has a savings account	16	19	16	5	27
Travels once a year	24	9	12	19	32
Travels once a year *and* spends over US$1,000	61	48	43	26	60
Has a mortgage loan	13	4	12	6	10
Owns a small business	3	2	4	3	3
Helps family with mortgage	13	1	8	7	12

her sense of belonging through material and symbolic practices. Belonging to an HTA is one practical yet substantive way to stay connected with the home country. However, it is important to stress that HTA membership is only one kind of association among organized diasporas; there are many kinds of domestic organizations working for Latinos in the US. Moreover, HTAs should be understood in the broader sense as organizations that include religious or professional groups not only working in the hometown but in philanthropy in the home country.

Within this context of Latino or diaspora community-based philanthropic institutions, membership is not as large as some insist. A survey of Latino groups from twelve Latin American and Caribbean countries showed that, on average, 8 percent of people who send remittances belong to an HTA (Table 3).

Table 3: Remittance Senders Who Belong to an HTA

Country	%
Guyana	29
Jamaica	16
Ecuador	10
Haiti	10
Honduras	7
Colombia	6
Nicaragua	4
El Salvador	4
Mexico	4
Dom. Rep.	3
Guatemala	3
Bolivia	1
Average	8

The numbers vary from group to group with people from the Caribbean showing the highest participation rate (Orozco 2005a). Although these percentages seem low, they reflect three critical issues. First, not everyone is involved in some kind of voluntary association, outside of religious membership. Second, HTA membership is one among many available kinds of memberships in the polity (Orozco 2000). Three, belonging to an HTA may reflect specific patterns associated with political culture, family links, material circumstances, cultural identity, and integration.

An analysis of the survey data shows that those who belong to HTAs differentiate themselves from other migrants in that they are better off economically, have greater ties with the home country, and are older (see Table 4). They are US citizens, but they still visit the home country more often and help the family back home. These members mix their commitments to both homes, signifying a transnational membership.

Table 4: Features of Remittance Senders and Membership in an HTA

Type of Activity	Belongs to HTA	
	Yes %	No %
Is over forty years of age	60	44
Visits country once a year or more	56	30
Helps family in home country with other obligations	55	20
Has been in the US more than ten years	44	29
Remittance sender is a US citizen	38	22
Sends over US$350	31	18
His or her average income is	$32,733	$20,659

This pattern of belonging as an affirmation of a transnational identity is relatively important among Central Americans. Although the percentage of those belonging to HTAs may be small, their contributions are important to the well-being of their communities of origin.

CENTRAL AMERICAN HOMETOWN ASSOCIATIONS AT WORK

This section surveys the experience and practices of HTAs in Guatemala, El Salvador, and Honduras, focusing on the membership structure of the organizations, types of projects and the process by which they are identified, fundraising efforts, project implementation, and other issues. The section also looks at examples of government programs that support HTA projects and at the potential of HTA partnerships with other philanthropic organizations.

GUATEMALAN ASSOCIATIONS

Guatemalan migrants have often been organized. In the 1980s migrants formed political units that mobilized against military regimes and human rights violations and, in the 1990s, promoted the peace process, indigenous rights, and democratization. More recently, this community has sought to further its political ties and increase its philanthropic activism.

The number of Guatemalan associations is uncertain. In 2004, an innovative but ill-funded government initiative within the Ministry of Foreign Affairs was created. This was the Office of the Vice-Minister of Migration and Human Rights, charged with acting as a liaison to the Guatemalan diaspora, building a relationship with it, and understanding its needs. The office identified a significant number of community leaders in contact with Guatemala and created a directory of 164 organizations based mainly in California, New York, and Illinois.[1]

Most Guatemalan associations have relatively small core groups of members that meet on a regular basis. These active

---

1. The author conducted interviews with these organizations in order to identify the range of organizational capacity and involvement with their home country issues.

members often make up the organization's board of directors, president, secretary, and treasurer. As membership is on a voluntary basis, some groups report that it is sometimes difficult to hold regular elections to select the board and officers due to the time constraints of their working-class members. As a result, those members who are able to serve in leadership positions often volunteer for posts. Associations have anywhere from five to twenty active members, but often have a much larger individual donor base throughout the Guatemalan community. For example, one association in Delaware boasts a general membership of around 250 people. Most of these groups have been created since 1991 in response to compelling needs in Guatemala, such as natural disasters, or to provide needed representation to the Guatemalan immigrant community in the United States, especially to those Guatemalans of indigenous descent.

Like other HTA groups, such as those from Mexico or El Salvador, membership is mostly comprised of migrants from a common community or region in Guatemala. As a result, the international activities of these groups are then focused on these municipalities, and association leaders in the United States maintain close ties to community leaders and organizations in their hometowns. Some groups have also made it part of their mission to assist Guatemalan migrants in the United States with anything from legal to social services, in which case participation is not limited to those immigrants from a particular community.

Guatemalan HTAs often have activities for their communities both in the United States and in Guatemala. Corn Maya, Inc., is an example of an HTA with a transnational focus—the group is involved in activities serving Guatemalans of indigenous descent both in the community of Jacaltenango in Guatemala and in Jupiter, Florida, where the group is based. In Guatemala, HTA projects are mostly focused around health, education, and disaster relief. Some recent activities carried out by Guatemalan associations have included gathering in-kind donations such as blankets and clothing for victims of Hurricane Stan and toys or school supplies for local students, providing prenatal care for women, and assisting in the development of infrastructure such as roads. Groups also promote cultural links between Guatemalans at home and abroad through activities such as the sponsorship of visits by Guatemalan musicians to the United States. They also fund the repatriation of remains for immigrants who have passed away in the US but wish to be buried in their hometown.

All of the associations interviewed reported that they rely heavily on the recommendations of local community groups and leaders in their respective target regions in Guatemala when identifying future projects and activities, with final project selection decisions being made by the board after it has evaluated need and feasibility. To that end, boards of directors maintain close contact with local groups, churches, and municipal governments in order to assess the needs of the community. Corn Maya's board of directors, for example, maintains a regular dialogue with community leaders and organizations in Jacaltenango, as well as with potential partners both in the United States and in Guatemala. The organization stresses that these partnerships are essential to the success of their projects. Groups often team up with the same local entities as they implement their projects. For example, Comite Ixchiguan in Delaware has become involved in conflict resolution efforts focusing on a border conflict between two municipalities that has left three residents wounded and ten homes destroyed. The group has been working alongside the local municipal government to establish a dialogue between key players in the conflict.

Guatemalan associations undertake a variety of different fundraising approaches, with varied success. Some groups noted that fundraising is a challenge for them, while others seem to produce a better return. In general, groups tend to raise anywhere between US$2,000 and US$8,000 a year. Some common fundraising activities include soccer tournaments, dinners, and other events within the Guatemalan community, in addition to individual membership dues. Some groups have looked outside the Guatemalan community for fundraising, using media to attract attention to their cause or soliciting grants from institutional donors. One group appealed to local television and newspapers for help in the aftermath of Hurricane Stan in 2005, pulling in donations for disaster relief from outside the Latino community and educating the public about the situation in Guatemala.

All groups comment that they are constantly searching for new donors and partners. In particular, one group noted that a single project, the donation of a used ambulance, took the association two years to complete because of the difficulties they had raising funds. In contrast, Corn Maya, with an active membership of only twenty people, has been able to plan a new Community Resource Center in Jupiter for the Guatemalan community in Florida with the help of Catholic Charities. One of Corn Maya's largest projects in Jacaltenango, the construction of an orphanage, was also sponsored in part by Catholic Charities of Jupiter. Building on its experience in Florida since its founding in 1991, the group is now attempting to forge new partnerships in Jacaltenango, such as with the Guatemalan microfinance organization in Salcaja.

The Guatemalan HTA experience suggests the value of HTAs' local connections and knowledge for appropriate project selection in home countries. It also demonstrates that HTAs can be much more effective when larger, wealthier philanthropic organizations agree to partner with or fund them.

Salvadoran Associations

Salvadoran HTAs are well-known among Central Americans. According to the Salvadoran Ministry of Foreign Affairs, there are some 200 Salvadoran HTAs distributed throughout various parts of the United States, with the largest numbers in California and the Washington, DC, area. The Salvadoran government has been especially active in diaspora outreach. A recent study on Central American transnationalism said that "the Salvadoran government as compared to the other governments in the region, both central as well as local, has a much more institutionalized response to international labor migration" (Eekhoff 2003).

Despite the limited resources available in a poor country like El Salvador, the government has sought to adapt to changing circumstances and promote policies toward their diaspora communities. In the past two years the government has also established a Vice-Ministry of Foreign Affairs for relations with the diaspora. The vice-minister is one of the most active, committed, and engaged public officials in the region. The government outreach strategy has focused predominantly on education and community outreach, but has not addressed political matters such as the right to vote abroad and broader representation of the community.

Interviews were conducted with the leaders of twenty Salvadoran associations based in Los Angeles and Washington, DC. Questions were asked about organizational structure, range of projects and activities, resources invested, and extent of interest in partnering with other organizations. The majority of the HTAs interviewed were created in the early 1990s.

Most Salvadoran associations have a well-defined structure, involving a board and a few active members, typically numbering around ten. They often work with a parallel board in their home community. This group, often consisting of the relatives of HTA members, sends ideas for projects and oversees the disbursement of funds. For the most part, Salvadoran HTAs rely solely on events and donations to support their activities.

Salvadoran HTA members come together because they have shared connections to a common community and political history. Frequent visits keep members in close communication with association members or family members in the hometown, as well as maintain their connection and drive to better their home community. While it may seem obvious to note, most HTAs are limited in scope because their goal is to help only one particular community in El Salvador. There are instances of partnerships with HTAs from other towns, but their focus is almost always on their place of origin. Also, they are volunteer organizations and are limited by the amount of free time available to their mostly working-class members.

Salvadoran HTAs tend to form after a disaster, such as Hurricane Mitch; around a cause, such as lack of a high school; or at the urging of a prominent member of their home community, such as their pastor. For example, Chinameca's parish priest was the catalyst for the creation of the Comunidad Unida de Chinameca in 1991. The priest asked his former church members to form a committee in the US to finish installing a water system in the local school. The Comunidad Unida de Chinameca began by constructing the school's water tower, as well as twelve restrooms. From there, they went on to construct a laundry facility and a recreational park for the town, as well as painting and putting a roof on the local church. Members travel constantly to Chinameca to oversee these projects.

Another example is COPRECA (El Comité Pro Paz y Reconstrucción de Cacaopera en Los Angeles), which works in Cacaopera, El Morazan, and with the Salvadoran community of Los Angeles. Founded in 1992, the club initially worked on reconstruction of sections of the town destroyed by the war. The members have worked on the construction of a health clinic and wells, bought an ambulance for the town, and raised money for medical and emergency donations. COPRECA has rebuilt the church, the school floor and basketball courts, and created a radio station and a clothing factory run by women. It has also distributed rope-fiber trees and vegetable seeds to help with reforestation and the re-establishment of the rope-making industry. Their latest project was a children's daycare center.

Salvadoran HTAs work on a range of projects that often involve a binational exercise of activities carried on in both countries. On the Salvadoran side, the majority of projects seems to focus on health and education. In health, the funds are invested in building health clinics and in medicine and ambulance donations. For education, the funds are invested in libraries, school water systems, school supplies, and school repairs. One of the future projects of the Comunidad Unida de Chinameca is the construction of a new trade school to train students to be electricians, plumbers, mechanics, and welders. Another category is charitable and infrastructural projects: the construction of laundry facilities, recreational areas, stadiums, and church renovations. In addition to carrying out projects in El Salvador, some organizations work on the US side to promote cultural and religious identity. Some of these activities include cultural events (dances, Independence Day celebrations), scholarships, religious events, youth motivational talks, and sports and recreation.

The decisions on project selection and implementation result from consultation among board members. In some cases, the organizations report being approached by people (both private citizens and elected municipal leaders) and organizations in El Salvador and petitioned to work on specific projects. In the case of the Comunidad Unida de Chinameca, as word of their work spread, petitions for help began to rain in. The groups who do not have a team in El Salvador ask the townspeople about their needs and try to meet them. One group described the number of community-based petitions as overwhelming, forcing the board to whittle down the projects to the ones most in-line with their goals, as well as most feasible. Salvadoran HTAs, much like their Mexican counterparts, are small organizations whose binational character allows them to choose projects based on the most urgent needs of their home communities. The needs of the town are identified by those close to the HTAs. The ideas for COPRECA's projects, for example, come from the citizens of Cacaopera and involve the labor of the community.

Efforts to raise funds translate into various kinds of activities, including raffles, pageants, and dinners arranged for the migrant communities. Donations in kind are also commonplace to support these activities. Many have a community base of fifty to over one hundred people who participate in their fundraising events. Most groups raise less than $15,000 a year for projects, but a few raise more. The Comunidad Unida de Chinameca gathers around $30,000 annually, raised mostly through banquets. Even when the total is greater, it does not necessarily all go to El Salvador; instead, the money may be used for activities supporting Salvadoran culture in the United States.

COPRECA began raising money through a monthly quota for its members and then moved on to raising money through dances. COPRECA has worked with the national government and the local mayor on both its reforestation project and the construction of a water tank. A government office helped teach townspeople how to take care of the seeds and seedlings. The Los Angeles city government also funded their motivational talks for Salvadoran Americans in the Los Angeles area; there are plans to continue this series with health education talks.

Founded in 1993, the Comité Unidos por Intipuca in Washington holds fundraising parties in the area to support their works in Intipuca, La Union. Their biggest project is fundraising for and organizing the travel of 300 to 400 people to Intipuca every March 1. They bring their *reina* (queen) to participate in the contest in El Salvador. The *reina* is chosen by the number of votes that she sells, which is also a fundraising mechanism. The Comité raises around $25,000 a year. They have been working for eight years on the construction of a stadium and have raised around $200,000 for the project, of which the Salvadoran national development agency, the Social Investment and Local Development Fund (FISDL), has given them $110,000. The Comité has worked with both FISDL and the mayor's office. They lobbied the government to reinstate a *bachillerato* school in the town; five years ago they worked with the FISDL to rebuild a bridge that was destroyed by Hurricane Mitch. Their newest project is the construction of a "casa de cultura," which also has the support of FISDL.

HTAs have established partnerships with organizations of all kinds. These groups include the national government, municipality, churches, other nonprofits, and businesses. Comunidad Unida de Chinameca, for example, received donations of construction material from the French embassy to build a wall for the Red Cross building in the town, with the town participating by donating labor. The Comunidad has corporate sponsorship for some of its events, as well as local business sponsors in the US. However, the group had a negative experience working with the government in reconstruction projects after the earthquake, and does not currently work with the government to complete their projects. Despite this example, local mayors and FISDL are among the main liaisons for project implementation (depending on HTA political affiliations or lack thereof). Additionally, some Salvadoran HTAs are closely connected with other Salvadoran organizations, through groups like El Rescate or CARECEN or through umbrella HTA groups like Comunidades Unidas Salvadoreñas, which have been essential to the lobbying power of the HTAs on their home government.

To take advantage of the success that Salvadoran HTAs have had in the design and implementation of projects in El Salvador, FISDL partnered with the General Directorate within the Ministry of Foreign Affairs, which was created in January 2000 to serve as the main official link between the government and the Salvadoran community. Together they developed a formal program through which HTAs abroad compete for matching funds from the national government to complete development projects. The program is known as "Unidos por la Solidaridad."

Through it, HTAs submit applications describing the project and funds required and FISDL reviews them for feasibility and responsiveness to community needs. In order for a project to participate in the partnership, FISDL has various requirements, some of which include: the project must conform to the municipal government's plan for civic participation; the HTA must match at least 10 percent of the project costs; the municipal government must be solvent; only social infrastructure projects are included; and projects must cost at least US$30,000 (FISDL 2004).

FISDL maintains a liaison approach through the program "Conoce tu municipio," which provides information to HTAs about the status of their hometown, as well as the projects FISDL has undertaken in individual towns. Of the forty-five projects that HTAs have partnered with FISDL on, twenty-eight have benefited the provinces of La Union (eleven), La Paz (ten), and Chalatenango (seven). Ahuachapan, La Libertad, Morazan, San Vicente, and Santa Ana have had one project each, although Sonsonante has had none to date (Table 5). The average cost of a project undertaken in these partnerships is $278,690, but varies with the department or partnership (from $1,210,350 in Usulutan to $40,000 in Ahuachapan).

Salvadoran HTAs, on average, gave 16 percent of the support, both in financial donations and in-kind support, but the percentage ranges from 1 percent in San Salvador to 57 percent in Usulutan. In the department of Cabañas, where HTAs have partnered with FISDL on three projects, HTAs have put up $99,000 (9 percent of total funds) to match the FISDL $780,000 (69 percent of total funds). The average cost of each project in Cabañas has been $380,000.

Of the forty-five projects, seventeen deal with infrastructure, fourteen with recreation, and six with health. The Cuscatlan-origin HTAs (SALA, LA, and Asociación Adentro Cojutepeque) have sponsored two projects with FISDL. In Cojutepeque they worked to remodel and furnish a recreation area for the town.

Table 5: FISDL-HTA Partnership Projects in US$

Department	Projects	HTA Funds	FISDL Funds	Total Project Costs	Avg. Cost Project	HTA Donation %	FISDL Funds %
La Union	11	$306,317	$2,394,217	$3,627,383	$329,762	8	66
La Paz	10	$62,500	$782,255	$1,366,122	$136,612	5	57
Chalatenango	7	$109,570	$408,653	$682,514	$97,502	16	60
Cabañas	3	$98,788	$778,278	$1,133,534	$377,845	9	69
San Miguel	3	$66,046	$336,622	$446,561	$148,854	15	75
Cuscatlan	2	$22,000	$184,262	$254,903	$127,451	9	72
San Salvador	2	$6,000	$387,798	$638,946	$319,473	1	61
Usulutan	2	$1,384,222	$1,025,049	$2,420,699	$1,210,350	57	42
Ahuachapan	1	$4,000	$21,000	$40,000	$40,000	10	53
La Libertad	1	$14,518	$134,587	$149,105	$149,105	10	90
Morazan	1	$4,972	$342,540	$497,155	$497,155	1	69
San Vicente	1	$36,779	$30,092	$66,871	$66,871	55	45
Santa Ana	1	$18,298	$93,930	$121,987	$121,987	15	77
Total/Average	45	$2,134,010	$6,919,282	$11,445,780	$278,690	16	64

Source: FISDL, Proyectos de "Unidos por la Solidaridad" con Salvadoreños en el exterior (FISDL 2004).

In Suchitoto, Cuscatlan, SALA worked with FISDL to repair and install streetlights on an access road to the Port of San Juan. As a measure of the program's success, by June 2004 the associations had raised a total of US$4.53 million, double the amount they had committed through January 2004. With the new administration of President Saca, a new program was inaugurated with a call for proposals that led to the approval of twelve new projects amounting to US$3.1 million, sixty percent of which was committed by the Salvadoran community living abroad (Ministerio de Relaciones Exteriores de El Salvador 2006).

Another case where institutional relationships and partnerships have occurred with government involvement is the participation of the International Fund for Agricultural Development of the United Nations (IFAD) in co-financing development projects with HTAs. IFAD has a widespread rural project network in the Latin American and Caribbean region and has been working on projects concerning the relationship between rural development and remittances in El Salvador. As well as working to determine the role of remittances from the United States to Latin America, especially as untapped capital, IFAD has been working with the World Bank and Salvadoran HTAs in the US. It aims to further sensitize them to the conditions of rural Salvadoran communities and identify potential cooperative projects for which HTA and IFAD resources might be pooled. For example, IFAD has worked with a Los Angeles HTA supported by El Rescate and a Virginia-based HTA to privately construct a local high school. Besides providing 53 percent of the funding, IFAD's main contributions were technical assistance and help obtaining the support of the Ministry of Education for the project.

What IFAD has done is incorporate HTA initiatives into its Rural Reconstruction and Modernization Program, which in turn encourages migrants and migrant associations to invest in income-generating projects in their home countries. By matching migrant funds, IFAD has provided technical and financial assistance for projects in targeted Salvadoran communities.

HONDURAN ASSOCIATIONS

It is uncertain how many Honduran associations exist. From a compilation of associations thirty were identified, four of which were interviewed for this analysis. Their activities are similar to those of the other groups. Like other HTAs, Honduran groups are also led by a board of directors as well as presidents, secretaries, and treasurers who are elected on an annual or biannual basis. Groups have between fifteen and one hundred members who meet on a regular basis. However, given the binational nature of many of the groups' activities, whereby they work to provide services both to local Honduran immigrants as well as communities in Honduras, locally based volunteers and clients could number into the hundreds. Honduran groups, as expected, are made up of members from a specific town or municipality in Honduras, although some have expanded their focus to include several municipalities, either on their own or in partnership with other HTAs. One New York–based group, Travesia Nueva Ola, was founded specifically to represent immigrants from Travesia within pre-existing Honduran umbrella organizations in the area. Other groups have come together around other common causes, such as Afro-Latino culture or an interest in investment.

Honduran organizations tend to keep in close communication with their hometown communities in Honduras in order to best understand what their needs are. They cite churches, local government entities, and community groups as important contacts for their work. Decisions on project selection are then usually made by the board of directors, although some groups do indicate a more formal process. One association interviewed, for example, sends a representative to their target community in Honduras every two years to hold community focus groups. The club then meets back in the United States to discuss the findings and vote on new projects.

Like other associations in the region, activities tend to concentrate on health, education, infrastructure, and disaster relief. Honduran associations have also become involved in innovative campaigns to link the Honduran community in the United States to their homeland. The group Unidad Hondureña de Florida recently organized a voter registration drive for immigrants wishing to vote in the last Honduran presidential elections and personally delivered voter registration cards to officials in Honduras to make sure that they would be accepted. The Organización Hondureña de Palm Beach, also based in Florida, secured in-kind donations from local Honduran-owned painting businesses for use in construction projects throughout San Pedro Sula. Other projects include assistance with school supply drives, the construction of community centers and computer labs, the donation of medical supplies, the repatriation of remains, and investment in tourism projects.

While all organizations reported willingness to partner with other groups, such as neighboring HTAs and umbrella groups like the Garifuna Coalition, several indicated their hesitation to work directly with local Honduran municipalities. Some groups indicate a fear of corruption, and others have had negative experiences with local government. However, that is not true for all associations. For example, one New York group is currently working with the government in San Rosa de Aguan to rebuild a bridge, and another received funding for a school repair project from the government of Travesia.

Fundraising efforts on the part of Honduran associations are often creative and have a strong cultural focus. Fundraisers have included trips to the beach and to casinos, a Mother's Day buffet and other dinners, dances, pageants, and other cultural performances. Most Honduran groups raise less than $10,000 a year. Many groups also rely on the individual donations of their members. For example, the members of the New Horizon Investment Club in New York pool their personal contributions for collective investment in stocks or real estate.

Ten Garifuna Honduran immigrants in New York City founded the New Horizon Investment Club in 2000 with the idea to combine their resources in order to learn how to invest in the stock market and then assist in the economic development of the Honduran community in New York City. New Horizon is a member of the Garifuna Coalition in New York and strives to empower Garifunas and Afro-Latinos in general with investing knowledge. Since its inception, the organization has grown to over one hundred members who convene for monthly meetings to deposit their investments and discuss possible stocks. In order to diversify their investments, in 2004 the group decided to make its first real estate investment, in the form of a five-unit apartment building in the Bronx.

More recently, New Horizon has become interested in the idea of leveraging remittances to boost economic development in tourism along the north coast of Honduras. To this end, the organization has developed a strategic alliance with the National Garifuna Tourism Chamber, which is comprised of Honduran entrepreneurs involved in the tourism industry. New Horizon has been active in negotiating investments in these tourism-related activities through funding from the Multilateral Investment Fund as well as the United Nation's International Fund for Agricultural Development. In addition, the organization is a co-sponsor of an upcoming Garifuna Annual National Conference in La Ceiba, Atlantida on the north coast of Honduras. The event will involve many local Garifuna organizations and entrepreneurs and will serve to promote tourism in this region of Honduras.

Transparency and corruption are important issues for many of these groups. One Miami organization personally delivers all of its donations on monthly trips to Honduras and brings back photos and testimonies from the beneficiaries to share with its members. They commented that many people prefer to donate to development projects in Honduras through their association rather than through other vehicles, because they can be confident that the donations will be going to the right place.

HOMETOWN ASSOCIATIONS AND DEVELOPMENT

Are the practices of HTAs compatible with economic development? Do the attributes and properties of an HTA intersect with those of development players and development work in a way that promotes long and sustainable development? If so, what conditions allow for HTAs to arrive at development solutions for their home country?

An association's development impact is measured against four criteria: projects' self-sustainability, matching of local basic needs, ability to promote community ownership, and potential for replication outside the local environment. However, in order to achieve such impact, HTAs alone cannot guarantee success.[2] To be most successful, policies and conditions mostly external to the HTA need to exist. First, development and government agents must respond to the input of HTAs when working on projects that can enhance local development. They must engage and communicate with HTAs and be willing to partner with them and allocate resources. Second, the capacity of the local economy to absorb migrant foreign savings, particularly those associated with community donations, is central to achieving local development.

---

2. HTA development performance is measured against their ability to adequately adopt projects that adhere to basic development operational impact criteria.

Table 6: Four Macro Determinants of HTA Development Impact

HTA Impact	HTA Capacity	Donor/Government Interaction	Productive Base
Correspondence	Capacity building	Interest and willingness to partner	Efficiency levels, modernization
Sustainability	Org. strength	Allocation of resources	Diversification/concentration of production across sectors, quality of entrepreneurship
Ownership	Partnership	Engagement and communication with HTAs	
Replicability	Long-term durability		Available technology tools
	Resource capability		Governments enabling environment to motivate an interaction between investment and production

HTA Development Promotion Capacity

HTAs are primarily philanthropic groups whose work some-times overlaps with economic development, but not always. The philanthropic work is instrumental to solidifying relationships with the community and promoting well-being. HTA develop-ment delivery capacity depends on the interplay of five elements: capacity building, quality of the organization, capacity to partner, durability, and resource capability, as defined below.

- Capacity building: Process of strengthening capacity to iden-tify priorities, resources, and implementation

- Organizational nature: How an organization operates its activities and functions

- Partnership and collaborative capacity: Ability to carry out projects in collaboration with other institutions

- Long-term durability: Organization's institutional capacity to last for at least five years

- Resource capability: Ability to raise enough resources to deliver adequate projects

Most Central American HTAs exhibit some but not all of these features, thus limiting their development delivery capacity. Al-though the majority of these groups are organizationally strong, and their projects have much needed short-term effects in their communities as they address local needs, they lack many of the other features that can enable them to become feasible develop-ment players. Few institutions identify priorities that are com-mensurate to the needs of the community, their resource stock is intermittent and, while extremely valuable, is generally small in nature and not enough to impact greater activities in any of the areas in which they work.

Some associations are models of success. For example, Salvadoreños Associados de Maryland and the New Horizons Investment Club are institutions that gradually learned to build partnerships with government institutions, assess local impact, identify priorities in their areas of interest, and strengthen their organizational base. They reached a maturation point at which they graduated from grassroots activism to proactive non-profit development mobilization.

Although development promotion capacity among HTAs is mixed, their regular involvement and activism over time provide lessons for improvement. Moreover, their interaction with outside institutions, donors, governments, or private sector groups strengthens their capacity to do development work.

DONOR, FOUNDATION, AND GOVERNMENT INITIATIVES

HTA interaction with larger bodies and institutions can be critical to their success. First, the experience of development agents adds value to HTA work. Second, HTAs are motivated to engage in such partnerships because their funding is matched and there is confidence in their positive performance. The cases of initiatives by the Inter-American Foundation, the Multilateral Investment Fund, the United Nation's International Fund for Agricultural Development, FISDL, and the Pan American Development Foundation all illustrate that leveraging opportunities leads to development results and also helps strengthen HTAs' ability to deliver.

A case where institutional relationships and partnerships have occurred with donor participation is the International Fund for Agricultural Development of the United Nations (IFAD). IFAD has had a role in co-financing development projects with HTAs. IFAD worked with a Los Angeles HTA, supported by El Rescate (a local Los Angeles NGO) and a Virginia-based HTA, to privately construct a local high school. Besides providing 53 percent of the funding, IFAD's main contributions were technical assistance and help obtaining the support of the Ministry of Education for the project. IFAD has incorporated HTA initiatives in its Rural Reconstruction and Modernization Program, which in turn encourages migrants and migrant associations to invest in income-generating projects in their home countries. By matching migrant funds, IFAD has provided technical and financial assistance for projects in targeted Salvadoran communities.

For example, in a joint operation with the Multilateral Investment Fund of the Inter-American Development Bank, IFAD funded a New Horizons Club project to conduct training and investment feasibility assessment of the Club's capacity to invest in the Atlantic coast of Honduras. Moreover, New Horizons also received funding to learn about the work performed by twenty other Honduran HTAs, to disseminate the lessons they learned and to identify opportunities for collaboration with donors.

There exist other successful initiatives by donors, foundations, and governments, some of which have even been behind the establishment of new HTAs. The Inter-American Foundation established a grant program through the Salvadoran-based NGO CARECEN International. CARECEN targeted twenty-one communities in three municipalities and promoted the creation of new HTAs in those communities where no migrant associations had previously existed. As a result, HTAs grew from three active migrant associations to fifteen, designing a total of twenty-one development projects identified for HTA funding. Moreover, municipal governments became involved; one municipal government committed funding for up to 30 percent of each project within its jurisdiction.

The work of CARECEN with HTAs and local communities in El Salvador benefited from lessons learned through the Inter-American Foundation's previous work with HTA community development projects. These lessons included the importance of strong citizens' groups and a focus on community-driven collaboration with local governments in building sustainable partnerships and projects. The Inter-American Foundation has taken active steps toward building the capacities of such community groups, both in the US and El Salvador, to effectively work together through training workshops and the work of community organizers. While CARECEN admits that working with HTAs has been a challenge, they have seen positive long-term results with important implications for the role of HTAs as partners in local development (Pyle 2006).

Another important case is the work of the Pan American Development Foundation in El Salvador through a USAID funded program, ALCANCE (Alliance of Communities Supporting Children and Their Continuation in Education). This program partnered with twenty-one HTAs to focus on rural Salvadoran primary school children by improving access to education and leveraging HTA involvement in education. One of the components of ALCANCE "established a $25,000 one-to-one matching fund, where one dollar invested in the program by the HTA was matched with an ALCANCE dollar from the private sector, up to $1,000 per school." Some of the results of this partnership with HTAs included the direct benefit to 12,056 children attending seventy-seven schools, and nearly $220,000 in cash and in-kind donations by HTAs (PADF 2005).

In addition to ALCANCE, the Pan American Development Foundation also works in partnership with Banco Agricola of El Salvador to sponsor the transnational development fund "Manos Unidas por El Salvador." This initiative matches funding for community-based projects in El Salvador through a competitive selection process. Migrant groups in the Washington, DC, and Los Angeles areas are eligible for between $5,000 and $40,000 in matching funds for projects supporting infrastructure development. This demonstrates, yet again, the role the private sector can play in migrant-led development initiatives (PADF 2006).

These donor initiatives resulted primarily from direct outreach by HTAs to develop partnerships with donors by demonstrating their synergies in local community projects. More importantly, the partnerships are an important invitation to HTAs to improve their capacity to support development projects. These partnerships have also had demonstration effects on other groups, donors, and HTAs, who may explore possibilities for further work.

LOCAL ECONOMIES' CAPACITY TO ABSORB SAVINGS/MIGRANT DONATIONS

Although remittances and other economic exchanges primarily go to the poor, these interchanges alone are not a solution to the structural constraints of poverty. Remittances offer temporary relief to families' poverty, but seldom provide a permanent avenue into financial security, unless leveraging policies are implemented. To do this, structural reforms regarding inequality in Latin America as well as specific policies for integration and financial democracy for sending and receiving households are necessary.

It is important to understand that the social and productive base of an economy significantly defines the ways in which migrant foreign savings will effectively function in that economy. Family remittances, migrant investment, and community donations need to be understood as exactly what they are: foreign savings. As with any other source of foreign savings, like aid, trade, or investment, community donations interact with the structure of the local economy. The extent to which such structures absorb those savings is the first question for development practitioners. This means that it is important to analyze the productive forces in an economy, the efficiency levels, how modern it is, what level of diversification/concentration of production exists within the various sectors, how entrepreneurship operates and is enabled, what technology tools exist or are missing, and the extent to which governments provide an enabling environment to motivate an interaction between investment and production.

A recent comparative study of four semi-rural communities in Latin America showed that the productive bases of their economies were unable to fully absorb these funds and the need to implement such strategies and policies was urgent (Orozco 2006a). The study also exposed the relative fragilities of the local economies, with high costs of living that make it difficult for remittance recipients to save and mobilize those savings.

In each community the entrepreneurial class caters little to the demands of remittance recipients, and its form of operation is relatively primitive. From the perspective of financial intermediation, a critical asset accumulation sector, financial institutions were not shaping the demand by supplying financial products, with some exceptions. Moreover, governments and civil society do not provide recipient families with adequate support networks to help them cope with the realities of migration. As a result, nearly one third of recipients reported that they too were considering leaving their communities in the near future and migrating abroad.

If an economy and its supply side are unable to produce in a competitive context, the labor force will depress and eventually a portion will migrate in order to provide for their families. The beneficiaries of money sent from abroad may only do so much with that money insofar as the local economy provides an effective supply for the demand of services and products.

CONCLUSION

Taking diasporas into account when designing a development strategy is more than justifiable for donors. The presence of millions of immigrants who are regularly connected to their homelands, as well as the impact that those connections have on local economies and communities, should not be overlooked.

However, only a few donors or foundations have engaged in experimental partnerships, and institutionally there remains to be found a strategy that links donor work with diasporas. There may be several reasons for this situation. First, some development experts do not believe that migrants are capable of participating in development schemes. Second, because of the limited knowledge that exists about organized diaspora groups, some donors have uninformed expectations about what results these groups can achieve. There are problems of symmetry between donors and diaspora organizations that need addressing. Third, a new line of communication with migrant organizations is critically important. Both diaspora organizations and donors need to find a space for interaction and communication to bridge the divide that separates them by virtue of their social conditions. Many conferences and policy discussions about migration, remittances, and HTAs exclude migrants and their predominantly volunteer groups from the debate. This silences an entire group and reduces its chances of effectively participating in development. Fourth, the performance of HTAs is often mixed, due to uneven ability to work on concrete development projects.

When donors, foundations, and even private sector institutions do interact and partner with HTAs, successful projects emerge. Governments and donors should seriously consider approaching HTAs as partners in development, while providing them with the means to better achieve their goals, including promoting better economic opportunities in the host countries. However, overall responsibility for development promotion should still rest on governments, not on diasporas. Many Central American diasporas continue to be part of an impoverished underclass of migrants whose livelihood is defined by precarious, low-paying jobs and society's disregard of their social, economic, and legal status. Therefore, a transnational development approach is a critical consideration in this age of globalization and transnational communities.

References

Chinchilla, Norma and Nora Hamilton. 1991. "Central American Migration: A Framework for Analysis." *Latin American Research Review* 26, no. 1:75–110.

De la Garza, Rodolfo, Manuel Orozco, Harry P. Pachon, and Adrian D. Pantoja. 2000. "Family Ties and Ethnic Lobbies." In *Latinos and U.S. Foreign Policy,* edited by Rodolfo de la Garza and Harry P. Pachon. New York: Rowman and Littlefield.

Direccion General de Atención a la Comunidad en el Exterior, Ministerio de Relaciones Exteriores, San Salvador, El Salvador (http://www.comunidades.gob.sv/Sitio/Img.nsf/vista/Documentos/$file/DGACE.pdf).

Direccion General de Atención a la Comunidad en el Exterior, Ministerio de Relaciones Exteriores, San Salvador, El Salvador, "Comunidad en Accion" (http://www.comunidades.gob.sv/comunidades/comunidades.nsf/pages/revista).

Dunkerley, James. 1994. *The Pacification of Central America.* London: Verso.

[Andrade-] Eekhoff, Katharine. 2003. *Globalization of the Periphery: The Challenges of Transnational Migration for Local Development in Central America.* El Salvador: FLACSO Programa.

Fink, Leon. 2003. *The Maya of Morgantown: Work and Community in the Nuevo New South.* Chapel Hill: University of North Carolina Press.

FISDL. 2004. *Programa Unidos por la Solidaridad.* San Salvador, January (http://www.fisdl.gob.sv).

Galtung, Johan. 1990. "Cultural Violence." *Journal of Peace Research,* vol. 27, no. 3:291–305.

La Prensa Grafica. "Departamento 15" (http://www.laprensagrafica. com/dpt15).

Lozano, Monica with Bryan Roberts and Reanne Frank. 1999. "Transnational Migrant Communities and Mexican Migration to the United States." *Ethnic and Racial Studies* 22, no. 2, March:238–266.

Ministerio de Relaciones Exteriores de El Salvador. 2006. Comunidades en el Exterior (http://www.comunidades.gob.sv/).

Moreno, Jenalia. 2006. "'Your Heart in Your Pueblo': Bread Upon the Water." *Houston Chronicle,* March 7.

Orozco, Manuel. 2000. "Latino Hometown Associations as Agents of Development in Latin America." Washington, DC: Inter-American Dialogue, June.

———. 2003a. "The Challenges of Democratization." *The World & I,* March, pp. 26–33.

———. 2003b. "Hometown Associations and Their Present and Future Partnerships: New Development Opportunities?" Report commissioned by the U.S. Agency for International Development. Washington, DC: Inter-American Dialogue, September.

———. 2003c. "Remitting Back Home and Supporting the Homeland: The Guyanese Community in the U.S." Working Paper commissioned by the U.S. Agency for International Development GEO Project, January 15.

———. 2005a. "Hometown Associations and Development: Ownership, Correspondence, Sustainability and Replicability." Pp. 157–179 in *New Patterns for Mexico: Observations on Remittances, Philanthropic Giving, and Equitable Development*, edited by Barbara J. Merz. Cambridge, MA: Global Equity Initiative, Asia Center, Harvard University: Distributed by Harvard University Press.

———. 2005b. *Transnational Engagement, Remittances and Their Relationship to Development in Latin America and the Caribbean*. Institute for the Study of International Migration, Georgetown University, July.

———. 2006a. "Between Hardship and Hope: Remittances and the Local Economy in Latin America." Report commissioned by the Multilateral Investment Fund. Washington, DC: Inter-American Dialogue, August.

———. 2006b. "Parties and Elections in Central America." In *The Elections of 2000*, edited by Mary Kirtz, Mark Kasoff, Rick Farmer, and John Green. Akron: University of Akron Press.

Pan American Development Foundation (PADF). 2005. *ALCANCE: Alliance of Communities Supporting Children and Their Continuation in Education*. Publication prepared for the U.S. Agency for International Development, Washington, DC: PADF, June.

———. 2006. *Transnational Development Initiative*. Washington, DC: PADF, August (www.panamericancommunities.org).

Pieterse, Jan Nederveen. 2004. *Globalization and Culture*. New York: Rowman and Littlefield.

Popkin, Eric. 1999. "Guatemalan Mayan Migration to Los Angeles: Constructing Transnational Linkages in the Context of the Settlement
Process." *Ethnic & Racial Studies* 22, issue 2, March:267–289.

———. 2005. "The Emergence of Pan-Mayan Ethnicity in the Guatemalan Transnational Community Linking Santa Eulalia and Los
Angeles." *Current Sociology* 53, issue 4:675–706.

Pyle, Katheryn Smith. 2006. "The IAF and Transnational Communities
in El Salvador." *Grassroots Development: Journal of the Inter-American
Foundation* 27, no. 1:16–21.

Ratha, Dilip and Samuel Munzele Maimbo, eds. 2005. *Remittances:
Development Impact and Future Prospects*. Washington, DC: World
Bank.

Robinson, Jenny. 2002. *Development and Displacement*. Oxford: Oxford
University Press.

Rosenau, James. 2003. *Distant Proximities: Dynamics beyond Globalization*.
Princeton: Princeton University Press.

Salvadoran Ministry of Foreign Affairs. Communities Abroad (http://
www.comunidades.gob.sv/).

Sheffer, Gabriel. 2003. *Diaspora Politics: At Home Abroad*. Cambridge:
Cambridge University Press.

Smith, Barbara Ellen. 2005. Marcela Mendoza and David H. Ciscel.
"The World on Time: Flexible Labor, New Immigrants, and Global
Logistics." In *The American South in a Global World*, edited by James
L. Peacock, Harry L. Watson, and Carrie Matthews. Chapel Hill:
University of North Carolina Press.

Striffer, Steve. 2005. "We're All Mexicans Here: Poultry Processing, Latino Migration, and the Transformation of Class in the South." In *The American South in a Global World*, edited by James L. Peacock, Harry L. Watson, and Carrie Matthews. Chapel Hill: University of North Carolina Press.

Telford, John, Margaret Arnold, and Alberto Harth with ASONOG. 2004. "Learning Lessons from Disaster Recovery: The Case of Honduras." *Disaster Risk Management Working Paper Series No. 8*. Washington, DC: The World Bank, June (http://www.worldbank.org/hazards).

Vélez-Ibáñez, Carlos, and Anna Sampaio with Manolo González-Estay. 2002. *Transnational Latina/o Communities: Politics, Processes and Cultures*. New York: Rowman and Littlefield.

Vilas, Carlos. 1994. *Between Earthquakes and Volcanoes: Market, State, and the Revolutions in Central America*. Translated by Ted Kuster. New York: Monthly Review Press.

INDEX

AAHOA. *See* Asian American Hotel Owners Association

AAPI. *See* American Association of Physicians of Indian Origin

Abacha, Sani, 159

Abiola, Hafsat, 159

activism: political, 101

Acumen Fund, 43

advisory councils, 31

Afewerki, Issaias, 162

affluence, 121. *See also* wealth

Afghanistan, 94, 95, 104, 112

Africa, 5, 8–9, 17, 41, 76, 78, 101, 104, 151, 163, 195; within continent migrations, 152–54; labor migration in, 154–55; philanthropic institutions in, 167–70; remittances to, 157–62; skilled emigration rates in, 12–13; social and economic equity in, 170–73. *See also various countries*

African Methodist Episcopal Church, 167–68

African Virtual University, 160

Afro-Caribbeans, 188

Afro-Guyanese, 195–96, 197

agriculture: in Central America, 218–19

Ahuachapan (El Salvador), 234

AIDS epidemic: in Africa, 12

AIF. *See* America India Foundation

airlines: bombing plots, 112–13

Al Barakat Bank, 165

Albanians, 96, 98

ALCANCE. *See* Alliance of Communities Supporting Children and Their Continuation in Education

Algeria, 113

Alliance of Communities Supporting Children and Their Continuation in Education (ALCANCE), 245

Alliances: with elites, 44–47; and

255